Fastest, Highest, Strongest

Fastest, Highest, Strongest presents a comprehensive challenge to the dominant orthodoxy concerning the use of performance-enhancing drugs in sport.

Examining the political and economic transformation of the Olympic Movement during the twentieth century, the authors argue that the realities of modern sport require a serious reassessment of current policies, in particular the ban on the use of certain substances and practices. The book includes detailed discussion of:

- The historical importance of World War II and the cold war in the development of a high-performance culture in sport.
- The changing Olympic project: from amateurism to a fully professionalized approach.
- The changing meaning of "sport."
- The role of sport science, technology and drugs in pursuing ever-better performance.
- The major ethical and philosophical arguments used to support the ban on performance-enhancing substances in sport.

Fastest, Highest, Strongest is a profound critical examination of modern sport, of interest both to students and scholars in the field of sport studies, as well as sociologists, political scientists, policymakers, sports administrators, and athletes themselves.

Rob Beamish is Associate Professor and Head of the Department of Sociology at Queen's University, Canada.

Ian Ritchie is Associate Professor in the Department of Physical Education and Kinesiology at Brock University, Canada.

D1262472

Routledge critical studies in sport

Series editors: Jennifer Hargreaves and Ian McDonald
University of Brighton

The Routledge Critical Studies in Sport series aims to lead the way in developing the multi-disciplinary field of sport studies by producing books that are interrogative, interventionist and innovative. By providing theoretically sophisticated and empirically grounded texts, the series will make sense of the changes and challenges facing sport globally. The series aspires to maintain the commitment and promise of the critical paradigm by contributing to a more inclusive and less exploitative culture of sport.

Fastest, Highest, Strongest

A critique of high-performance sport

Rob Beamish and Ian Ritchie

Routledge
Taylor & Francis Group

NEW YORK AND LONDON

First published 2006
by Routledge
270 Madison Ave, New York, NY 10016

Simultaneously published in the UK
by Routledge
2 Park Square, Milton Park, Abingdon, Oxon OX14 4RN

Routledge is an imprint of the Taylor & Francis Group, an informa business

© 2006 Rob Beamish and Ian Ritchie

Excerpt from Animal Farm by George Orwell,
© 1946 by Harcourt, Inc. and renewed 1975 by Sonia Orwell,
reprinted by permission of the publisher.

Typeset in Goudy by
GreenGate Publishing Services, Tonbridge
Printed and bound in Great Britain by
MPG Books Ltd, Bodmin

All rights reserved. No part of this book may be reprinted or reproduced
or utilised in any form or by any electronic, mechanical, or other means,
now known or hereafter invented, including photocopying and recording,
or in any information storage or retrieval system, without permission in
writing from the publishers.

The publisher, editor and typesetter make no representation, express or
implied, with regard to the accuracy of the information contained in this
book and cannot accept any legal responsibility or liability for any errors
or omissions that may be made.

Library of Congress Cataloging in Publication Data
Beamish, Rob.
Fastest, highest, strongest : a critique of high-performance sport /
Rob Beamish and Ian Ritchie.
        p. cm. – (Routledge critical studies in sport)
   Includes bibliographical references and index.
     ISBN 0–415–77042–4 (hardback) – ISBN 0–415–77043–2 (pbk.)
        1. Doping in sports. 2. Olympics. I. Ritchie, Ian, 1964– .
II. Title. III. Series.

RC1230.B45 2006
362.29–dc22

                                                        2006001561

British Library Cataloguing in Publication Data
A catalogue record for this book is available from the British Library

ISBN10: 0-415-77042-4 (hbk)
ISBN10: 0-415-77043-2 (pbk)
ISBN10: 0-203-96785-2 (ebk)

ISBN13: 978-0-415-77042-2 (hbk)
ISBN13: 978-0-415-77043-9 (pbk)
ISBN13: 978-0-203-96785-0 (ebk)

Contents

Foreword		vi
Preface		viii
Acknowledgements		xii

Introduction   1

1 From Coubertin's dream to high-performance sport: the shifting dynamics of Olympic sport   11

2 Steroids: Nazi propaganda, cold war fears, and "androgenized" women   31

3 "Sport," German traditions, and the development of "training"   46

4 From Stalingrad to Helsinki: the development of German sport systems   66

5 "Something had altered in the faces of the pigs …:" converging sport systems in the GDR and FRG   85

6 Ethics reconsidered: the spirit of sport, the level playing field, and harm to the athlete   105

Conclusion: the brave new world of high-performance sport   136

Notes   145
Index   187

Foreword

In *A Contribution to the Critique of Hegel's Philosophy of Right*, Karl Marx argues that "To be radical is to grasp the root of the matter". Without doubt, *Fastest, Highest, Strongest: A Critique of High-Performance Sport* is a truly radical text. It is an empirically informed, penetrating critique of the structure and culture of high-performance sport that lays bare one of the most controversial and intractable issues to have plagued sport in the post-war period: performance-enhancing drugs. Copious amounts of time and space have been devoted to the problem of doping in sport by policy-makers, the media and academics. Often the "debate" is polarized around one question: are you for or against drug taking in sport? But, as Beamish and Ritchie explain, doping is symptomatic of the quest to be the fastest, highest or strongest in high-performance sport. It is a package deal. If one accepts the culture of high-performance sport, it makes little sense to ask the "for" or "against" question. The key is to situate the use of performance-enhancing substances in the totality of the sport–culture–society nexus.

Based on a critique of the romanticized and highly ideological notions of Olympian internationalism, and framed by a concern with the human rights of athletes, *Fastest, Highest, Strongest* situates the use of performance-enhancing drugs in its socio-historical context. Drawing on original archival research, Beamish and Ritchie set out their critique of an incoherent doping policy which itself is an expression of the contradictions between sporting ideologies, capitalist modernity and the culture of high-performance sport. However, the authors do not allow the complexities of analysis to detach them from an engagement with the pragmatic world of sport policy. Beamish and Ritchie outline three general criteria that should shape the debate on performance-enhancing substances: first, the starting point has to be an understanding of the socio-historical reality of performance enhancement as the basis for formulating policy, rather than the ideologically mystifying notion of the "spirit of sport". Second, given the reality of high-performance sport, a frank discussion needs to occur about the safeguards required to protect athletes' health. And third, athletes themselves must be centrally involved in any policies related to their training and work conditions. This is a text that takes the debate on drug taking in sport to new and more meaningful levels.

Fastest, Highest, Strongest powerfully exemplifies the rationale for the Routledge Critical Studies in Sport series. In the series, our intention as editors is to tackle some of the big questions facing sport and society, to question assumptions about sport, to critique established ideas, and to explore new ones. We are keen to encourage the production of texts that are empirically grounded and socially relevant, challenging and innovative, in particular through their engagement with issues concerning relations of power and discriminatory practices. The series as a whole aims to challenge complacency and encourage reflection, and should assist students, researchers, policy-makers and professionals to make sense of the changes, challenges and crises facing sport. The guiding philosophy for the series can be summarized as:

- Interrogative: challenging common sense ideas and exposing relations of power in the world of sport.
- Interventionist: highlighting the relationship between theory and practice and providing arguments and analyses of topical and polemical issues.
- Innovative: seeking to develop new areas of research, and stimulating new ways of thinking and studying about sport.

In *Fastest, Highest, Strongest: A Critique of High-Performance Sport*, Rob Beamish and Ian Ritchie have certainly produced a text that is interrogative, interventionist and innovative. We are proud to include it in the series. Our hope is that this book will provoke and stimulate discussion both inside the academy amongst students, teachers and researchers, and outside amongst policy-makers, athletes and journalists. Ultimately the aim of this book and of our series as a whole is to spark dialog across the academic–non-academic divide in the world of sport, to help develop a more humanistic and empowering vision for sport.

Jennifer Hargreaves and Ian McDonald
University of Brighton
Series Editors

Preface

The seeds of this study date to long before we began this as a joint project and well before the first words were written. Though never the primary, or even a major impetus for writing this book, the events surrounding Ben Johnson and the 1988 Seoul Summer Games did, nevertheless, play a critical role for several reasons.

First, although athletes had tested positive for banned substances before Johnson, and drug controversies in high-performance sport had come and gone many times – and will continue to do so into the future – Johnson's performances leading up to, and at the Games, crystallized the key issues lying at the center of high-performance sport in the modern era. Johnson's 100 meter victory in 9.79 seconds clearly demonstrated the phenomenal athletic feats that high-performance athletes can achieve, but his positive test left people wondering how and why an athlete would so single-mindedly pursue the outer limits of athletic performance.

The official response to Johnson's positive test was the Canadian government's Order in Council PC 1988–2361 on 5 October 1988, which established a commission "to enquire into and report on the facts and circumstances surrounding the use by Canadian athletes of drugs and banned practices intended to increase athletic performance." Despite its extremely public profile, the commission could not monopolize the analysis of performance enhancement in world-class sport. Sport scholars focused on the central issues, journalists presented various sides of the arguments concerning performance-enhancing substances, and numerous Canadians formed their own views on Johnson, Canada's high-performance sport system, and the modern Olympic Games. The commission, created in the wake of Johnson's positive test and the federal government's mishandling of the event in its earliest hours, placed high-performance sport and performance enhancement under public scrutiny in ways they had never been before.

In 1987, Rob Beamish had completed a three year study of Canada's high-performance sport system from the perspective of the athlete, co-authored a monograph based on the results of that study and overseen 10 workshops carried out with nationally carded Canadian athletes, in both official languages, across the country. His response to "the Ben Johnson scandal" was shaped by that background and his position differed significantly from that of the mainstream. In November 1989, Rob was asked to engage in a debate with Richard Pound, then Vice-President of the International Olympic Committee, in the Stikeman, Elliott Speaker Series in the Faculty of Law at Queen's University; the topic of debate was the International Olympic Committee's list of banned substances.

Following a six month appointment in the Institute for Sport History at the Freie Universität, Berlin, Rob presented more developed arguments about the banned list and the shortcomings of the Dubin Commission at the annual meetings of the Canadian Association for Sociology and Anthropology and in the School of Physical and Health Education at Queen's University's seminar series. The notes from the debate and those two papers were then set aside as Rob returned to Berlin for another six months in 1991 and shifted the focus of his research energies to the collapse of the Berlin Wall and the transformation of East Germany. Serving as Associate Dean (Studies) in the Faculty of Arts and Science at Queen's from 1995 to 2001, Rob was further removed from an ongoing analysis of high-performance sport although he continued studying and publishing material on sport systems from the perspective of the athlete during that hiatus from full-time scholarship.

During this time period, after completing his doctoral studies which included social and historical accounts of Olympic policies and the ethics of banned substance use, Ian Ritchie began his teaching career at Queen's University where he taught undergraduate and graduate courses in sport sociology, history and policy; the issue of banned substance use played an important role in many of those courses. Ian's professional engagement with the issues of banned substance use and Olympic policies continued with presentations at Queen's University's School of Physical and Health Education seminar series and at the annual meetings of the North American Society for the Sociology of Sport, during lively and often heated debates in the United States, Canada, the Netherlands and elsewhere, in addition to published commentaries on the topic including in Canada's national newspaper the *Globe and Mail*. It was during this period that Rob and Ian first began to share their positions on the use of performance-enhancing substances, and discussions about collaborating on a book began.

Throughout the time teaching courses, through public debates and in continuing to study the issue after moving to Brock University, what was always so striking to Ian was the perpetually large gap that existed between the perspectives of those who studied the topic in a careful and informed manner in disciplines such as history, sociology, policy studies, legal studies, and philosophy, and the perspective of those involved with the creation and administration of banned substance policies, especially in the International Olympic Committee and, more recently, the World Anti-Doping Agency.

Overcoming this perpetual gap is one of our goals in this study. Our commitment to the study's central objective – examining performance-enhancing substances within the socio-historical reality of high-performance sport as it has been constituted in the latter half of the twentieth century – has guided our work from the start of our professional relationship. We hope that the arguments we present will demonstrate the importance of locating banned substance use in particular, and high-performance sport in general, in their full sociological and historical contexts so that their reality will be understood more clearly, and a more open, informed and democratic debate about "drugs" and, more importantly, the real world of high-performance sport may be initiated.

Like all projects of this sort, the end product conceals the many years of labor and no less an amount of patience as we worked through multiple versions of the manuscript towards its completion. Equally significant, it conceals how many people, through critical comments and reviews of the manuscript, helpful and informed discussions, and general encouragement or personal support, made the end product possible. From Routledge we are grateful for the work Samantha Grant and Kate Manson put into this study. They saw the manuscript through its review and editing stages to its final production. Samantha and Kate were diligent while also providing thoughtful comments and encouragement throughout. Series editors Ian McDonald and Jennifer Hargreaves were particularly supportive of the study; they believed in it from the start and provided invaluable critical comments that had a significant impact on the final product. Finally, we thank those who anonymously reviewed the manuscript, providing us with encouragement, helpful critique, and important food for thought. In responding to their criticisms, the manuscript has been strengthened in many important respects.

Adele Mugford, with the help of a generous grant from the School of Physical and Health Education at Queen's University, and Ryan Beamish, also funded through Queen's, provided important research assistance – Adele during the early stages of the book's preparation, Ryan during the final phases. We appreciate their industriousness, patience, and attention to detail during their long hours in the library.

Several people played significant roles in carefully reviewing or editing various parts of the manuscript, engaging and challenging us in critical discussions of different themes, or providing support in important but too often invisible ways. Our appreciation in that respect goes out to Greg Jackson, Don McQuarie, Sandra Peters, Kelly Lockwood, Cathy van Ingen, Mary Louise Adams, and David McDonald. Danny Rosenberg, Chair of the Department of Physical Education and Kinesiology at Brock University, and Joan Westenhaefer and Lynn O'Malley in the Department of Sociology at Queen's University, provided valuable assistance and "protection" so the manuscript could be completed.

Ian would like to personally thank family members and very close friends for lifelong support and companionship. Long-term projects of this sort often entail the greatest sacrifices by those who are closest, yet at the same time these people made the work so much easier and enjoyable due to their love and friendship. Thank you to Claire Binnie, Alan Ritchie, Jill Beaupre, Ken Ritchie, Michael Murphy, Andrew Leger and Rebecca Mancuso.

Rob would like to thank his "sisters" in the Faculty Office for six unforgettable years and their belief, support and encouragement in his decision to return to academic life. Scholarly work is time-consuming and solitary; Nada, Travis and Ryan Beamish have always given him the freedom, love and joy needed to sustain him in those sometimes lonely hours. In addition, they have supported his presentation of unorthodox views, even though they might not share them and yet still be called upon to defend them through "guilt by association." Rob regrets causing that burden but will forever treasure the bond that keeps them in his corner through thick and thin.

Acknowledgements

Chapter 1: material reprinted by permission of Sage Publications Ltd from Rob Beamish and Ian Ritchie, "From Chivalrous 'Brothers-in-Arms' to the Eligible Athlete: Changed Principles and the IOC's Banned Substance List" in *International Review for the Sociology of Sport* 39: 4 (2004) 355–71. (c) 2004 International Sociology of Sport Association and SAGE Publications.

Chapter 2: material reprinted by permission of Taylor & Francis from Rob Beamish and Ian Ritchie, "The Spectre of Steroids: Nazi Propaganda, Cold War Anxiety and Patriarchal Paternalism" in *The International Journal of the History of Sport* 22: 5 (2005) 775–93. See http://www.tandf.co.uk/journals/titles/09523367.asp

Chapter 3: material reprinted by permission of Taylor & Francis from Rob Beamish and Ian Ritchie, "From Fixed Capacities to Performance-Enhancement: The Paradigm Shift in the Science of 'Training' and the Use of Performance-Enhancing Substances" in *Sport in History* 25: 3 (2005) 412–33. See http://www.tandf.co.uk/journals/titles/17460263.asp

Chapter 5: Excerpt from *Animal Farm* by George Orwell, Copyright © George Orwell, 1945, by permission of Bill Hamilton as the Literary Executor of the Estate of the Late Sonia Brownell Orwell and Secker & Warburg Ltd; and Copyright © 1946 by Harcourt, Inc. renewed 1975 by Sonia Brownell Orwell, reprinted by permission of the publisher.

Introduction

In 1998, only a decade after Ben Johnson's dramatic disqualification in the premier event of the Seoul Olympics, three incidents put performance enhancement in world-class, high-performance sport back into the spotlight. Following several years of suspicion and the 1994 disqualification of seven swimmers at the Asian Games in Hiroshima, a number of newspapers reported that Sydney customs officials had discovered 13 vials of the synthetic human growth hormone (hGH) somatropin (norditropin) in a bag apparently belonging to Yuan Yuan of the Chinese national swimming team.[1] Detained briefly, the team continued its flight to Perth and despite the controlled nature of hGH the police did not lay any charges. Further investigation by the International Swimming Association led to Zhou Zhewen's statement that he had packed the vials of growth hormone. Zhewen and Yuan received 15- and four-year suspensions respectively.[2]

Just two months later, on March 9, 1998, Reims customs officials found 104 doses of erythropoietin (EPO) in the TVM cycling team's van.[3] Four months further on, just days before the start of the Tour de France, Festina's team masseur Willy Voet was stopped at the Franco-Belgian border on July 8 with more than 400 ampules of EPO and other performance-enhancing substances in his car.[4] The police investigation soon expanded to other Festina officials. TVM returned to the spotlight on July 23 when police arrested and charged team director Cees Priem and a team doctor, Andrei Mikhailov, for "transporting poisonous substances and the possession of dangerous merchandise."[5] Unlike the swimming incident in January, the Tour discoveries led to criminal prosecution.[6]

If observers were surprised by the French officials' unprecedented action against Festina, International Olympic Committee (IOC) President Juan Antonio Samaranch's commentary on the events astounded the world of high-performance sport. In comments published in the Madrid daily *El Mundo*, picked up by the press around the world, Samaranch stated that the doping list should be drastically reduced. The list, as was reported in the various press accounts, currently included substances that were dangerous to athletes' health as well as those that artificially improved performance. "Doping is everything that, firstly, is harmful to an athlete's health and, secondly, artificially augments his performance," the *New York Times* quoted Samaranch as saying. "If it's the second case, for me, it's not doping. If it's the first case, it is."[7]

Samaranch's comments were truly remarkable given the unyielding stance on the use of selected performance-enhancing substances the IOC had taken in the last 25 years of the twentieth century. Was Samaranch signaling a new IOC position? Had the IOC given up the "war on drugs" or was Samaranch simply trying to protect Spanish cyclists from legal sanctions? Perhaps Samaranch was resigned to the logical outcome of contemporary world-class, high-performance sport. Whatever his reasons were, these three sets of events created a unique opportunity to re-examine the most fundamental issues related to the use of particular performance-enhancing practices and substances in world-class sport.[8]

One trial and two important conferences followed. In early February 1999, the IOC held a "World Conference on Doping in Sport" in Lausanne and in May 1999, Duke University's School of Law held "The Duke Conference on Doping."[9] The trial of the Festina officials took place in 2000.

While the conferences featured some frank assessments of banned substance use in high-performance sport and examined important issues in the testing for those substances, the presentations were seriously limited. Even though John MacAloon and John Hoberman were critical of the current practices, their analyses neither engaged with, nor examined in detail, the reasons selected performance-enhancing substances were proscribed in the first place. As supporters of prohibition, neither man questioned the rationale for the ban nor examined the socio-historical conditions of world-class, high-performance sport at the turn of the twentieth century and how they have changed over the past 100 years.[10] No one at the conferences or in the Festina trial examined the real work world of high-performance sport in its current form.[11]

In view of the outcry that followed Samaranch's pronouncements and suffering from scandals of its own, the IOC finally followed the steps that critics had recommended in the past; the IOC supported the establishment of the World Anti-Doping Agency (WADA) as an independent body to monitor the use of performance-enhancing substances in the Olympic Games. WADA was given expansive powers; it set global standards, supported the development of the laboratory technology required to detect the substances athletes use, and established a universal code that became binding on all International Sport Federations (ISFs). WADA's strategic plan also included media campaigns, educational programs, research development, and increased ties with other like-minded organizations.[12]

WADA's major accomplishment to date was the development and ratification of the *World Anti-Doping Code*.[13] During a three-day summit in Copenhagen in March 2003, representatives from 65 sport federations and 73 governments met to discuss and endorse the *Code*. The new *Code* established random, out-of-competition testing for all athletes in Olympic sports including those drawn from professional leagues like Major League Baseball and the National Hockey League. Summit participants also stipulated that any national government wishing to send teams to the Turin Winter Games in 2006 must have passed legislation enshrining the *Code*'s policies prior to the Games.[14] By August 2005, 175 countries had adopted the *Code* as had all 29 IOC-recognized ISFs, 65 National Anti-Doping Organizations and all 202 National Olympic Committees.[15]

In September 2003 WADA announced that after two years of intensive research and debate it had produced a new comprehensive list of prohibited substances. Though largely identical to the IOC's previous list, there were changes.[16] The most highly publicized were the removal of caffeine and pseudoephedrine, an ingredient found in many remedies for the common cold. A more significant change – the addition of topical or inhaled corticosteroids, which could only be used after January 2004 if an athlete received an exemption via the "therapeutic use simplified process form" – received less comment, while marijuana remained on the list although its performance-enhancing potential for sport is dubious.[17]

Celebrating WADA's new approach to enforcing the ban on selected performance-enhancing substances, Arne Ljungqvist stated that "[w]e must adjust our list to modern thinking and to changes of attitude and changes of knowledge."[18] Ljungqvist felt no need to justify the continued policing of athletes' performance-enhancing practices, nor did he feel that athletes and the public deserved a statement of the principles upon which WADA based substance prohibition in general or had chosen to ban specific substances on the list. For WADA it would be business as usual – with increased vigilance.

No sooner had WADA revised its list when the intrigue in performance enhancement deepened. A reporter from the *Mercury News* informed the United States Anti-Doping Agency (USADA) that a person with highly sensitive information wanted to come forward. Track coach Trevor Graham alleged that a number of high-ranking athletes in several sports were using an undetectable steroid distributed by Victor Conte, through his Bay Area Laboratory Co-operative (BALCO). He gave the USADA a syringe containing a clear liquid which Don Catlin, director of the drug testing centre at the University of California, Los Angeles, identified as a synthetically produced designer steroid which he named Tetrahydrogestrinone (THG).[19] Graham also alleged that Conte's client list included a number of high profile American and international athletes.[20]

Terry Madden, the USADA's chief executive, declared that

> This is a far cry from athletes accidentally testing positive as a result of taking contaminated nutritional supplements. Rather this is a conspiracy involving chemists, coaches and certain athletes using what they developed to be "undetectable" designer steroids to defraud fellow competitors and the American and world public who pay to attend sports events.[21]

While so much attention was centered on BALCO, two less publicized incidents took place. In January 2004, the Canadian Centre for Ethics in Sport announced that a sample of AAA midget hockey players in the province of Quebec would be tested for performance-enhancing substances.[22] The main concern behind the testing was the league president's claim that as many as 25 percent of the players were using drugs.[23] With the announcement, other minor and junior hockey leagues in Canada reported they were considering similar tests in the future.[24]

Four months later, Major League Baseball announced that

> [i]n response to reports of steroid abuse by baseball players in the Dominican Republic, Major League Baseball ... would begin a drug-testing program for the Dominican Summer League with all players being subject to testing when the league commences in June.[25]

This decision came in the wake of allegations that young Dominicans were using cheap veterinary drugs, including steroids intended for animals, to enhance their ability to compete in the burgeoning market of Latino prospects for Major League Baseball.

Events came full circle in the summer of 2004. Just prior to his entry in the 2004 Tour de France, French police searched the Biarritz home of British time trial specialist David Millar and seized two empty syringes containing traces of Eprex, a common form of EPO.[26] The seizure followed a six-month investigation of the prestigious French cycling team Cofidis. Charged with the illegal possession of toxic products, Millar admitted on July 1, 2004 to Judge Richard Pallain that he had used EPO once in 2001 and twice in 2003.[27]

Two central points emerge from this brief history. First, despite the IOC's decision to formally prohibit the use of selected performance-enhancing substances in 1967, the introduction of tests for those substances in 1976, and the increasing surveillance of athletes over the past decade, the use of banned performance-enhancing substances continues. More important, Madden is correct in his assessment that positive tests are not the result of inadvertent use; the use of performance-enhancing substances by world-class, high-performance athletes involves sophisticated teams of individuals with particular knowledge and expertise. Their use is calculated. Despite repeated, high-profile, moral condemnations, important constituents within the real world of high-performance sport continue to act in accordance with the predominant forces, actions and decisions which fundamentally animate the objectives of world-class sport today.

Second, as WADA expands its powers and national governments accommodate themselves to its demands, world-class athletes live and work in an environment where their lives are increasingly monitored and regulated. An ever expanding culture of surveillance pervades the world of sport from the heights of Olympia down through to the rank and file developmental levels; every athlete is viewed with suspicion. Nevertheless, despite the increasing control over athletes' lives and the growing resources employed to monitor their behavior, the IOC, the ISFs, WADA, and the police and judiciary have not curtailed the use of performance-enhancing substances in high-performance sport.

Nineteen ninety-eight provided an opportunity to dramatically rethink the issue of performance enhancement in the world of sport. No significant changes took place; increased surveillance and repression followed and so did "the BALCO scandal" as well as "the Cofidis affair." The central goal of this study is to place the use of performance-enhancing substances within a comprehensive discussion of the socio-historical reality of contemporary world-class, high-performance sport. Within this context, it seeks to stimulate a reconsidered approach to the debate about performance enhancement in modern sport and the use of performance-enhancing substances and practices.

Performance enhancement and the Olympic Movement

The use of a performance-enhancing substance is one single decision within a large, complex set of historically created, and socially situated, actions and relationships. One cannot understand the use of performance enhancers outside of the historically developed relationships which human agents have constituted over the last 100 years and continue to constitute on an ongoing basis today. This study presents a detailed, critical examination of the real world of high-performance sport as it has developed over the last century generally, but most specifically, in the post-World War II period. It identifies the social forces and relationships that make up that social world. The stark truth is that the widespread use of performance-enhancing substances in the latter half of the twentieth century and on into the present is the direct result of a particular set of social and political circumstances and decisions in which winning and the scientifically and technologically assisted pursuit of the linear record became the overriding objectives within several well-funded, extremely sophisticated, high-performance sport systems. Furthermore, the use of certain performance-enhancing substances – including those that were later prohibited by bureaucratic fiat – was, and remains, an integral component of the goals and mission of the individuals who constitute those sport systems. The use of performance-enhancing substances is part of the internal logic that drives the comprehensive high-performance sport systems that developed over the last half-century and their use will continue unabated as long as the social and political relations of sport remain in their current trajectory and winning is the thing that really matters.

This study's most important findings concern the ways in which larger political and social events shaped the decisions and actions of those who laid the foundations for the contemporary world of high-performance sport. Idealism, ideology, war, conquest, the pursuit of geo-political power, wealth, personal interest, and the dominating influence of technical rationality all combined to constitute the world in which athletes today make their decisions. The study does not advocate the use of performance-enhancing substances nor does it exonerate anyone in high-performance sport from the decisions they make on a daily basis irrespective of the circumstances in which they find themselves. It does, however, clearly indicate that the current approach to banning certain substances is not only ineffective but dangerously counterproductive. Change will only occur when the dominant relations and logic of the world of high-performance sport are altered.

While most of the analysis to follow focuses on the particular socio-political circumstances that led to the use of performance-enhancing substances and the unquestioned pursuit of the linear record, this study also indicates the fundamental discrepancy that exists between the rationale and perspective policy makers adopt to formulate and legitimate the prohibition of selected means of performance enhancement and the real historical forces that constitute world-class, high-performance sport today. A set of unique social and political forces led to the systematic pursuit of performance enhancement in the modern era, but those who ban certain substances and practices have relied on a "trans-historical," "universal" conception of "sport." Because one is a real world of human practice and struggle and the other does not exist, and never has, the current approach to solving the so-called "moral crisis" of "doping in sport" will never work.

The policy implications this study contains are profound and far reaching; they are discussed in the final chapter. Two points, however, are of immediate importance. First, any policy prohibiting selected substances by separating "doping," on the one hand, from "sport," on the other, is misguided. The frequently held assumption that the "essential nature of sport" automatically precludes certain performance-enhancing substances and practices and allows others reinforces the mistaken belief that the "ethics" of performance enhancement are self-evident. No discussion is required. That naïve – or calculated – position shifts the focus away from the real historical conditions of modern sport and leaves policy makers to draw upon "principles" that are derived from the "universal essence of sport." The resulting solutions are reactionary responses and they limit real discussion even further. For those who are genuinely interested in the problems associated with performance enhancement in the contemporary world of sport, the events since 1998 – or 1988 – signal the need to broaden the analysis beyond the false idealism of the last half-century. It is time to begin with a detailed, socio-historical analysis of the real conditions that led to, and continue to shape, the contemporary world of high-performance sport.

This leads directly to the second point. The question of why athletes use proscribed performance-enhancing substances is too narrow; the question policy makers need to address concerns performance enhancement in its full socio-historical context. The practices constituting sport today are dominated by instrumental rationality, the quest for victory, the pursuit of the linear record, and the desire/demand to push human athletic performance to its outer limits. If that is the world of sport we want, the advanced nations of the world are well along the road to its full development. If there is a different construction of sport that people wish to see and pursue, then they have to address the current social reality in order to know where to make change. There are no answers in an appeal to "sport."

Performance enhancement: a sociological analysis

The primary focus in this study is the Olympic Movement because it is the most important, influential and visible force in modern sport. The IOC itself has played a pivotal role in the development of modern sport in four ways. First, it has held out an image of sport that contrasts – or contrasted – with the entertainment world of professional sport. The IOC proffered an image of sport as an ennobling, uplifting, educational undertaking. This is the IOC's brand.

The purity of the IOC's brand required it to curtail some of the inherent tendencies in the competitive undertakings called Olympic sport. To maintain its product's purity, the IOC restricted the type of athletes who could take part in its Games and the practices it would allow. As a result, the IOC, now through WADA, has been the leading regulator of certain performance-enhancing practices. While those restrictions once included the sex of the participants, their occupations, the number of days they could train, and the remuneration they could receive for time lost away from work, they now focus on minimum performance standards to qualify for participation and on the policing of certain pharmaceutical agents. WADA has become a huge multinational enterprise entrusted with the restriction of certain performance-enhancing substances in IOC sanctioned sporting events.

Through the ISFs and National Olympic Committees (NOCs), the IOC exerts far reaching influence. Through the NOCs, IOC policies influence national high-performance sport systems and reach down to provincial or state, regional, and local school or club programs and organizations. The majority of the sport hierarchies in the world lead to the IOC at the top. In short, the IOC and the Olympic Games are among the most influential forces in sport today; they merit close attention and analysis.

Finally, as the guardian of the most successful global sporting spectacle – the Olympic Games – the IOC has been deeply embroiled in some of the world's most significant political events. Certainly the Games of 1936, 1972, 1976, 1980 and 1984 are all recognized for their geo-political importance. In the material that follows, the extent to which global politics shaped the Games and, more important, contoured the nature of world-class, high-performance sport in the modern era, will become fully apparent. Rhetoric aside, Olympic sport has always been both "political" and "Political."

The following chapters are organized around different themes or issues related to performance enhancement as it has emerged in the real world of high-performance sport in the modern era. The study begins with a focus on the principles and objectives Pierre Coubertin placed at the foundation of his Olympic project. Coubertin revived the Games to bring the youth of the world together in a chivalrous bond of brothers-in-arms so that in the cauldron of athletic competition they would develop the character traits needed to lead Europe out of its spiritual and moral decline. These fundamental principles justified the IOC's strict regulation of the practices it would permit in its Games. The chapter traces challenges to those principles during the first half of the twentieth century, through the politically and commercially motivated assaults of the post-World War II period, to their demise in 1974. The cold war years from the mid-1940s to 1974 are brought into sharp focus because this period marked the emergence of a growing emphasis on performance and victory which challenged, and eventually undermined, the Movement's fundamental principles. The chapter demonstrates that from 1952 onwards, the emphasis on performance enhancement, fueled by cold war ideology and the use of selected performance-enhancing substances on both sides of the iron curtain, led to the eventual all-out pursuit of the linear record.

From their outset, the Olympic Games have traded heavily in myth, symbolism and imagery. Coubertin saw the Games as an elaborate, inspiring ceremony that would lift the human spirit. In contrast to his dream of sporting competition "radiant with sunlight, exalted by music, [and] framed in the architecture of porticoes," Fascism in Europe evoked, and relied upon, symbols of power, domination, dark determination, and absolute victory at any cost.[28] Chapter Two explores how the long shadow of the Nazi war machine and the social and political paranoia of the cold war fueled the deepest suspicions people hold about the Games, the nature of high-performance sport in the modern era and, in particular, the use of steroids and other performance-enhancing substances. It was in the inaugural cold war confrontation in 1952 that rumors of steroid use began. Totalitarian symbolism conjured fears of "Frankenstein athletes" and east bloc females unwillingly subjected to the androgynous effects of steroids for the communist cause. Uncertain of the extent to which the Soviets would go in the pursuit of victory and recognizing the threat east bloc female athletes posed to the notion of "appropriate" female athleticism, this chapter demonstrates that the simultaneous introduction of "sex tests" and the list of banned substances and practices was not coincidental. The impact this period had upon the western psyche explains some of the deep anxieties that continue to haunt those who fear the use of performance-enhancing substances in high-performance sport today.

Most arguments defending the restriction of performance-enhancing practices rely upon "sport" as an abstract, universal entity. By looking at a single country, over time, Chapter Three undermines that basic assumption. Sport, it turns out, can only be understood within its specific, socio-historical context, as material drawn from the German Turners, the Workers' Sport Movement and the Bourgeois Sport Movement in Germany, as well as the "coordinated" sport of Nazi Germany, sport under "Real Existing Socialism," and the bourgeois sport of West Germany demonstrates. Beginning with turn of the century ideas in German physiology and medicine, this chapter also documents how the concept of "training" changed through the 1920s and 1930s, due to influences of the Harvard Fatigue Laboratory and Fredrick Winslow Taylor's Scientific Management, through to the current domination of science, technology and instrumental rationality today. World-class, high-performance sport in the twenty-first century is now an intensive, exhausting occupation where athletes are fully embroiled in sophisticated training regimes utilizing scientifically developed technologies that create long-term physiological and personality changes as they progress through the high-stakes, winner-takes-all road to the pinnacle of world-class sport.

Chapters Four and Five use the high-performance sport systems of the German Democratic Republic (GDR) and the Federal Republic of Germany (FRG) as case studies in the development of high-performance sport in the east and west from the post-World War II period to the present. Chapter Four focuses on the war in the eastern front to set the appropriate context for how East Germans felt about Soviet occupation, Stalin's plans for Germany, and Walter Ulbricht's ability to pursue his own interests in the GDR while cultivating an independent East German pride. Sport was a major vehicle for that latter objective. Sport in the FRG, the chapter documents, developed entirely differently as the western Allies imposed Directive Number 23, "The Limitation and Demilitarization of Sport in Germany," to build a decentralized, thoroughly democratic, federated sport system in West Germany.

Chapter Five details how far world-class, high-performance sport moved from Coubertin's original project. Despite their differences, high-performance sport in East and West Germany required an increasingly full-time commitment as both systems came to rely on professionalized athletes, ever more sophisticated scientific knowledge and cutting-edge expertise to reach the podium at the Olympic Games. The IOC's decision to hold the 1972 Games in Munich was a major catalyst for the transformation of international sport in the FRG, the GDR and worldwide. A second theme in the chapter concerns the GDR's unprecedented investment of resources, personnel, and research activity in high-performance sport. Although many attribute that nation's success to the use of performance-enhancing substances, this chapter offers a very different scenario. Finally, the material presented makes the case that although television and various commercial interests significantly shaped world-class sport in the 1970s and 1980s, it was the immediate and long-term political goals of the GDR and other nation-states that played at least as decisive a role in shaping high-performance sport today. The legacy of World War II reaches much further than many realize.

Most critiques of performance-enhancing substances centre on the ethics of their use. The IOC, ISFs, and WADA use straightforward proscriptive generalizations to justify their policies of prohibition but the real historical development of high-performance sport systems and the performance-enhancing practices associated with them involve complex social forces that are unmoved by moral condemnation. Chapter Six examines the main ethical arguments used to justify and uphold the IOC's ban – certain performance-enhancing substances are unethical because their use violates the "spirit of sport," they eliminate the "fair and level playing field," and they are a danger to the health and well-being of athletes. When examined within the context of the real world of high-performance sport, each of these propositions fails to meet its burden of proof. Winning and the scientific, technologically assisted pursuit of the linear record have become the central ethos of the Olympic Games. Policies concerning performance enhancement will only be meaningful and effective if they recognize that world-class athletes are engaged in an enterprise that is marked by an unqualified zeal for victory, where record breaking performances are pursued by full-time, professional athletes, and training and competition are part of an all-encompassing, year-round occupation.

In addition to enumerating the policy implications that evolve from this study of performance enhancement in modern sport, Chapter Seven presents a phenomenological examination of the work world of high-performance athletes. World-class, high-performance sport, the chapter shows, is not for the uncommitted. While Coubertin sought to establish a chivalric, international brotherhood-in-arms through his revival of the Olympics, just over a century later the Games are contests among athletes who have fully dedicated a major portion of their entire being to the pursuit of Olympic gold. Cut, hardened, powerful, resolute, and combat-ready, Olympic athletes enter the highly competitive arenas of world-class sport as it has grown out of the legacy of World War II, the cold war struggles between east and west, the domination of scientific rationality and the pressures of commercial and consumer cultures in the modern era. Performance enhancement can only be understood and changed on the basis of that socio-historical reality.

1 From Coubertin's dream to high-performance sport

The shifting dynamics of Olympic sport

To complete its "intellectual journey," a sociological analysis must examine the intersection of personal biography and the history of social structure.[1] Nowhere is this truer than in the serious study of high-performance athletes and their use of performance-enhancing substances in world-class sport at the present time. Unfortunately, few investigations of performance enhancement complete this journey. Instead, well-entrenched biases, personal values and vested interests guide much of the work on drugs and sport, which is only to be expected since the decision to proscribe selected means for improving athletic performance was the result of complex political negotiation in the first place. The restriction of certain substances is governed by three different groups, which may not always share the same objectives – the IOC, the different ISFs and WADA.[2]

Leaders in positions of legitimate authority have the right to structure and enact policies and to impose sanctions on those who violate them. Those leaders may even feel morally and ethically justified in their actions despite widespread disregard for their regulations. Nevertheless, a policy's ongoing legitimacy ultimately rests on how internally consistent it is with an organization's fundamental principles and the actual social practices that arise from them. When policy diverges from principle and practice, it can only be enforced for so long before it meets growing resistance and concerted opposition.

This chapter examines the principles and vision Baron Pierre Coubertin used to found and justify his revival of the ancient Olympic Games. It shows how his philosophy became tied to the ideal of the amateur athlete at the turn of the century and indicates some of the early challenges Coubertin's principles faced. The analysis indicates how the IOC responded to the challenges that arose throughout the first half of the twentieth century and on into the post-World War II era before abandoning the Movement's founding principles in the 1974 change to Rule 26 of the *Olympic Charter*. The discussion demonstrates how that single decision undermined the legitimate, principled restriction of performance-enhancing substances and practices.

The second focus of this chapter is the social construction of high-performance sport from the beginning of the cold war to the 1970s. The growing emphasis on performance and victory during this period challenged, and eventually undermined, the Movement's fundamental principles while also creating the conditions in which the use of performance-enhancing substances became widespread in east and west bloc countries.

The main thesis in the ensuing argument is that Coubertin's original principles justified the prohibition of performance-enhancing substances, but the 1974 change to Rule 26 of the *Charter,* and the reasons for that change, removed the central, principled foundation upon which the list of banned substances was based. The list's legitimacy was open to question after 1974. In tracing this complex and important history of the Games' fundamental principles and linking it directly to the question of performance-enhancing substance use, the chapter presents the first component of an argument concerning why the grounds for the IOC's decision to ban selected means of performance enhancement no longer hold.

Baron Pierre Coubertin and the principles of the ancient Games

Baron Pierre Coubertin's primary motive for initiating the modern Olympic Games was to establish an educationally oriented project that would reverse the spiritual and moral decline he, and others, attributed to the growing materialism of nineteenth century industrial capitalism. "At the end of the nineteenth century, a century that was profoundly evolutionary but filled with illusory projects," Coubertin wrote in 1929, "continental Europe, and France in particular, needed educational reform urgently." Male youth lacked "drive and passion," it was "living in greyness" and it required the "garden to cultivate the will that organized sports provide."[3]

In his final speech as IOC President, Coubertin argued that the educational philosophy in Europe had allowed "the present generations to stray into the impasse of excessive specialization, where they will find nothing but obscurity and disunity." "They believe" he continued,

> they are very powerful because they have great appetites, and they believe they are very wise because they have a great deal of scientific data. In reality, they are poorly prepared for the troubles ahead. Intelligence is smothered by knowledge, critical minds are debased by an overwhelming mass of facts, and adolescents are trained into the mentality of the anthill, surrounded by the artificial and the accepted, with categories and statistics, a fetish for numbers, an unhealthy search for detail and the exception.[4]

To change the fate and future of Europe, Coubertin believed that educational reform was required and it should follow the principles found in the muscular Christianity of England's Canon Charles Kingsley and the Reverend Thomas Arnold as well as the ceremony and religious spiritualism of the ancient Olympic Games.[5] In contrast to the mind–body dualism that dominated educational philosophy in nineteenth century Europe, Coubertin promoted the classical Greek idea that humans are comprised of mind, body and character. Since the Greeks believed that character "is not formed by the mind, it is formed above all by the body," sport and physical activity, according to Coubertin, had to play a major role in reviving the spirit, drive, and passion of European youth.[6]

Coubertin believed that a revival of the Olympic Games would engender "a marvelous solidification of the human machine;" the Games would foster "a delicate balance of mind and body, the joy of a fresher and more intense life, the harmony of the faculties, a calm and happy strength" provided they had a sound philosophical foundation, pursued lofty goals, and followed a religious, ceremonial format similar to the ancient Games.[7] Without a sound foundation the Games would "decline into commercialism and into the mud"; they would be indistinguishable from numerous other world championships.[8] In stark contrast to the "simple athletics" which Olympic sport "encompasses and surpasses," the Games were to be a lofty, uplifting experience that built character, spirit, and vision. Coubertin's image of the revived Olympic Games is compelling:

> The athlete enjoys his effort. He likes the constraint that he imposes on his muscles and nerves, through which he comes close to victory even if he does not manage to achieve it. This enjoyment remains internal, egotistical in a way. Imagine if it were to expand outward, becoming intertwined with the joy of nature and the flights of art. Picture it radiant with sunlight, exalted by music, framed in the architecture of porticoes. It was thus that the glittering dream of ancient Olympism was born on the banks of the Alphaeus, the vision of which dominated ancient society for so many centuries.[9]

For Coubertin, the Games would rise far above the fray of day-to-day life at the turn of the century in Europe and constitute a noble calling for Europe's future leaders. "We hope to build a temple" Coubertin wrote, "while a great free-for-all will be held on the plain. The temple will last, and the free-for-all will pass."[10]

Athletes, according to Coubertin, would have to choose between the sacred and the profane. The pure sport of the revived Olympics would bolster the souls of its participants; the Games would be like a religion with their own cathedrals, dogmas, and service. "But above all" they would involve "a religious feeling" in which athletes embraced "the spirit of chivalry – what you here [in England] so pleasantly call 'fair play'."[11]

The Olympic temple and the spirit of Olympism had no room for sport that was tainted by commercialism or an overly competitive zeal. Ribbons, trophies and prize money were for the fair grounds of the world; the Games were for those who chose to cultivate the spirit of Olympism. Coubertin stated that "fair or temple sportsmen must make their choice; they cannot expect to frequent both one and the other ... let them choose!" This image of a sacred sport experience, taking place amid pageant and circumstance, was central to Coubertin's vision.

Shifting away from religion, Coubertin also wanted the athletes of the Games to form "an *aristocracy*, an *elite*" which would "also be a *knighthood*" – "'brothers-in-arms', brave energetic men united by a bond that is stronger than that of mere camaraderie, which is powerful enough in itself." The Games would be chivalrous where "the idea of competition, of effort opposing effort for the love of effort itself, of courteous yet violent struggle, is superimposed on the notion of mutual assistance."[12]

"Athletae proprium est se ipsum noscere, ducere et vincere – it is the duty and the essence of the athlete to know, to lead and to conquer himself." This motto, which Coubertin drafted along with the better-known maxim "Citius, Altius, Fortius," encapsulates the "whole lesson in manly athletic education." "The transposition from the muscular to the moral sphere, the basis of athletic education," is captured clearly and concisely in the Latin dictum.[13]

The only athletes who appeared to have the potential to embody, exhibit, and further the principles of Coubertin's Olympic Movement were the amateur athletes of the late nineteenth and early twentieth centuries. The amateur, aristocratic athletes were the only group that could approach sport purely as a means for self-improvement and they appeared to have the requisite background to become future European leaders. As a result, the amateur athlete became the fundamental element of Coubertin's Games.

The extent to which the "amateur athlete" became the central pillar of the Movement missed Coubertin's main point. His image and plan were more subtle and profound; they can only be understood with reference to classical Greece and nineteenth century England – societies for which, Barrington Moore points out, the conceptions of privilege and the gentleman were extremely important.[14] In both societies it was felt that "only a limited number of persons were believed capable of achieving full aristocratic status." In both societies, Moore notes, "the 'real' ruler–gentleman was a qualitatively distinct form of humanity." This was the type of leader Coubertin sought to shape and build within the crucible of the Olympic Games.

"Anyone who studies the ancient Games will perceive that their deep significance was due to two principal elements: beauty and reverence" Coubertin wrote.

> If the modern Games are to exercise the influence I desire for them they must in their turn show beauty and inspire reverence – a beauty and a reverence infinitely surpassing anything hitherto realized in the most important athletic contests of our day. The grandeur and dignity of processions and attitudes, the impressive splendour of ceremonies, the concurrence of all the arts, popular emotion and generous sentiment, must all in some sort collaborate together.[15]

Given the emphasis he placed upon the classical conception of the "ruler–gentleman" and the importance beauty, pageantry, and reverence played in his image of the Games, Coubertin was not persuaded that the amateur athlete of the late nineteenth and early twentieth century was necessarily the type of participant he sought for the Games. In his memoirs, Coubertin candidly noted, "My own conception of sport has always been very different from that of a large number – perhaps the majority – of sportsmen." "To me," he continued,

sport was a religion with its church, dogmas, service ... but above all a religious feeling, and it seemed to me as childish to make all this depend on
whether an athlete had received a five franc coin as automatically to consider the parish verger an unbeliever because he receives a salary for looking
after the church.[16]

Honor, rather than one's amateur status, was the criterion Coubertin wanted to
determine who could take part in the Olympic experience. "We must establish
the tradition," he wrote, "that each competitor shall in his bearing and conduct
as a man of honour and a gentleman endeavour to prove in what respect he holds
the Games and what an honour he feels to participate in them." The Games
would be a spectacle in which the arts, with their color and integrative capacities, would provide "a worthy setting for the Games, a setting in which athletes
shall move well prepared to assist in the great festival, and shall be conscious of
the special glory it confers on them." And to confirm the integrity of the Games
and the athletes' commitment to their genuine spirit, Coubertin would "revive ...
the [ancient Games'] ceremony of the oath."[17]

Because he could not gain the IOC's full agreement on the role that classical
athletic honor would play in deciding eligibility for the Games, Coubertin ultimately accepted the restriction of the Games to amateur athletes as a first step. For
Coubertin, the amateur restriction was far less limiting than he wanted – "amateur"
was simply a category of status. Honor was a commitment of the individual to specific values, goals and objectives and an element of the chivalric code which was
central to the traditional European values that he sought to re-establish.

Immediate challenges to Coubertin's principles

In the pursuit of popular recognition for his new Movement, Coubertin was forced
to deal almost immediately with challenges from existing sporting traditions that
were incompatible with, or rivals to, his proposals. In preparation for the inaugural 1896 Games in Athens, British, German, American and French officials all
resisted the IOC's amateur restriction. Officials from those nations wanted to use
the Games as a vehicle to demonstrate the national strength and vigor of their
respective countries. Each felt they could best achieve that goal by bringing the
world's best athletes together – amateur or not. The IOC's restrictions excluded
too many of the world's top competitors and threatened to make the Games, in
the eyes of different national sports leaders, a second-rate competition.

Coubertin also faced challenges over the nature of the events featured in the
Games. Leaders of the German Turner Movement and the French Gymnastics
Movement, who supported non-competitive, mass demonstrations of tumbling,
pyramid building, and synchronized acrobatics, argued that their sport forms rep-
resented Coubertin's ideals better than the competitive games of England which
Coubertin supported.[18]

Commercial interests were the strongest influences that Coubertin had to confront in launching his project. In the first few decades of the twentieth century,

the "universal market," where all aspects of human life, including sport and leisure activities, were turned into commodities that could be bought and sold, was already well established. The tension between the logic of the market and Coubertin's ideals for the Games was obvious from the outset. "No matter what the intentions of the founders of the modern Olympics," Richard Gruneau and Hart Cantelon point out, "the actual possibilities open to them were limited by the nature of the economic system as a whole and the network of social institutions associated with it."[19] In a market economy, any large-scale undertaking would have to rely at least somewhat on commercial interests. Land was required, facilities had to be constructed, finances had to be raised; the Games could not insulate themselves from the material world of commerce and finance. Without the financial largesse of wealthy businessman George Averoff, for example, the ancient stadium where the first modern Games were held would not have been renovated in time.[20]

In contrast to Coubertin's vision of the Games as a force that would combat the crass materialism of the market, organizers of subsequent Games also formed agreements with commercial powerbrokers and the Games were "drawn into the economic struggles of modern nation states."[21] The Games of Paris, St. Louis and London (1900, 1904 and 1908 respectively) were all held in conjunction with international exhibitions celebrating advancements in technology, science, industrial capitalism, and modern culture more generally – the very forces Coubertin blamed for the demise of the great traditions of Europe.

Coubertin's aim for non-commercial sport fell not only short of the mark but in a most tawdry fashion. In 1928, despite the IOC's vehement protests, the Amsterdam organizers sold rights packages to various companies, including Coca-Cola, which allowed advertising within the stadium and on various buildings in the vicinity of the Olympic venues.[22] The decision transformed Coubertin's sacred Games into a colossal billboard that celebrated the profane world of modern commerce. To show how far the Games were dragged from Coubertin's lofty dreams, from the 1930s through to the early 1950s the IOC and the United States Olympic Association fought American bread maker Paul Helms over the use of the Olympic name and five-ring insignia which he used to advertise his bread.[23] Contrary to the impression of many, the Games' struggle against commercialism was a major concern from the Movement's earliest days.

With respect to the "amateur question" itself, the restriction of Games participants to amateur athletes was equally problematic and one of the Movement's earliest struggles centered on the issue. As a truly international sport with a rabid following, soccer was excluded from the first Olympiad because it was already well on the way to complete professionalization by the turn of the twentieth century. The Fédération Internationale de Football Association (FIFA) could not stage world-class soccer at the Games while conforming to the IOC's code of amateurism, but the sport was too popular internationally to be excluded from the Games indefinitely. When only 17 teams could take part in the 1928 Games, FIFA proposed a scheme of "broken time payments" – payments to players for lost wages while competing – to enable better players and more teams to take part in 1932. Backed by the powerful International Amateur Athletic Federation (IAAF) and its firm adherence to a strict code of amateurism, the IOC rejected FIFA's proposal, so soccer was excluded from the 1932 Games. FIFA countered the snub by initiating its own world championship, the World Cup, in 1930. By 1936 a compromise was possible. The IOC wanted soccer and FIFA had no concerns about the amateur quality of the teams at the Games because it meant that the Olympics would not overshadow FIFA's World Cup. The Games provided an opportunity for the best amateur players to compete while the World Cup featured the best soccer in the world.[24] Holding firm to its principles, the IOC had successfully addressed the first, serious challenge to the fundamental premises that it had embodied in the amateur athlete.

Even though FIFA's breakaway was a unique event and most ISFs complied with and supported the Amateurism Code, constant tensions within the Games kept bringing the issue back onto the IOC's agenda. In the era of capitalist empire building, National Olympic Committees (NOCs) had already begun to use the Games as an indicator of national strength and vitality, which resulted in complaints that other NOCs were using athletes who did not conform to the requirements of amateurism. Before World War I, for example, the British complained that American athletes were not amateurs and in the 1930s there were complaints about the professionalized training procedures employed by the Germans.[25] Commenting years after the event, British sports administrator Jack Crump complained of German training methods in Berlin in 1936.

> We had the impression that we were competing against a scientifically organized machine. For example, after each event the German athletes were taken into a room and their blood pressure and other tests were taken. It was all very serious and highly planned and to my mind the antithesis of amateur sport.[26]

Despite the continued debate around the concept of amateurism, the IOC, in concert with the ultra-conservative IAAF, held firm to the central principle of Coubertin's Games.[27]

Olympic principles and the reality of cold war sport

The modern Games have always faced the divisive tension between its lofty principles and the logic of athletic conquest. In 1908 Coubertin contrasted his Olympic principles with "a second and quite different point of view – that of organized competition. Athletics for the sake of winning something." Coubertin recognized that the cult of victory was a "dangerous canker with which we have to reckon."[28] True to his fear, as the Olympics grew in status, winning became an overriding concern as countries increasingly viewed the Games as a powerful propaganda vehicle, and commercial interests became more involved with the Games. At the same time, the scientific rationality that dominated so many spheres of twentieth century life gradually made its presence felt in the realm of sport. In the immediate post-World War II period, these three factors threatened to change the Games irrevocably unless the IOC could stem the tide.

At the IOC's first post-war conference in 1946, Swedish delegate Bo Ekelund forcefully argued that the distinction between amateur and professional athletes should be abolished.[29] Avery Brundage led the defense of Coubertin's principles by strongly attacking the excesses of sport and the crass materialism to which it was being reduced. He saw these excesses as "purely a divertissement."[30] A year later, at the Stockholm Session of the IOC, as Chair of the Amateur Commission Brundage wanted to formally enshrine the Movement's central philosophy in the *Olympic Charter*. Brundage wanted the *Charter* to clearly define the category of athlete who could participate in the Games and thereby exclude those who were motivated by the cult of victory and end the practices that had already begun to "corrupt" the Movement in the pre-World War II period. "An amateur is one whose connection with sport is and always has been solely for pleasure," Brundage contended, "and for the physical, mental or social benefits he derives therefrom and to whom sport is nothing more than recreation without material gain of any kind, direct or indirect."[31] Echoing Coubertin's basic principles, Brundage firmly believed and preached that the amateur code, "coming to us from antiquity, contributed to and strengthened by the noblest aspirations of great men of each generation, embraces the highest moral laws. No philosophy, no religion," he continued, "preaches loftier sentiments."[32] This was the spirit of Olympism; it was an accurate reflection of Coubertin's ideal; but it also increasingly conflicted with the socio-historical conditions of sport in the post-World War II era.

Although the Americans had been accused many times of sending "professional" athletes to the Games, and their approach to international sport was criticized for its apparent win-at-all-costs philosophy, it was the return of the Union of Soviet Socialist Republics (USSR) to the Games in 1952 that initiated the greatest challenge to Coubertin's principles. As competitive as the Americans were, the Soviets were fully committed to winning Olympic gold.

Immediately after World War II, the USSR was determined to "overtake the most advanced industrial powers [of the world]" in all realms of social life, including sport.[33] Under Stalin, for whom ethical considerations rarely mattered, the Council of People's Commissars of the USSR established, in October 1945, a financial reward system based on athletes' performances. The Soviets also developed a sport infrastructure that included housing and training facilities where top-level athletes could concentrate on systematically planned training regimes to improve their performances.[34] The Soviets did not, however, seek immediate inclusion in the Games even though there was a certain pragmatic willingness within the IOC to include the USSR in the Olympic family. Instead, the USSR engaged in a number of manoeuvres which kept the IOC and selected ISFs off balance and guessing about Soviet intentions.

The sport reward system contravened IOC and most ISFs' regulations and despite communications between the Soviets and Brundage from the IOC, and Sigfrid Edstrøm, president of the IAAF, the USSR did nothing to make its system conform to the requirements of amateurism. Nevertheless, in August 1946, a team of athletes from the Soviet Union arrived to compete at the European Championships even though they had no standing with the IAAF and violated its eligibility requirements. David Burghley, acting IAAF head, granted the USSR permission to compete. A similar incident occurred at the 1946 World Weightlifting Championships. Each incident gave the Soviet system increasing legitimacy despite its financial reward system and its centralized, state planning.

In January 1947, the USSR formally applied for membership in the International Wrestling Federation and the IAAF, but attached several conditions, including the adoption of Russian as an official ISF language. Brundage warned Edström in a January 21, 1947 letter that the political organization of the Soviet sport system and the payments to athletes violated the Games' principles. In any application for membership in an ISF, Brundage advised, the Soviets "must not be given any special consideration and their athletes must not be admitted to international or Olympic competition unless we are positively certain they are amateurs. Any other course," he emphasized, "will invite disaster."[35] Following almost a year of negotiation, Burghley, on behalf of the IAAF, admitted the USSR in December 1947 after its officials agreed to eliminate the Soviet's financial reward system and assured the ISF that its athletes held real jobs outside of their athletic endeavors.[36]

The USSR did not meet all of the IOC's criteria for participation in the Games in time for the 1948 London Games but the Soviets were ready by 1952.[37] For two very different, but interrelated reasons, the Helsinki Games were a momentous transition point in the history of the Olympic Movement. First, Avery Brundage was elected to what became a 20-year term as President of the IOC. Of all IOC leaders, Brundage was the most impassioned defender of Coubertin's fundamental principles and vision for the Games.

Second, the drama of a no-holds-barred athletic confrontation between the two emerging, post-World War II superpowers arose with the USSR's entry into the Helsinki Games. The direct antithesis to Coubertin's lofty aspirations, the ensuing east–west confrontation animated and changed the Games forever. Brundage, however, adopted the position that Coubertin would have also taken. The Games, he argued, were the beacon that could guide the superpowers to the successful resolution of their differences. "Sport," Brundage noted at the end of several speeches at the time,

> which still keeps the flag of idealism flying, is perhaps the most saving grace in the world at the moment, with its spirit of rules kept, and regard for the adversary, whether the fight is going for or against. When, if ever, the spirit of sport, which is the spirit of fair play, reigns over international affairs, the cat force, which rules there now, will slink away, and human life emerge for the first time from the jungle.[38]

At the Helsinki Games, the drama of the first superpower confrontation unfolded before a world audience. Despite the Soviets' early, almost insurmountable lead in the opening days of the Games, the Americans overtook them on the last day of competition. While the east–west confrontation brought tremendous excitement to the Games, it also initiated the most formidable challenge to Coubertin's founding principles. The cold, calculated pursuit of victory emerged as a dominating principle from the 1952 Games.

Aside from the importance placed on the USA–USSR confrontation, two additional features of the competition were extremely important. The first was the Soviet women's domination of their American counterparts. Even though the American media could minimize the importance of the women's events for one Olympiad, and hail US victories in the men's events, in the overall struggle between political systems it was total medals and total points that counted and the Americans could not ignore either the Soviet women or their own. The nature, importance, and approach to women's sport changed fundamentally from those Games onwards.

The three golds, three silvers and one bronze the Soviets won in weightlifting was the second outcome of significance. Those seven medals were a major catalyst in the rapid and widespread use of synthetic steroids in world-class, high-performance sport. Watching the Soviets carefully, American weightlifting coach Bob Hoffman told Associated Press that he knew the Soviets were "taking the hormone stuff to increase their strength."[39] At the 1954 World Weightlifting Championships, Hoffman and team physician John Ziegler satisfied themselves that the Soviets were using testosterone.[40] In the heightened patriotic climate of the time, Ziegler returned to the USA and with assistance from Ciba Pharmaceutical Company, oversaw the development of the synthetic steroid methandieone (brand name Dianabol).[41] Ziegler then gave Dianabol to the weightlifters at the York Barbell Club in Pennsylvania.[42] "The news of anabolic steroids spread through the athletic community like wildfire" Bob Goldman notes, "and soon drugs and stories of drugs became the chief topic of conversation at training camps and the subject of articles in all of the sports magazines."[43] The American weightlifters had quickly levelled the playing field and, as Yesalis and Bahrke indicate, by the mid-1960s "most of the top-ranking throwers began using anabolic steroids." The list cited in Yesalis and Bahrke included Randy Matson, the 1968 Olympic champion and world-record holder in the shot put, 1964 Olympic shot put champion Dallas Long, 1956 Olympic gold medal hammer thrower Harold Connolly, and world-record holding decathlete Russ Hodge.[44]

Despite the fact that steroids would eventually become the most sinister performance-enhancing substance because they appeared to transform human physiology in the pursuit of victory, it was Danish cyclist Knud Jensen's death, allegedly from an overdose of nicotinyl alcohol in combination with amphetamines, at the 1960 Summer Games that led the IOC to vigorously reassert the fundamental principles upon which the Games were based.[45] Jensen and other cyclists' crass embrace of an unqualified commitment to victory had pulled down the ancient Greek pillars upon which Coubertin's lofty ideals were set and dragged the Games "into the mud" of crass materialism and commercial gain. The shadow of the cult of victory loomed ominously above the Movement.

Rule 28 of the *Olympic Charter*, the death knell of Coubertin's principles

The IOC moved quickly to reassert the Games' central principles at the 1961 Athens session by trying to formally control the type of athlete who could participate in the Games. Brundage hoped that a bureaucratic regulation could safeguard Coubertin's principles. At the 1962 Moscow session, Brundage succeeded in his quest to entrench Coubertin's principles in the *Olympic Charter* by restricting the Games to amateur athletes.[46] At the same time, with the use of performance-enhancing substances by male and female athletes spreading on both sides of the iron curtain, the IOC knew that it still had to address the growing drive for Olympic victory at any cost; the Olympics had to be drug-free. To this end, Brundage established the IOC's first Medical Committee to investigate drug use in sport and to recommend how the IOC could ensure the integrity and purity of the Games.

At the 1964 Tokyo meetings, the Medical Committee recommended that the IOC condemn drug use, introduce testing, have athletes sign a statement that they were drug-free, and sanction individuals and National Sport Organizations implicated in drug use.[47] Three years later, the IOC defined what it would henceforth term "doping." The addition of Rule 28 to the *Olympic Charter* formally prohibited "the use of substances or techniques in any form or quantity alien or unnatural to the body with the exclusive aim of obtaining an artificial or unfair increase of performance in competition."[48] While the action was decisive, it only partially met the recommendation of the head of the IOC Medical Commission, Sir Arthur Porritt. He argued that "only a long-term education policy stressing the physical and moral aspects of the drug problem" would stop athletes from using performance-enhancing substances.[49]

Educating athletes about the physical risks of substance use, in the wake of Jensen's death and the 1967 Tour de France death of Tommy Simpson, appeared almost unnecessary, yet the creation of a list of banned substances satisfied those who believed athletes' health would be protected by regulating their activities. If performance-enhancing substances were forbidden, and if athletes complied, their health would not be at risk.

The moral dimension of Porritt's concerns stemmed directly from Coubertin's fundamental principles and image of the Games – morally sound athletes competing in the spirit of chivalry and fair play so that brothers-in-arms would be united by bonds that were stronger than those of mere camaraderie. The overly competitive zeal demonstrated in the use of performance-enhancing substances fell outside the Movement's moral code. This was the educational message Porritt wanted Olympic athletes to receive.

Finally, the change to the *Charter* directly addressed the most extreme manifestations of scientific rationality and the cult of victory that increasingly threatened to undermine and debase the Olympic project. The legitimacy of Rule 28 and the IOC's opposition to the social forces of world-class, high-performance sport rested in the Movement's continuing claim to Coubertin's heritage, his philosophy of Olympism, and its fundamental principles, irrespective of whether or not the IOC articulated that rationale.

As precise and restrictive as the IOC tried to be, its bureaucratic solution could not hold back the actual social practices that existed, and were gaining force, in the world of high-performance sport even as they diverged further and further from the regulative Amateurism Code and the ban on certain substances. The USA and the USSR were not the only countries pursuing victory with increasingly single-minded determination.

On October 1, 1948, Walter Ulbricht, the first General Secretary of the Central Committee of the Socialist Unity Party (Sozialistische Einheitspartei Deutschlands–SED), decided to use sport as one of the major vehicles for raising the profile of the German Democratic Republic (GDR) internationally and to build national pride domestically.[50] Initially, Ulbricht used all four of the main, national level, Communist Party organizations – the Association of Free German Trade Unions, the Cultural Association for the Democratic Renewal of Germany, the Free German Youth, and the Democratic Women's Association of Germany – to actively shape the direction of sport in East Germany but the task was soon assigned to Erich Honecker as head of the Free German Youth.[51] Freshly returned from Moscow, Honecker embraced the same system that Stalin was developing in the USSR.

Honecker began with the resources of pre-World War II sport associations that were struggling to re-establish themselves and numerous industry-related sport associations (Betriebssportgemeinschaften), to initiate the rise of the East German sport system out of the ashes of a defeated Germany. In 1949, the SED established the State Committee for Physical Culture and Sport (Staatliches Komitee für Körperkultur und Sport–STAKO) and made it responsible for the rapid improvement of the GDR's athletes.[52] Specific sports such as track and field, swimming, gymnastics, boxing, cycling, wrestling, rowing, soccer, volleyball, basketball, and handball were singled out for particular emphasis.

In 1951, the GDR had established the German Institute for Physical Culture in Leipzig where coaches were trained, athletes developed, and research into performance enhancement was systematically conducted. The 1952 article, "Let's Learn from Soviet Union's Scientific Physical Education," which appeared in the official SED periodical *Einheit* [Unity], confirmed that the GDR's centralized program would adopt the Soviets' approach to the systematic pursuit of performance enhancement. By 1957, Honecker was in a position to focus even more resources upon world-class, high-performance sport and he placed the entire East German system in the hands of Manfred Ewald and the newly established German Gymnastics and Sport Federation (Deutscher Turn- und Sportbund–DTSB).[53] From that point on, the East Germans sought to extend themselves beyond not only the west but also the Soviet Union in world-class sport.[54]

Never complacent, the Soviets continued to develop their system throughout the 1960s as the Americans appeared increasingly vulnerable in world-class sport. Alongside the addition of sports boarding schools in 1962, the Soviets expanded their athlete talent pool and ranked an incredible 17 million athletes at various levels from local to regional to national. Some 400,000 athletes were included in the USSR's top rankings by 1965.[55]

In the west, it was politicians and sports leaders in the FRG who felt the most pressure to compete with the scientifically rationalized, performance oriented systems of the USSR and the GDR. At first, the FRG relied on its industrial and financial strength, its larger population base and the historical strengths of its voluntary, club-based sport system to provide the athletes needed to keep pace with the GDR. As international performances improved and training committ- ments extended in terms of daily time investment and the number of years required to compete successfully at the international level, the FRG's German Sport Federation (Deutscher Sportbund–DSB) recognized the need for change to improve West Germany's competitive position in world-class, high-performance sport. The first step was the formation of partnerships between corporations and high-performance athletes so they would not have to make undue career sacri- fices while committing themselves to world-class sport. The German Track and Field Association, for example, initiated a "Friends of Athletics" association in 1963 so that former track and field athletes could help current athletes secure sponsorships or other financial support. The German Gymnastics Association ran a similar program.[56]

The defeat of a number of West German athletes seeking spots on the com- bined FRG–GDR Olympic team in 1964 indicated that West Germany was quickly losing ground to East Germany. In view of the political symbolism associ- ated with an ascendant GDR just three years after the erection of the Berlin Wall, Friedel Schirmer, national coach for decathlon and Chair of the Sports Advisory Board of the Social Democratic Party's National Executive Committee, advanced several recommendations for sport development in the FRG. His "Theses Towards the Advancement of Physical Education and Sport" were quickly embraced by the Social Democratic Party. The FRG's other major politi- cal party, the Christian Democrats, also added a sport assistance program to its general platform.

The IOC's decision to hold the 1972 Games in Munich forced the FRG to provide further support for its athletes as the pursuit of gold medals took on heightened political significance. In 1967 the West Germans introduced The German Sport Assistance Foundation which oversaw an athlete ranking and reward system, and in 1969, the first West German sport boarding schools were opened.[57] These developments represented the first attempt in the west to coor- dinate an entire high-performance sport system to challenge east bloc rivals. In addition, the FRG's sport system would serve as a model for other western nations such as Canada, Australia and even the USA.[58]

Television, commercial interests and the Olympic ideal

Although government planning and coordination would become increasingly significant in shaping the world of high-performance sport, the market economy in the west was robust enough throughout the 1960s to attract and reward sport-ing goods manufacturers and athletes who were successful in their respective competitive arenas. Long before Nike was a major player, the Dassler brothers, Adolf (Adi) and Rudolf (Rudi), competed with each other as heads of the rival Adidas and Puma shoe manufacturers.[59] Similarly, a host of German and French ski manufacturers strove for superiority as they used the Winter Games to adver-tise their products to a world audience.[60]

Sporting goods manufacturers used the Games to broaden their markets and the best athletes in the west needed money to compete against the comparatively well-funded east bloc athletes. The best western athletes, television coverage, and the lucrative ski and shoe industries came together at the Games to form partnerships that would seriously undermine Brundage's efforts to keep the Games pure. "Under-the-table" performance fees and additional remuneration for winning medals and breaking records attracted the top athletes to interna-tional competitions; those athletes increased the size of television audiences and more viewers meant increased advertising revenue. All of these combined to stimulate the professionalization of high-performance sport in the cold war era.

The importance of television to the Games was discovered in the pre-World War II period. Nazi Germany, as part of its national propaganda campaign, had provided domestic television coverage in public viewing halls in parts of Berlin for the 1936 Games, but up to the mid-1950s the IOC had no official television policy and did not profit from television in any direct way. The 1956 Games in Melbourne changed the relationship between the Games and television forever. The Melbourne Olympic Organizing Committee (MOOC), seeking a new source of revenue, had the private media company, Fremantle Overseas and TV Incorporated, negotiate television rights packages with international networks. In response, broadcasters from the USA, Canada, Great Britain, and several European countries formed a cartel to protest MOOC's initiative and argued that the Olympic Games should be available to international media free of charge. Fremantle held firm and the television cartel chose to boycott coverage of the Games, leaving very limited exposure through the networks outside the cartel. MOOC kept the profits that were generated from the packaged highlights they sold to networks not covering the Games.[61]

From 1956 on, television rights became a divisive issue as IOC members were attracted to the potential for Olympic revenue while remaining concerned about the possible challenges the commercial medium might bring to the Movement's ideals. Brundage attempted to get the best of both worlds by carefully revising the *Olympic Charter* to permit the negotiation of television rights within a framework that would protect Coubertin's principles. In 1958, Rule 49 of the *Charter* was modified to permit the Organizing Committee of the Olympic Games to negoti-ate television rights for each Olympiad with the IOC holding final approval and the right to determine how the revenue would be distributed. The rule change allowed the IOC to benefit financially from television revenues but left the Organizing Committees exposed to any image problems that arose through dis-putes over the negotiations.[62]

The *Charter* revision permitted Brundage to keep the IOC out of direct negotiation with the new commercial television interests but allowed it to reap the
financial benefits of the market forces that were progressively influencing the
Movement. "This increase in commercial value [of TV rights]" Brundage wrote
in 1966, "can be of great use to the Olympic Movement if it is distributed properly ... [but] it can also be a great danger if Olympic ideals are not maintained."[63]
The genie in the television revenue bottle was more powerful than Brundage had
anticipated, as the commercial forces of television rights and sponsorship revenue, along with the political forces of the cold war, would radically reshape the
Movement in the last decades of the twentieth century.[64]

The amateur code and performance-enhancing substances in the post-war Games

With respect to amateurism, although there were no major changes to the
"Amateurism Code" at the 1964 Tokyo meetings, the pressures of the real world
of high-performance sport forced the IOC to extend the time athletes could
attend training camps from three to four weeks in any single year. At the 1967
meetings, Soviet delegate Constantin Andrianov opened up the eligibility
debate again when he noted that the IOC had argued about a definition of amateurism for more than 50 years. "The IOC," Andrianov maintained,

> endeavours to prove to the world its own point of view without taking into
> account the requirements of life and conditions in which modern sport is
> developing. This is one of the most knotty questions and it seems necessary
> to find a new approach to this problem, renouncing antiquated formulas of
> the amateur status, formulated at the end of the nineteenth century.[65]

"We should be able to muster sufficient courage" Andrianov continued, "and
in the face of modern requirements, to determine the new rules of amateur status, and not to cling to the former ones, which ... are very often violated."[66] He
then proposed "that the IOC should work out new eligibility rules for the
Olympic Games."[67]

Brundage held firm knowing that the Movement's fundamental principles
were embodied in the type of athlete Coubertin had originally admitted to the
Games. Even in the face of IOC–NOC joint commission reviews of the "eligibility question" in 1969 and 1970 and a proposal to rename Rule 26 as the
"Eligibility Code," Brundage barely wavered. Giving with one hand, Brundage
agreed to rename Rule 26, but he held decisively firm with the other by ensuring
that the criteria contained in the "Eligibility Code" were as restrictive as any previously employed by the IOC. As a result, the new code had a special section
clearly excluding many of the financial support strategies that were proliferating
in both the east and west. "Individuals subsidized by governments, educational
institutions, or business concerns because of their athletic ability" the new Code
stated,

are not amateurs. Business and industrial concerns sometimes employ athletes for their advertising value. The athletes are given paid employment
with little work to do and are free to practise and compete at all times. For
national aggrandizement, governments occasionally adopt the same methods and give athletes positions in the Army, on the police force, or in a
government office. They also operate training camps for extended periods.
Some colleges and universities offer outstanding athletes scholarships and
inducements of various kinds. Recipients of these special favours which are
granted only because of athletic ability are not eligible to compete in the
Olympic Games.[68]

With regard to the use of performance-enhancing substances, the IOC sought to
use its bureaucratic, regulative powers to eliminate this growing practice among
world-class athletes. At the Tehran meeting of 1967, the IOC adopted drug and
sex testing and generated its first list of banned substances which included alcohol, pep pills, cocaine, vasodilators, opiates, and hashish.[69] Formally and publicly
the IOC was attempting to ensure that Olympic athletes were not those who had
been corrupted by a professionalized, victory-at-all-cost orientation to sport; those
who were would be excluded from participation or detected and ejected from the
Games. While completely out of touch with the training regimes of world-class,
high-performance athletes in certain sports, the drug ban was consistent with the
Movement's fundamental principles – as fragile as they had become.

The IOC did not have a suitable test for anabolic, androgenic steroids until
1973 and did not test for them until the 1976 Games. In that interval, the shift
within world-class sport to an all-out assault on the linear record left the ban
with little more than moral authority.[70] Even though the record of steroid use in
the west is not as well documented as it is in the east, there is substantial evidence of the widespread use of performance-enhancing substances by the late
1960s. Pat Connolly, Charlie Francis, Charles Dubin, Werner Franke and
Brigitte Berendonk, and Terry Todd and Jan Todd all indicate that steroid use
was prevalent, if not pervasive, among numerous athletes in the west.[71]
Decathlete Tom Waddell's estimate that more than a third of all the male athletes attending the pre-Olympic training camp at Lake Tahoe in 1968 were using
steroids is typical of that period.[72]

In the context of east bloc sport systems, evidence released from the Ministry
for State Security (Ministerium für Staatssicherheit – Stasi) after the dissolution
of the GDR documents a tightly controlled and scientifically administered program of performance enhancement that first emerged in the 1960s. By the early
1970s it was fully integrated into the GDR's high-performance sport system and,
by 1974, official state policy.[73]

1974: the Olympic watershed

The 1969 and 1970 reports from the IOC–NOC joint commissions documented
the complete transformation of high-performance sport during the post-World

War II period. Research showed that from 1950 to 1970 the time track athletes, for example, spent training had doubled and in some events even tripled. The training regimes of the late 1960s and early 1970s significantly increased the physical demands placed on athletes. The workload grew as one or more of five different variables were altered. Coaches changed the total volume of training, they increased the intensity in each session, some compressed more work into shorter time frames or increased the duration of work in training intervals, or reduced the recovery time between intervals.[74] In the eight years from 1960 to 1968, the average training distances for male swimmers in the USSR grew from 594.7 km to 1,064.0 km per month and the time devoted to high tempo work was augmented from 18.0 percent to 57.4 percent of a workout. The Soviet women increased their distances from an average of 482.4 km to 1,045.0 km and the percentage of each practice dedicated to high tempo work grew from 18.5 percent to 59.0 percent of a workout.[75] In addition, research indicated that performance increases were directly linked to the demands of training and the development of annual training plans in which the intensity of training varied allowing for more concentrated work in certain periods and more technically related work in others.[76]

In addition to a growing intensity in training, there was a trend towards initiating serious, systematic training at earlier and earlier ages. Based on the trend towards increased specialization at younger and younger ages, Tomasz Lempart argued that optimal success came from the introduction of systematic training during athletes' elementary school years.[77] These trends in athlete development had no connection at all to the virtuous, inspirational, character-building, chivalrous contests "of effort opposing effort for the love of effort itself, of courteous yet violent struggle" that Coubertin envisaged for his project.

The period from 1972 to 1974 was the watershed of the Olympic Movement. By 1970, it was increasingly obvious that the Olympic Games were absolutely and resolutely different from Coubertin's original vision. Downhill skiers in the Winter Games were the most "brazen in their subversion of Olympic rules," according to Brundage and represented the greatest threat to the Eligibility Code.[78] At the 1972 Sapporo Winter Games, in the midst of growing claims of hypocrisy and the clearest statement of eligibility in years, the IOC's Eligibility Commission had no choice but to disqualify Austrian skier Karl Schranz from the Games.[79] Schranz had not only received endorsement money – a practice common among skiers and other athletes at the time – but in a media interview in the Olympic Village, he stated that he earned $40,000 to $50,000 annually through appearance fees and endorsements.[80]

The "code of silence" on endorsement money was broken; the myth of the amateur athlete in world-class, high-performance sport in the latter third of the twentieth century was shattered. The IOC was at a major crossroad. Steps to genuinely exclude athletes who did not meet the criteria of the Eligibility Code would carry heavy financial costs; pretending the Code was enforced when it was not, would simply discredit the Movement. One interview, in an Olympic Village, toppled the central pillar of Coubertin's Movement.

The IOC decided to adjust to the reality of world-class sport rather than defend and maintain the Movement's founding principles. At the 1974 meetings a new Eligibility Code was introduced. "To be eligible for participation in the Olympic Games," Rule 26 now stated,

> a competitor must observe and abide by the Rules of the IOC and in addition the rules of his or her ISF as approved by the IOC, even if the federation's rules are more strict than those of the IOC [and] not have received any financial rewards or material benefit in connection with his or her sports participation, except as permitted in the bye-laws to this Rule.[81]

On the surface, the Rule appeared as restrictive as ever, but it crossed the threshold of the Movement's cardinal principles in three ways. First, athletes could, under the *Charter*'s bye-laws, receive financial reward and material benefit for their athletic prowess. Not only was the fundamental nature of the athlete taking part in the Games no longer an issue, the type of athlete taking part in the Games was the direct antithesis of the athletes Coubertin wanted at the Olympics. The IOC had cast aside the fundamental reason for reviving the ancient Olympic Games.

Second, the IOC had given the ISFs control over eligibility. Since ISFs determined standards of eligibility annually (not just once every four years), and various ISFs had strong incentives to admit increasingly professionalized athletes to their championships, the restrictions to fully professionalized, world-class, high-performance athletes were gone.

Third, the Eligibility Code no longer stated, reflected or reinforced Coubertin's essential principles. The Games were not centered any longer on the "chivalrous athletic effort" that could be "intertwined with the joy of nature and the flights of art." The "glittering dream of ancient Olympism ... born on the banks of the Alphaeus, the vision of which dominated ancient society for so many centuries" had been replaced by a regulation that recognized commercial interests, an unqualified zeal for competition, and full-time professional athletes. The IOC had adapted its *Charter* so that the Games would feature the best athletes in the world for whom sport was a full-time, year-round occupation. Winning and the conquest of the linear record were the new foundation of the Olympic Movement. The scientifically rational, technologically assisted pursuit of the limits to human physical performance was accepted as the central ethos of the Games: open access to the finances and, by association, other means needed in that pursuit was irrevocably recognized as legitimate.

Olympic principles and performance-enhancing substances

The 1974 change to Rule 26 of The *Olympic Charter* and the actual practices that constituted world-class, high-performance sport by the 1970s are directly relevant to the prohibition of performance-enhancing substances in several important ways. First, as this chapter documents, Baron Pierre Coubertin founded the modern Olympic Games as a far reaching, innovative, educational program that would end the growing materialism of industrial capitalism and return Europe to its traditional values. His Games were a means to a majestic end and never ends in themselves. Coubertin's project was premised upon the unique experience young men would gain by taking part in athletic competition that exuded beauty and inspired reverence – "a beauty and a reverence infinitely surpassing anything hitherto realized in the most important athletic contests of our day." The intense experience of the Games, appropriately controlled and tempered, would forge "an *aristocracy*, an *elite*" that would "also be a *knighthood*" – "'brothers-in-arms', brave energetic men united by a bond that is stronger than that of mere camaraderie." The chivalric code would reign supreme and the "the idea of competition, of effort opposing effort for the love of effort itself, of courteous yet violent struggle," would be "superimposed" on the principle of "mutual assistance."[82] The Games would produce a new, educated elite for Europe.

The history of the Olympic Games and western Europe unfolded vastly differently from how Coubertin had hoped it would. In fact, Europe followed the path Coubertin had feared and wanted to prevent. Commercial interests grew; narrow-minded nationalism flourished; sport became just another part of the growing world market. The principles of Coubertin's Games were not only at variance with the reality of European life in the mid- to late-twentieth century, but also unable to shape it in any meaningful way.

Recognizing it could not control or alter the real world of high-performance sport and wanting to continue to have the best athletes in the world at the Olympic Games, the IOC abandoned the cardinal principles of Coubertin's Olympic Movement and adapted the Games to the social realities of contemporary, world-class sport. The 1974 change to Rule 26 of the *Charter* proved that no principle or formal rule, no matter how central or sacrosanct to the Movement, was immutable.

Second, the rules regulating substance use were never themselves central to the Movement, although they were a corollary of Coubertin's original, lofty principles. The use of performance-enhancing substances, within the environment Coubertin wanted to create, was cheating. But it was also cheating to pursue sport on a full-time basis, to receive funding or state support, or to adopt a win-at-all costs attitude towards the Games.

Once the IOC cast aside the Games' fundamental principles, it also surrendered the philosophical grounds for justifying the prohibition of particular performance-enhancing substances. After 1974, the IOC formally opened the Games to world-class, high-performance athletes for whom sport was a full-time occupation. Even though those athletes had participated in the Games for years, they had been cheats before 1974. From then on, they were legitimate participants. The IOC accepted, with the 1974 change to Rule 26, the real social world of high-performance sport that had developed in the post-World War II era. The newly accepted world consisted of state funding, comprehensive, scientifically based, year-round training, an unreserved zeal for victory, an intense, personal commitment to the pursuit of medals, and a resolute drive to push performances

to the outer limits of human potential. The use of performance-enhancing substances is legitimately part of that world even though the IOC refused, and
continues to refuse, to admit such a reality.

Commenting on the IOC's perpetual "battle" against "doping," former IOC
executive member and current WADA President Richard Pound quoted Sir
Winston Churchill: "Never give in, never give in, never, never, never – in nothing, great or small, large or petty – never give in except to convictions of honour
and good sense."[83] Pound's comments reflect a common conviction among leaders in positions of authority who feel morally and ethically obligated to enact and
reinforce the policies upon which their organization's power rests. But an organization's legitimate authority is genuine only as long as it is consistent with its
history, principles and practices. The IOC's history demonstrates a radical dis-
juncture between the principles it has espoused, those that it currently enshrines
in its *Charter* and its practices since the end of World War II. The IOC's position
on performance-enhancing substances is just one example of its own internal
contradictions in the present day. While there may be reasons to limit the use of
selected performance-enhancing substances and practices, the IOC, in 1974, cast
aside any rationale that could be made in principle.

2 Steroids

Nazi propaganda, cold war fears, and "androgenized" women

The manifesto of the Communist Party opens with a dramatic and chilling image: "Ein Gespenst geht um in Europa – das Gespenst des Kommunismus [A specter is stalking Europe – the specter of communism"]. But the first English publication of the manifesto must have eased the fears of the bourgeoisie as Helen Macfarlane translated Marx's forewarning as: "A frightful hobgoblin stalks throughout Europe. We are haunted by a ghost, the ghost of communism."[1]

After the fall of the Berlin Wall and the disintegration of the USSR, it seems that Macfarlane may have been more prescient than Marx – communism, Soviet style at least, appears to have been not much more than "a frightful hobgoblin." But in international, high-performance sport there are still specters that stalk about western Europe and North America, none more chilling to the leadership of the IOC, WADA, or the ISFs than the hyper-masculinizing powers attributed to anabolic, androgenic steroids.

Western Europe and North America were first haunted by anabolic steroids when it was rumored that National Socialist (Nazi) Germany was creating hyper-masculinized, ultra-aggressive combat soldiers by injecting the Schutzstaffel (SS) troops with steroids. After World War II, the steroid specter continued to stalk western Europe and North America as allegedly testosterone-enriched male and androgenized female communist athletes dominated the Olympics' strength events. But was the specter of anabolic, androgenic steroids a ghost that should have struck such fear, or was it merely a frightful hobgoblin that should have been laid to rest long ago?

From the beginning, the Olympic Games have been an intense, deliberately manipulated medium of powerful cultural images, mythology, symbols, and meanings, so it is not surprising that words such as "drugs," "banned list," and "steroids" carry potent, symbolic significance which reaches well beyond the precise objects these nouns represent.[2] Their meaning entails a strong element of fear, which is much deeper than some general, "intuitive" uneasiness that substance use violates vaguely held notions of what is natural, authentic, and pure in sport. The symbolic power of the Olympic Games, tied as it is to larger historical events that stretch from the "Nazi Olympics" of 1936 through to the cold war Games of the 1950s and 1960s, has forged frightening images of "drug use" in high-performance sport which continue to haunt people today.

This chapter examines the critical years from Hitler's rise to power in 1933 to the cold war confrontations of the USA and the USSR, when the Olympic Games experienced an unprecedented and dramatic growth of partisan politics within the Movement. It was in this period that rumors of steroid use by Olympic athletes began. The fears associated with use of steroids by athletes were intensified by three factors: reports that the Nazis had used steroids to heighten troop aggression during World War II; claims during the cold war that "the communists" were using steroids to build their totalitarian regimes in a manner similar to the way the Nazis had allegedly used them; and finally, allegations that east bloc female athletes were forced to accept the androgenizing effects of anabolic steroids and other hormone treatments to win Olympic medals and further the communist cause.

The 1936 Games, the long shadow of World War II and the Nazi war machine, and the paranoia of the cold war are the sources of the deepest suspicions people hold about the Games, the nature of high-performance sport in the modern era and, in particular, the use of steroids and other substances to boost athletic performance. The impact this period has upon the modern psyche in the west merits careful examination because it is centrally relevant to the irrational fears people hold about athletes using steroids. Only through the careful consideration of the repressed anxieties engendered during this period can the status of current substance prohibition be fully and accurately evaluated.

Olympic politics, Nazi symbolism, and propaganda

Symbolism was a powerful, constitutive element of the modern Olympic Games and even Pierre Coubertin consciously manipulated it to launch his project. "In contrast to the usual practice," Coubertin wrote of his preparations for the first 1894 Congress, "I wanted the principal solemnity to take place the first day to attract and captivate public attention."[3] To demonstrate that it was more than "an ordinary sports conference," Coubertin insisted that the meetings take place in the Halls of the Sorbonne because "under the venerable roof of the Sorbonne the words 'Olympic Games' would resound more impressively and persuasively."[4]

Although the Games continued to be symbolically exploited for certain cultural and political goals in the decades after their inception, it was the 1936 Games in Nazi Germany and the long shadow cast by World War II that were the sources of the darkest symbols which still color how people think about the competitive side of the Games and the nature of high-performance sport in the modern era.[5] In the 1936 Games, the Nazi's cold, calculating Ministry of Public Enlightenment and Propaganda carefully manipulated the Games' symbols to convey finely crafted images of power, lineage, victory and domination – themes that had a favorable reception among the post-World War I German population while also portraying an ominous future for the rest of Europe.[6] The Games were not, however, an isolated project for Joseph Goebbels' Ministry; they were just one part of an ongoing, multifaceted program of political propaganda.

In his classic study of German film and the psychological dispositions it reflected – "those deep layers of collective mentality which extend more or less below the dimension of consciousness" – Siegfried Kracauer argued that post-World War I film in Germany was infused with a "nihilistic gospel" where history was presented as "an arena reserved for blind and ferocious instincts, a product of devilish machinations forever frustrating our hopes for freedom and happiness."[7] Reflecting on their World War I experiences in the German army, screenplay writers Hans Janowitz and Carl Mayer wanted to overturn the dominant, nihilistic *Weltanschauung*, "stigmatize the omnipotence of state authority" and "penetrate the fatal tendencies inherent in the German system." In their screenplay *Caligari*, the protagonist "stands for an unlimited authority that idolizes power as such, and, to satisfy its lust for domination, ruthlessly violates all human rights and values." Cesare, a somnambulist entrusted to, and controlled by, Caligari, represents the common man "who, under compulsory military service, is drilled to kill and to be killed." In the original screenplay, Caligari's exploitation of Cesare is exposed by a student named Francis and "reason overpowers unreasonable power, insane authority is symbolically abolished."[8]

In shooting the film, despite Janowitz's and Mayer's protests, director Robert Wiene inverted the entire meaning of the screenplay by placing the Caligari plot within a larger framing story in which Francis is a patient in an insane asylum. After following the original narrative, the framing story shows a highly agitated Francis accusing the director of being "the dangerous madman Caligari." Once Francis is subdued, the asylum doctor puts on horn-rimmed spectacles and then, looking like Caligari, examines the patient. Removing his spectacles, in a mild and reassuring voice, he tells his assistants that Francis believes him to be Caligari. "Now that he understands the case of his patient, he will be able to heal him." "With this cheerful message" Kracauer writes, "the audience is dismissed."[9] There is nothing in the film version of *Caligari* for Germans (or others) to fear in the post-World War I nihilism that gripped much of Europe or an omnipotent state with unlimited, centralized power and authority.

Kracauer argues that the framed version was "more consistent with the attitude [of what the less educated felt and liked] than the original story."[10] Putting the story into a frame "faithfully mirrored the general retreat [of most post-World War I Germans] into a shell" while it "preserved and emphasized this revolutionary story – as a madman's fantasy." The film suggests that

> during their retreat into themselves the Germans were stirred to reconsider their traditional belief in authority. Down to the bulk of social democratic workers they refrained from revolutionary action; yet at the same time a psychological revolution seems to have prepared itself in the depths of the collective soul. The film reflects this double aspect of German life by coupling a reality in which Caligari's authority triumphs with a hallucination in which the same authority is overthrown.[11]

From his early wayward existence in Vienna, through his experiences on the front lines and hospitals during World War I, to his political orations in the beer halls of Bavaria, Adolf Hitler remained closely attuned to the sentiments, fears, and aspirations of the masses in Germany and Austria.[12] Hitler had extensive, first-hand knowledge of the psychological dispositions that Kracauer would later analyze in *From Caligari to Hitler*. Knowing the strength of the traditional belief in authority but aware of how German defeat in World War I had brought it into question, "the drummer" beat away continually at three themes in his rise to power. The German army was not defeated on the battlefields of the Great War; the "wire pullers" who formed the Weimar Republic's first government had stabbed the army in the back by signing a humiliating, unacceptable armistice. Germany's strength lay in the history and racial superiority of the German Volk. Finally, Germany needed a great Führer to return the empire to its former, natural, and justified glory.[13] Power, pride, racial purity, and struggle–combat (Kampf) constituted the central core of Nazi ideology.[14]

Hitler's life experiences made him keenly aware that he could capture and shape the beliefs, hearts and souls of the masses by well-crafted and carefully choreographed propaganda. For Hitler, propaganda was "not just a necessary evil, a question of justifiable lies, of warranted exaggeration." For the Führer, propaganda was an art.[15] As a result, massive political rallies, large-scale sporting events, feature films, radio programs, advertising, political posters, and assiduously organized art exhibitions delivered precisely constructed, carefully crafted images that consolidated Germany's links to its heroic Nordic past and the strength and purity of the Aryan race. The message celebrated a visceral, semi-erotic adulation of the Führer and demonstrated the growing power of the Third German Reich.[16] That image was projected across Germany and throughout Europe.

The 1936 Games gave Hitler a unique opportunity to weld the Promethean symbolic power of the Games to create the specter he wanted looming over Europe.[17] In pursuit of that goal, the Nazis refined some of their well-developed techniques for influencing public opinion. The Nazis had routinely exploited the new technologies of the mass media in spreading their propaganda domestically. Hitler's vast rallies relied on state of the art public address systems and were carried on radio and shown in cinemas across the country. The Nazis developed an imposing monumentalist style that adapted certain elements from Hollywood musicals to stage powerful, emotion-laden Gesamtkunstwerke – total works of art – in the huge venues of sports stadiums across Germany. Music, choreography, drama, and neoclassical architecture were blended into captivating, exhilarating, and emotionally draining experiences.[18] The 1934 Nuremberg Party Congress served Hitler and the Nazis as an elaborate dress rehearsal for the staging and filming of the 1936 Games. The similarities between the events themselves and Leni Riefenstahl's films *Triumph of the Will* and *Olympia*, leave no doubt about the Nazi party's overt exploitation of the Games for its own political purposes.[19]

At Nuremberg and in Berlin, the "stages" are organized in a pattern of images which show people flowing into huge geometric formations that symbolize the transformation of a formless mass into a disciplined, united force. Hitler's entrance through the wide aisles of the assembled masses to an elevated podium signifies his rise from a rank and file soldier to the nation's Führer who now dispenses divine wisdom to the people (das Volk). Through his various exchanges with the assembled crowd, Hitler is portrayed as the personification of the will of the people. Riefenstahl's editing of both films continually shifts the viewers' focus from the massed ranks of spectators, to the Führer, to the swastikas, reinforcing the Nazi's leitmotiv of "Ein Volk, ein Führer, ein Reich" (One Racially Pure People, One Leader, One Empire).[20] Both films suggest they are following the natural chronology of the events but are actually meticulously constructed narratives that present selective, well-crafted images and messages to the viewer. The climax to both events was identical. The closing ceremonies of the 1936 Games replicated Albert Speer's "cathedral of light" at Nuremberg. To close the Party Congress, Speer placed 130 powerful anti-aircraft search lights at 40-foot intervals around Zeppelin Field which shot sharply defined beams of light 25,000 feet into the night sky. Using the same technique in 1936, the columns of light went straight up and then, Mandell wrote about the Games' closing ceremonies, "the infinitely distant tops of the shafts gradually converged to enclose the darkened stadium in a temple composed entirely of glowing spirit."[21] The scene provided Riefenstahl with a powerful conclusion to *Olympia*, symbolizing the glory of Nazi Germany as well as the majesty of the Olympic Games.

The 1936 Games provided two additional propaganda vehicles that the Nazis exploited for domestic and foreign consumption. The first was the introduction of the torch relay which added a completely new, and symbolically important, opening to the Games and provided a different, though no less majestic, opening to *Olympia* to complement Hitler's "descent from the heavens" in *Triumph of the Will*. The torch relay – which rekindled memories of the imposing, symbolically rich images of the torch procession Goebbels had staged upon Hitler's January 30, 1933 appointment as Chancellor – allegorically linked the heroic age of Greece – the racially homogeneous apogee of ancient civilization – with the Third Reich to which the torch was now passed.[22]

Second, Nazism was a male-based cult that glorified youth, strength and conquest. It emphasized genetic and racial endowment in the natural, Darwinian struggle for the survival of the fittest. Riefenstahl's portrayal of the 1936 Games in *Olympia* was a finely crafted aesthetic in which the innate beauty and strength of the Games' competitive dimensions were linked to the natural supremacy of the white races so that the Nazis' ideology could be clearly seen and understood.

While some optimistically felt that Jesse Owens's four gold medals undermined Hitler's political objectives, the German total of 33 gold, 26 silver and 30 bronze medals, which easily topped the American 24, 20 and 12, ensured that the Führer's message was not lost on the sympathetic or undecided German viewer. Internationally, Hitler also enjoyed a propaganda victory. Shirer notes that the "visitors, especially those from England and America, were greatly impressed by what they saw: apparently a happy, healthy, friendly people united under Hitler – a far different picture than they had got from reading newspaper dispatches from Berlin."[23] Riefenstahl's artistic portrayal of the athleticism, natural grace and internationalism of the Games reinforced the feeling that Germany triumphed not only as the winning nation but as the most successful host ever of the international festival.

Cold war anxieties and the specter of steroids

The 1936 Games themselves, *Olympia*, and the intensive propaganda campaigns of Nazi Germany – by themselves or together – do not explain the deep psychological anxiety attached to steroid use in high-performance sport today. But as the image of the Nazi war machine's naked aggression and power linked itself to three additional historical realities, the deep-seated fear of steroid use by athletes becomes clearer. First, the legacy of World War II left profoundly engrained anxieties about the destructive potential science holds for those who use it in the unbridled pursuit of power. Second, the threat of communist totalitarianism, as it was portrayed in the west, and the remarkable and rapid success of east bloc athletes, created the fear that in its quest for world domination, the USSR would use the same cold, calculating, instrumental rationality that the Nazis had exploited in their quest for world supremacy. Finally, a visible, clearly articulated fear centered on the east bloc's female athletes. Widely rumored to be either men in disguise or women taking male testosterone, strong, successful female athletes from the USSR represented a serious challenge to notions of "natural gender" in the west. Each of these realities warrants careful consideration.

World War II was the most devastating conflict in human history. Its horrifying legacy included the "Battle of Britain" and the retaliatory razing of Dresden and Hamburg by fire bombs and carpet bombing; the marches on and sieges of Moscow, Leningrad and Stalingrad followed by Soviet retributions in the march on and into Berlin; as well as the brutalization of political opponents, gypsies, homosexuals, and the handicapped in the Nazi concentration camps. What really separated World War II from any other human conflict was the Nazi death marches and rationally calculated, mechanized mass murder of Jews in extermination camps – Chelmno, Sobibor, Treblinka, Belzec and later Auschwitz-Birkenau, and the American decision to use atomic bombs on Nagasaki and Hiroshima.[24] Those decisions demonstrated the catastrophic power residing in the unrestrained, systematic application of scientific instrumental rationality in the pursuit of political objectives.

Following his 20 years of imprisonment in Spandau, Speer, the last Minister of Armaments in the Third Reich, reflected upon his final statement at the Nuremberg Trials, what he had wanted to impress upon future generations, and the legacy left by the war in which he had played a leading role. "The criminal events of those years," he wrote,

> were not simply the result of Hitler's personality. The extent of the crimes was also attributable to the fact that Hitler was the first to be able to use means of technology that could multiply their impact.
> I thought about the consequences of unrestricted domination [Herrschaft] coupled with the power of technology – making use of it but also being dominated by it – might have in the future: this war, I indicated [at the Nuremburg Trials], had ended with remote-controlled rockets, supersonic aircraft, atom bombs, and a prospect of chemical warfare. In five to ten

years [by 1951–56] one could, with about ten men, annihilate in seconds a million people in the centre of New York, create widespread epidemics and destroy harvests with chemical weapons. The more technological the world becomes, the greater is the danger. ... As the former minister of a highly developed armaments system it is my final duty to state: a new world war will end with the annihilation of human culture and civilization. Nothing can stop unchained technology and science from completing its work of destroying humankind which they have, in such an insane manner, begun in this war."[25]

The grotesque possibility that post-war science and technology could give a demagogue such formidable, unbridled power was deeply engrained in the psyche of all who survived the war or grew up in its immediate aftermath.[26]

World War II also left a profoundly disturbing political legacy in the east–west confrontation of the cold war. Although the western democracies had never had a comfortable relationship with their communist ally prior to 1940, World War II had exacerbated the situation. The annexation of the Baltic countries and the disputes over a divided Germany were only part of the west's political problems with Stalin and the eastern bloc. The west itself was not unified – the harsh conditions of occupation exercised by the Nazis in France, northern Italy, Austria, and Scandinavia left different feelings towards Germany on the one hand and the Soviet liberators on the other. In addition, the leading role European communists had played in national resistance movements, combined with the decisive role that the Soviets had taken in the defeat of Germany, legitimized the Communist Party and the socialist movement in the eyes of many Europeans. Western governments felt vulnerable to the monolithic power of an aggressive Communist Movement while they simultaneously struggled with their own internal, political divisions and dissent. The immediate post-war period resulted in an international situation of muted confrontation, fought frequently through domestic and international propaganda battles, between two opposing and suspicious power blocs.[27]

Against this background, the USSR's highly successful entry to the Games in 1952 demonstrated that the west faced a strong, highly motivated and capable adversary, which had entered the Olympic Movement to be more than brothers-in-arms. Although divisive partisan politics had existed since the Games' revival in 1896, the post-World War II struggle between two great superpowers was of a different magnitude altogether. Following the appointment of Soviet delegates Constantin Andrianov and Aleksei Romanov to the IOC, the sessions were never the same. "In all spheres of international life, including the Olympic Movement," Romanov made clear, "there is a continuous struggle of the new with the old, of the progressive with the reactionary, and, as a mass social movement, international sport is in our time an arena of sharp political and ideological struggle."[28]

Little in the first dozen years following Soviet entry into the IOC reduced western concerns. Major geo-political events like the Korean War, Castro's victorious revolution in Cuba, the Soviet Union's launch of sputnik, the ongoing war in Vietnam, the deployment of Pershing missiles in Europe, the construction of the Berlin Wall, the failed invasion at the Bay of Pigs, and the Cuban Missile Crisis, all occurred within the time frame of three Olympiads following Soviet entry into the Games.

Although there was no doubt that the Soviets had some fine athletes, communist success had to be based on something more.[29] Immediately after their dramatic performance in the 1952 Games, rumors spread that the Soviets relied heavily on the systematic use of male testosterone or testosterone derivatives. These allegations touched on some of the western psyche's deepest anxieties in the post-World War II period. In a manner similar to the American use of Nazi scientists to develop the atomic bomb, the Soviets seemed to be using the same drugs the Nazis had reputedly given their troops to enhance aggression in the killing fields of the eastern front, to wage war against their next opponent. The brutal, unprincipled pursuit of global domination had not ended with the defeat of Nazi Germany. The powerful Soviet colossus appeared to be using similar means to reach the same end.[30]

One of the key references to the Nazis' alleged use of steroids was Dr. Nicholas Wade's unreferenced intervention into the debate on steroid use in athletics just as they had become a major IOC issue. "The first use of male steroids to improve performance is said to have been in World War II," Wade wrote,

> when German troops took them before battle to enhance aggressiveness. After the war, steroids were given to the survivors of German concentration camps to rebuild body weight. The first use in athletics seems to have been by the Russians in 1954. John D. Ziegler, a Maryland physician who was the U.S. team physician to the weight lifting championships in Vienna that year, told *Science* that Soviet weight lifters were receiving doses of testosterone, a male sex hormone. The Russians were also using it on some of their women athletes, Ziegler said.
>
> Besides its growth-promoting effect, testosterone induces male sexual development such as deepening of the voice and hirsuteness, which might account for the manifestation of such traits in Soviet women athletes during the 1950s.[31]

In fewer than 150 words, Wade tied together images of German military aggression, concentration camp horror, rampant Soviet ambition, the male hormonalization and masculinization of female Soviet athletes, and the expert testimony of an American physician.

The allegation of steroid use by Nazi troops was given further credence when Herbert Haupt and George Rovere (who relied on Wade) repeated it in the *American Journal of Sports Medicine* and Robert Windsor and Daniel Dumitru (relying on Haupt and Rovere and Wade) did the same in *Postgraduate Medicine*.[32] Virginia Cowart stated, without reference to Wade, Silverman, or Windsor and Dumitru, that "the first reported use of steroids in a non-clinical setting was during World War II when German troops took them to enhance aggressiveness." She continued "[i]t was only a small step to recognize that enhanced aggressiveness might be desirable in athletic competition, and the Russians took that step in the early 1950s."[33] Finally, J.E. Wright also made the claim in *Exercise and Sport Review*.[34] In her extensive critique of steroid use in East Germany, Berendonk also attributed steroid use to the Nazis. "In many general review articles," she wrote, "it was noted that during the Second World War, German army storm troopers had been doped with psychotropic testosterone just a few years after the first chemical identification, synthesis, and structural description of these compounds."[35]

Once made, these unsubstantiated allegations continued to appear in scholarly publications, medical periodicals, medical conference presentations, newspapers, and are now ubiquitous on the world wide web.[36] As late as 2001, Steven Ungerleider gave the following unreferenced account in *Faust's Gold: Inside the East German Doping Machine*:

> During World War II, Hitler issued vast quantities of steroids to the SS and the Wehrmacht so that his troops would better resist combat fatigue and be more ruthless in following any order. As early as 1941, Soviet Red Army observers had noted an unusually passionate fighting spirit among German soldiers, who often seemed eager to die for the glory of the Third Reich.[37]

It never mattered whether or not the rumors were true; what mattered, and continues to matter, is that opinion leaders like physicians, scientific researchers, policy makers, and journalists believed the rumors were true.[38] The discovery that communist athletes were using steroids became even more chilling to the west because it conjured visions of Nazi experimentation, the use of cold, calculated, scientifically manipulated power for aggressive means, and the lust for world domination. These dire images of Nazi power, which have remained so vivid partly because of the war but also Goebbels' success in carefully crafting and instilling them in the Nazi's pre-war Gesamtkunstwerke, were now easily transferred to Stalin's communist Russia and the USSR's quest for world domination at the Olympic Games and beyond. The specter of steroid-enhanced communism haunted Europe even more ominously than the Communist Party manifesto's image had a hundred years earlier.

Steroids quickly became more than a "Nazi drug;" they became the "atomic bomb" of the cold war. Steroid use by Soviet athletes represented the unprincipled use of science in pursuit of world domination without any concern for its human consequences.[39] The reputed benefits attributed to steroids would most certainly tip the balance of power in the cold war towards the USSR as it gained medals and international prestige at the Olympic Games. The image of steroid users changed from tall, blond, muscular, Aryan warriors committed to the Führer's will to power, to legions of swarthy, Rasputin-like Cossacks, dedicated to the goals of communism. The fear of the dictatorial control of human beings in the unrestrained pursuit of power was even more ominous in view of the USSR's reliance upon raw power throughout its history. When Ziegler indicated a Soviet informant had confirmed that the USSR's athletes, including their females, were using steroids, it seemed that the Soviet commitment to victory on the world stage had no bounds.[40] To compete in the brave new world of cold war, international sport, the west might have to sacrifice not only its youth, but women also would be among the casualties. The Olympic Games quickly became the most high profile site for sophisticated chemical warfare between the two superpowers.

Gender ambiguity and sex/drug testing

The Games of 1952 demonstrated that the USSR would rely heavily on the performances of its female athletes to defeat the USA. Three fears emerged from this reality. First, it was entirely plausible that Ziegler's source was correct: the Soviets were injecting female athletes with male hormones. That was a step most patriarchal, paternalistic sports leaders in the west did not want to take. Second, perhaps the Soviets were not that desperate and were simply disguising some male athletes as women and using the steroid rumor as camouflage. Since a number of female athletes from the USSR deviated from the dominant western perceptions of the "proper" or "natural" female physique, either or both scenarios seemed possible. Third, it could also be the case that world-class, high-performance sport for women had suddenly and dramatically become the same scientifically rational, technologically assisted, pursuit of the linear record as men's sport. While it turns out that the first and third possibilities were true and the second was not, the fear of all three existed in the popular consciousness of the day.[41]

To understand the strong symbolic significance these fears held, it is important to consider the longstanding history of the clear separation of the sexes that has characterized modern sport and the Olympic Games. The Olympic Movement has reflected and reinforced what Thomas Laqueur termed the "two-sex model."[42] Sport symbolically conveys the notion that the natural, and by association the social or cultural constitutions of men and women are determined by their bodies' respective biological, physiological and anatomical structures. "The 'logic' of the sport–body combination, the seemingly free play of bodies in motion, contributes to an illusion that sport and its bodies are transparent, set apart from politics, culture, and the economy" Cheryl Cole argues.[43] The seemingly ahistorical, apolitical nature of sport further reinforces the two-sex model because sport appears to confirm the natural differences that separate men from women in sport and all other competitive situations in social life.

Coubertin set the tone for the Olympic Movement's distinction between the sexes in his numerous justifications for excluding women from the Games. His arguments drew on the biological naturalism commonly held by many at the turn of the twentieth century.

> Respect of individual liberty requires that one should not interfere in private acts ... but in public competition, [women's] participation must be absolutely prohibited. It is indecent that the spectators should be exposed

to the risk of seeing the body of a woman being smashed before their eyes. Besides, no matter how toughened a sportswoman may be, her organism is not cut out to sustain certain shocks. Her nerves rule her muscles, nature wanted it that way.[44]

Coubertin's vision for the Olympic Movement was not an isolated one. Hoberman points out that there were several internationalist movements at the turn of the century that reinforced a certain idealized male type. The Boy Scout movement, which arose during roughly the same period as the Olympics, attempted to develop and fortify similar universal human traits. The "inventory" of characteristics reinforced by the different movements involved a Eurocentric orientation which claimed political neutrality. The wealthy and those with aristocratic connections determined the direction of the movements. They tended to express an interest in peacemaking or pacifism which was framed in a complex sense of national and international loyalty. The movements also advocated a "citizen of the world" type of supranationalism and relied on various symbols, flags and anthems to unify themselves.[45] The idealized chivalrous male figure was regarded as the embodiment of the international movements' goals and, as Chapter One demonstrated, this figure was crucial to Coubertin's idealized athlete. Gender exclusion was part of the founding ethos of the Games and would continue to pervade the Movement's constitutive practices for years to come.

Other institutional settings excluded women from sport or redirected them towards more "moderate" exercise. Physical education programs in the west have a long history of regulating activity on the basis of gender, the devaluation of girls' and women's activities, and the normalization of heterosexuality.[46] The form of regulation shifted over time and an interesting historical change in gender relations is evident in the dynamics of women's physical education programs in the USA.

In the early twentieth century physical education programs were often charged with creating "mannish" students, implying sexual deviance. The deviance that was feared, however, was an "aggressive heterosexual activity outside the norms of feminine respectability."[47] Female athletes were too mannish because they reputedly exhibited men's vigorous and overtly heterosexual drives. While many women in physical education departments identified with this image, they did not feel encumbered by it since it existed alongside more traditional notions of female decorum. Female athletes enjoyed the spirited experiences of companionship among female athletes and students too much to be dissuaded by the charge of mannishness.[48]

By the 1920s, however, physical education departments felt the strong chill of growing sentiments opposed to homosexuality and innuendo about the pathology of non-heterosexuality. Under the influence of turn-of-the-century sexology and the normalization of heterosexuality through the medical–scientific gaze, concerns with same-sex perversion began to be expressed in same-sex institutional settings. Factories, hotels, boarding schools, convents, and physical education departments all came under scrutiny. By the 1930s in the USA, non-heterosexual practices were labeled dysfunctional in medical terminology, and lesbian taboos were reinforced in institutional settings. Psychological tests for masculinity and femininity were developed and the presence of "lesbian characteristics" became the litmus tests for female masculinity.[49] The battery of testing techniques included psychiatric and psychological tests and methods, such as free association, questionnaires or interviews; endocrinological measurements of hormone levels; gynecological examinations, including measurements and sketches of breasts and genitals; even photographs were used for morphological descriptions of homosexuality.[50] Under the threat of these taboos, the emphasis in physical education programs changed from one of female companionship to one of heterosexual attractiveness and "moderation." The shift virtually suppressed all forms of aggressive, masculine competition for women.[51] A 1946 brochure of the Ohio Association for Health, Physical Education and Recreation bluntly stated: "the mannish concept of a physical educator is no longer acceptable."[52]

These normalizing practices continued into the post-World War II era and took on political significance internationally as the east bloc female athletes openly challenged western norms regarding "proper" female appearance. Images and perceptions of the sexual body played a vital role in national ideologies and in the inculcation of nationalistic feelings. Cold war imagery was constructed through ideals and symbols generated in relation to the trope of the body politic. During the cold war construction of "imagined communities," images of gender, sexual, and family relations became paramount and reached near-hysterical heights.[53]

In the USA, a super-heterosexualized cold war family became a "psychological fortress" against the fear of communist aggression from without, and communist infiltration from within. "The legendary family of the 1950s, complete with appliances, station wagons, backyard barbecues, and tricycles scattered on the sidewalks," family historian Elaine Tyler May points out, represented "the first wholehearted effort to create a home that would fulfill virtually all its members' personal needs through an energized and expressive personal life."[54] The catchword of the day was "domestic containment," whereby the consolidation of public policy and private behavior endeavored to secure a stable home and family, accentuate the benefits of American-style capitalism and its concomitant consumable goods and lifestyles, and maintain psychological security against the perceived threat of communist aggression and intervention. In this climate, communism, the atomic bomb, internal subversion and "non-traditional" women – and men – were particularly weighty threats.

> "[N]ormal" heterosexual behavior culminating in marriage represented "maturity" and "responsibility;" therefore, those who were "deviant" were, by definition, irresponsible, immature, and weak. It followed that men who were slaves to their passions could easily be duped by seductive women who worked for the communists. Even worse were the "perverts" who, presumably, had no masculine backbone.[55]

The intersection between sexual and domestic practices, on the one hand, and political ideology, on the other, made its way to the highest levels of cold war diplomacy. In the 1959 "kitchen debate," Vice-President Richard Nixon boasted about the superiority of the American home, its family life and its consumable household products. The idealized American housewife with her domestic role as housekeeper and mother was part of Nixon's claim to US superiority. Soviet women, working for the good of the communist system, Premier Nikita Khrushchev countered, were the mark of a superior social system.[56] While Rosie the Riveter had been persuaded to help the cause during World War II by working in munitions and supplies factories, she was encouraged to return to "domestic duty as usual" once the war was over. The dominant imagery of "normal" gender and sex roles returned, whereby heterosexuality, the nuclear family, and "gender-appropriate" behavior was reasserted and re-established.[57]

Within this context of cold war sexual rhetoric, Soviet and east bloc female athletes openly challenged the west's heterosexual imperative. Soviet athletes were portrayed as unfeminine, "Amazons," lesbians, or men in disguise. The crass treatment of Soviet female athletes is best exemplified in the western media's coverage of "the Press Brothers" – the gold medal shot and discus thrower Tamara Press and her sister Irina, a world record holding heptathlete. In an effort to fully discredit the Soviet approach to all things in social life, including world-class, high-performance sport, *Life* magazine published a feature article where the "muscular sisters" were juxtaposed in words and photographs with the "properly feminine" female athletes of the USA.[58]

The redefining of sexual norms in the post-World War II period set the stage for one of the strangest and arguably most misguided sport policies ever. Once again, it was the Nazi–Soviet specter that lurked in the background. At the 1936 Summer Games, Hermann Ratjen posed as "Dora" in the women's high jump although he later admitted to the deception and claimed the Nazis had forced him to it.[59] If Hitler was willing to go that far, why would Stalin not follow? In 1938, a European women's high jump champion was barred from competition because she had ambiguous genitalia, indicating that the Soviets might seek out special competitors to win at the Olympic Games.[60] Although there were very few cases of cheating, rumors combined with cold war-based sexual ideology fed into a heightened concern with the "politics of sex" in world-class sport. In an attempt to control the unrestrained ambitions of the communists, the IOC introduced a battery of imperfect, official procedures to check the sex of every female athlete.[61]

Determined to guarantee there was no room for deception, international sports officials introduced, in the 1960s, procedures that were alternately referred to as a "sex test," "gender verification," or "femininity control." Every female athlete who entered the Olympic program underwent a sex test right up until the 2000 Sydney Games, at which time the IOC finally bowed to criticisms that the test was unethical and ineffective.[62]

Defenders of the procedures employed the rhetoric of fairness and scientific objectivity to justify the tests. Comments from certain medical officials, however, revealed the three main motivations for their implementation. Testers feared they were needed because the unscrupulous communists would stop at nothing to achieve their goals; they tended to subscribe to the compulsory heterosexuality of post-World War II sexual ideology; and they exhibited their own degree of a generalized misogyny.[63]

During the administration of the first chromatin sex test at the 1968 Games, the chief tester told reporters that the women he tested showed various signs of masculinzation because of sports, and that sports had generally made them ugly.[64] R.G. Bunge commented in the influential *Journal of the American Medical Association* in 1960 that although he was "not one to fool around with classification," he had noticed that "Nature's capricious deviation" had, in some cases, resulted in certain "unfortunate individuals." Bunge rhetorically asked "how would a French female feel if she were beaten by a Bolivian contestant who had a vagina and testicles in her labial folds?" – a condition he later referred to as a "ball-bearing female." The author suggested that the chromatin sex test was necessary to prevent "genetic doping," a metaphor likely to have been made possible by the growing knowledge of drug use among athletes at the time alongside the known androgenic side effects of steroids.[65] Bunge's position is an early example of how the association of drug use with sexually ambiguous athletes – both challenged the "natural" order of sport and the idealized fair playing field.[66]

Robert Kerr, a California-based physician who assisted male athletes with their steroid regimes,[67] echoed Bunge's sentiments but expressed a slightly different set of concerns – the paternalistic protection of female athletes in the west from the escalating competition with the USSR. Winning was important, keeping up with the Soviet men was imperative, but protecting the American way of life as it was embodied in the post-World War II female ideal, was an even higher good. "We've been witnessing today, and for the last number of years," Kerr wrote,

> how our female athletes are being defeated in certain strength and power sports by Russian and East German women who just seem to have an edge – *a masculine edge. Right now we don't want our women to be defeminized in order to win, but in the next Olympics, or the next after that, will we still be willing to feel the same way?* I don't know, I hope in this case that we don't change.[68]

With the entry of the Soviet women to the Olympic Games, world-class, high-performance sport was challenging some highly sensitive, fundamental conventions in the post-World War II west.

The specter haunting Europe, the USA and the Olympic Games

The escalation of not just the importance of winning at the Games but also the growing "arms race" to ensure victory was changing the Olympic landscape dramatically as the 1950s gave way to the 1960s. Before the 1950s were over, the specter of Nazi drugs spreading throughout the Games, the growth of an uncontained communist ambition to dominate the world, and the prospect of legions of masculinized, Amazon female athletes from the east haunted the psyche of sports leaders in the western bloc. Sex and drug testing would, the IOC wagered, return the Games, and a world quickly spinning out of orbit, to the "normal world" of 1950s America.

The 1960s were even more unsettling than the previous decade. Haunting, vivid memories of the atomic bombs dropped on Hiroshima and Nagasaki came back into terrifying focus as President Kennedy confronted Khrushchev during the Cuban Missile Crisis of 1962.[69] The specter of what might have inhabited the Nazi storm troopers, Joseph Mengele, and other perpetrators of the Nazi death machine in Eastern Europe as their actions had been exposed to the world during the Nuremberg trials from 1945 to 1949, was raised again in the 1961 trial of Adolf Eichmann.[70] Finally when the American destroyer Madox was hit by North Vietnamese torpedoes in August 1964 and Operation Rolling Thunder marked the USA's full engagement in the war, the ghosts of communism were shown to be lurking everywhere, stopping at nothing, including the use of women and children, to gain its expansionist goals. Fear and uncertainty called out for dramatic action like the saturation bombing and napalming of North Vietnam by the American military.

The IOC took its own decisive action and simultaneously introduced into the *Olympic Charter* rules against steroids and other performance-enhancing sub-stances as well as mandatory sex testing. The fears stimulated by the growing commitment to victory at seemingly any price compelled the IOC to take action.

In the second last line of the communist manifesto, Marx wrote that "The proletarians have nothing to lose but their chains." Imprisoned by the specter of steroids, images of Nazi storm troopers, the anxieties of an expanding cold war, and patriarchal fears over the degradation of the female ideal, the banned list and sex testing were introduced. The chains of patriarchy have been loosened and compulsory sex testing removed from the *Charter*. The hobgoblin of steroids and other performance-enhancing substances seems still to haunt the IOC; change from within appears remote. Perhaps it is the athlete–workers of the world who must discard those final chains.

3 "Sport," German traditions, and the development of "training"

Everyone thinks they know what "sport" is. It is one of the most taken-for-granted words in our vocabulary. But WADA President Richard Pound is more circumspect than most people. To understand the use of performance-enhancing substances in sport, Pound notes that "you first have to understand something of the nature of competitive sport."[1] Pound's advice is sage because, as George Orwell wrote in "The Politics of the English Language," "the worst thing you can do with words is surrender to them. When you think of a concrete object," Orwell argued, "you think wordlessly, and then, if you describe the thing you have been visualizing you probably hunt about till you find the exact words that seem to fit it." However, when you think of something abstract you are more inclined, Orwell warned, "to use words from the start and unless you make a conscious effort to prevent it, the existing dialect will come rushing in and do the job for you, at the expense of blurring or even changing your meaning."[2]

In the single, simple word "sport" people include a host of physical activities ranging from pick-up road hockey or ultimate frisbee, to house league softball and basketball, through AAA minor hockey and NCAA football, to Major League baseball, Women's National Basketball Association and National Basketball Association basketball, National Hockey League hockey, and the Olympic Games. However, even though the practices of today's professional athletes could serve as the major reference point for the meaning of "sport," it is the transhistorical, essentialist conception of competitive physical activity that tends to dominate. In the vernacular, "sport" is frequently, easily and almost deceptively transformed into a mental image that portrays competitive physical activity as a non-work, competitive game freely played and enjoyed by its participants.

Of the 28 definitions contained in the *Oxford English Dictionary*, ranging from sport as a "pleasant pastime" through "jest and merriment," to the description of one who is "a good fellow" or "consumed with sport," the following is the primary definition of the abstraction "sport."

> a. Pleasant pastime; entertainment or amusement; recreation, diversion; b. Amorous dalliance or intercourse; c. Pastime afforded by the endeavour to take or kill wild animals, game, or fish. Freq. with adjs. referring to the result achieved; d. Participation in games or exercises, esp. those of an athletic

character or pursued in the open air; such games or amusements collectively; e. In proverbial phr. *the sport of kings* (latterly, influenced by sense 5), orig. applied to war-making, but later extended to hunting and horse-racing (also surf-riding); b. *spec.* A game, or particular form of pastime, esp. one played or carried on in the open air and involving some amount of bodily exercise; c. *pl.* A series of athletic contests engaged in or held at one time and forming a spectacle or social event.

On the etymology of the word, the *Oxford English Dictionary* indicates that "sport" was derived from the gradual, unintentional loss of the first two letters of the word "disport" which it defines as follows:

1. Diversion from serious duties; relaxation, recreation; entertainment, amusement. *Arch;* 2. Anything which affords diversion and entertainment; a pastime, game, sport. *Arch.;* 3. Merriment, mirth, fun. *Obs.;* 4. The making sport of. *Obs. Rare;* 5. Bearing, carriage, deportment. *Obs. Rare.* [3]

All of these definitions are derived from the vernacular in various societies at different points in time. Their use, in representing contemporary, world-class, high-performance sport is, however, highly problematic. The dominant conception of "sport," as casually understood, and defined in the *Oxford English Dictionary,* is a universal term that denotes an enjoyable, non-serious, sometimes competitive but always fair, physical activity that is freely undertaken and shaped by players who seek their own personal fulfillment as they conduct themselves as good sports. All of these notions are far removed from world-class track and field meets, high-performance wrestling matches, or international cycling races, for example, as they are practiced at the elite levels today.

The power and significance of the unreflective use of "sport" should not, as Pound warns, be ignored or underestimated, because its impact can be extremely far reaching. It is the vernacular, for example, that Chief Justice Dubin drew upon as he wrote his opening comments to the 1990 *Commission of Inquiry Into the Use of Drugs and Banned Practices Intended to Increase Athletic Performance.* "The use of banned performance-enhancing drugs" Dubin wrote, "is cheating, which is the antithesis of sport. The widespread use of such drugs has threatened the essential integrity of sport and is destructive of its very objectives."[4]

Similarly, WADA's new *Anti-Doping Code* employs a similar conception of "sport" to justify the prohibition of selected performance-enhancing substances.

Anti-doping programs seek to preserve what is intrinsically valuable about sport. The intrinsic value is often referred to as "the spirit of sport;" it is the essence of Olympism; it is how we play true. The spirit of sport is the celebration of the human spirit, body and mind."[5]

While the vernacular has its place, almost half a century of scholarship in philosophy, history, political science, and sociology has shown that in serious discussions of different physical activity forms, the use of transhistorical, essentialist conceptions of sport are wrong. Even though up until the late 1970s many sport scholars sought a single, unequivocal, "scientific" definition of "sport," that futile pursuit for the most part ended with the growing influence of social history and cultural studies.[6] Few scholars today maintain that "sport," as an unqualified abstraction, is particularly useful. No longer accepted by scholars as "an unchanging, transhistorical, and universal cultural form" that is "understood essentially the same way by all people in all societies," serious scholars discuss sport in the plural, as specifically located cultural activities that are "understood best as distinct creations of modernity, fashioned and continually refashioned in the revolutionizing conditions of industrial capitalist societies."[7]

Three specific examples discussed in this chapter demonstrate why this is the case.[8] The examples are important for two reasons. First, while prohibitions against the use of banned substances have relied on a transhistorical conception of sport, as the Dubin *Commission of Inquiry* and WADA's *Anti-Doping Code* demonstrate, the examples presented here show that such justifications are groundless. Second, the discussion of training paradigm shifts demonstrates just how much "sport" has changed over time. "Training" has changed by degree; however, more importantly, this chapter demonstrates that in the mid-twentieth century, it also changed in kind. The important paradigm shift in the ontology of human performance discussed here led to new ways of thinking about human capacities in which physical performance was pushed to its outer limits. This paradigm fundamentally reshaped high-performance sport in the second half of the twentieth century and continues to shape it today.

"Sport" and physical activity historically

Owing to its relatively late unification into a single state, Germany can serve as an excellent example of the pitfalls of studying "sport" solely in the abstract. Following unification in 1871, there were three different forms of sporting practice that competed with each other for pre-eminence during the late nineteenth and early to mid-twentieth centuries in Germany – the Turner Sport Movement, the English-influenced Olympic or Bourgeois Sport Movement and the Worker Sport Movement. In all three, physical performance was a central criterion of "sport" but there were significant differences concerning the types and goals of the pertinent physical activities.

Tracing its origin back to 1809 and Father Friedrich Ludwig Jahn's first Turner Association in Berlin, Turner Sport emphasized national pride, mass education, and health through specific sporting activities such as group drill, gymnastics with different apparatuses, and military tactical exercises.[9] Since the focus was upon group education and development, a record performance in a single event by an individual athlete was meaningless. Turner Sport competitions centered on participants engaging in a series of events where the objective was to maximize the number of athletes on a team who could exceed a particular, designated level of performance rather than looking for one single athlete who could outperform and thereby defeat all others. In addition, performance rested on the normal, everyday, general fitness level of the participants; it was not associated with a compulsory lifestyle (Zwangslebenweise) involving a special diet, an unusual expenditure of time or money on the competitive activities, or other specialized preparation. "Training," a pronouncement for the 10ᵗʰ German Turner Day Competition in 1887 declared, "is unworthy of a German Turner."[10] Finally, Turner Sport was almost the direct antithesis of the individualistic sporting activities of the English. Turner Sport was a social movement seeking to develop a healthy social whole in which the collective functioned as a cohesive, well-coordinated unit. This contrasted directly with the English public school's focus on the character development of individuals who would become a small cadre of elite leaders inspiring others through demonstrations of their personal strength, self-sacrifice, and unwavering determination.[11]

The emergent middle class in Germany supported the competitive, performance-oriented model of sport embodied in Coubertin's Olympic Games. In view of their individualistic, liberal world view, bourgeois sport enthusiasts in Germany emphasized the importance of individual effort and discipline that sport taught participants. A world-class country should not only compete on the world stage, it should also win: bourgeois sport participants sought to demonstrate the power of their new nation through athletic prowess. The credo of citius, altius, fortius encapsulated the goals and aspirations of bourgeois sport in Germany, and stood in stark contrast to the Turners and the Worker Sport Movement at the turn of the twentieth century. Individual discipline, delayed gratification, competitive zeal, and the pursuit of victory quickly characterized middle-class sport in Germany from the late 1800s onward.

In direct contrast to, and in competition with, bourgeois sport and the Turner Movement, a vibrant Worker Sport Movement developed in Germany toward the end of the nineteenth century.[12] Unlike the highly nationalist Turners, Worker Sport was internationally focused and was inclusive of both genders and all races. The Movement emphasized health through sport, socialist fellowship, worker solidarity, class consciousness, and the development of the working class's unique physical culture.

In contrast to Coubertin's project, Worker Sport was an alternative to the national chauvinism, individualism, and the obsession with individual records that was quickly characterizing bourgeois sport and the Olympic Games. In a manner similar to the Turners, Worker Sport enthusiasts wanted to achieve their collectivist world view through participation in less competitive activities like gymnastics, tumbling, pyramid-building, mass displays of physical artistry, hiking, swimming, and cycling.

Each of these three movements promoted "sport;" all three overlapped in the late nineteenth and the first half of the twentieth century; each of them promoted and supported physical activity as a means for infusing particular educational values. At the same time, each movement differed significantly in the types of physical activity it promoted, the educational lessons behind the activities, and the way in which performance would be assessed. These three examples demonstrate how much meaning is lost if one simply labels the activities of the Turner Movement, the Bourgeois Sport Movement and the Worker Sport Movement as "sport."

The poverty of the abstraction "sport" is also apparent in a second example drawn from German sport history. Through the careful analysis of texts and speeches, distinguished German sport historian Hajo Bernett has demonstrated, with specific reference to Carl Diem, how the central, defining characteristics of "sport" changed in Germany over four different historical periods.[13] During the Kaiserreich (1871–1918), when a strong sense of nationalism and Prussian militarism dominated the newly formed nation's consciousness, sport associations were formed which promoted opportunities for competitive sport. "Sport's operating principles of combat [Kampf] and victory" Bernett noted, could be seen as "analogues for the political pursuit of power." At the same time, the Darwinian principle of the survival of the fittest extended from everyday life into sport legitimating, on the basis of a natural law, the competitive zeal being fostered in and through sport. In 1908, already President of the Brandenburg Athletic Association as well as the Chairman of the German Sport Board for Athletics, Carl Diem "proclaimed with great conviction – 'Fight [Kampf] – then you must win!'" "The man who is developed in combat [Kampf]" Diem believed, "is the bearer of culture. Greatness is only achieved through a steadfast will."[14]

Few societies have been as fragmented as Weimar Germany (1918–1933). While most sport leaders, including Diem, continued to view and define sport in the Darwinian terms of combat, struggle, and triumph, other approaches made inroads into what was subsumed under the concept of "sport."[15] Philosophical and phenomenologically inspired investigations began to see sport in more diverse terms. By 1928, Diem had altered his conception of sport and then viewed it as play. Diem focused on players' freedom in an "elevated sphere of Being."[16] In sum, during the late-Weimar period, a critically analytical view of sport as play, rather than combat and struggle, assumed an increasingly important emphasis during the late 1920s and early 1930s.

The rise of the National Socialists to power in 1933 had a direct impact on sport in Germany. The socialist and democratic approaches that had emerged in the Weimar period were quickly suppressed as the Führerprinzip and Nazi policies dominated all aspects of German life. Sport organizations were taken over by the Nazi state; the "Aryanization" of German sports clubs began in December 1933;[17] sport theory supported the Nazi's bellicose, racist (völkische) worldview. Kampf – "the basic virtue of the Nordic–Germanic people" according to Meyer's Lexicon in 1936 – became the dominant focus of sport.[18] Carl Krümmel, Head of the Ministry for Physical Education in the Reich's Education Ministry, maintained that: "Naked, clear, fierce will dominates sport – where 'fierce' is understood in a positive fashion."[19]

Although Diem, in whom the Nazis placed no particular importance initially, continued to see both play and combat as constitutive parts of sport, the link between the two was quickly "coordinated" with the Nazi perspective.[20] In 1938, as director of the German Olympic Institute, Diem presented play and combat as basic principles of Nazi sport in an article published in *Paris Soir*. "Play, for us," Diem wrote, "is part of the powerful, united movement which Germany has, with such predominant power, welded together. Competitive sport [Kampfsport] is the counterpart."[21] Kampfsport was a vehicle for military preparation according to Diem. A year later, employing imagery drawn from sport and the Turners, Diem indicated that sport was the "Schwungsverstärker [strengthening impetus]" of the soldier. In Paris, Diem emphasized the "militaristic meaning of the Olympic Games" and accentuated those aspects of Coubertin's legacy in which sport was presented as "a means for cultivating militarily able-bodied men."[22] Similarly, in speeches on the Eastern Front in the 1940s, Diem spoke of the "soldierly essence of Olympic ideas" and in a September 1943 edition of *NS-Sport*, following one of Goebbels' most significant propaganda events, the declaration of total war, Diem evoked the sacred, clarion call of the Olympic Movement to inspire youthful conscripts to join the battle: "I call upon youth – to their military duty!"[23] Sport, Kampf, and Krieg (war) had never before been so perfectly coordinated with a nation's politics and ideology.

In divided, post-war Germany, the GDR linked sport to the Worker Sport Movement and the tradition of socialist physical culture, on the one hand, and the official party doctrine of Marxism–Leninism, on the other. Quickly subordinated to official state ideology, the Worker Sport tradition was opportunistically manipulated to meet and justify particular national objectives. The central importance of "labor" in Marxism–Leninism allowed the GDR's ruling Socialist Unity Party (Sozialistische Einheitspartei Deutschlands – SED) to easily link sport to work and performance, which later provided the Party with the ideological justification for committing itself to a completely state sponsored, high-performance sport system. The play dimensions of sport, Bernett demonstrated, were quickly subordinated to the work and performance elements of sport, with the former heavily criticized as elements of bourgeois sport ideology.[24]

In the Federal Republic of Germany (FRG), sport leaders reached back to the pre-Nazi period of the Weimar Republic and sought to re-establish the goals of that period. This meant that "sport" was defined in a number of very different ways by the social democratic and religious sport associations which began to flourish in the post-World War II period. The play element of sport was reincorporated into the notion of sport, but so too were performance-oriented, specialized, scientific understandings brought to the fore. For his part, Diem returned to an image of sport that emphasized play. Drawing upon the work of philosophers from Aristotle to Karl Jaspers, Diem wrote that sport "is earnestly undertaken, regulated, and intensified play."[25] The Olympic Games, Diem now insisted, were a "Peace Festival of Humanity."

Within a single country, over four different historical periods, and in four different socio-political contexts, the "essence," meaning, and significance of "sport" changed. In the case of Carl Diem, one can see the idea of sport undergoing several fundamental changes within the lifetime of a single individual sport scholar. In a different way, this example demonstrates the conceptual problems tied to the use of "sport" in the absence of specific historical and social contextualization.

The development of "training" in sport

Just as the forms of physical activity designated as sport have varied throughout history and the meaning of "sport" has changed under different historical circumstances and social conditions, so too has the way scholars, researchers, coaches and athletes approach their involvement in sport. Today, it is often taken for granted that there has always been a precise science in which world-class athletes, coaches, exercise scientists and others with expertise in various branches of sports medicine direct their efforts to enhancing athletic performance.[26] This section critically examines that assumption by focusing on the notion of "training" and documenting not only how it changed but that a fundamental paradigm shift in the "ontology of human performance" took place in the mid-twentieth century. The emergent paradigm fundamentally shapes high-performance sport and sport science today.

While scientists in the nineteenth and early twentieth centuries studied athletes, they did not do so to increase or enhance athletes' performance capacities. Scientific discourse was contoured by the law of the conservation of energy (the first law of thermodynamics). Moreover, in accordance with the conception of science at that time and the associated principle that scientific laws applied universally, the laws of one area were applied to others; this was especially true of the laws of pure physics. As a result, the first law of thermodynamics was applied to the scientific understanding of many realms, including how the human body operated.

In the 1830s and 1840s several European researchers – most notably Julius Robert von Mayer, James Prescott Joule, and Hermann von Helmholtz – worked simultaneously on theoretical aspects of the doctrine.[27] The first law states that energy can be transferred from one system to another but it cannot be created or destroyed. The total amount of energy in the universe is constant. Einstein's theory of relativity – $E = mc^2$ – describes the relationship between energy and matter precisely and indicates that energy (E) is equal to matter (M) times the square of a constant (C). The equation demonstrates that energy and matter are interchangeable and, if the quantity of matter in the universe is constant then the quantity of energy is also fixed.[28]

While the conservation of energy applied directly to non-organic matter was instrumental in the development of machines, its proponents also applied it to humans, comparing their biological and physiological functions to mechanical engines.[29] "As the power to work is without question the most important of the products of animal life," Mayer wrote in the 1850s, "the mechanical equivalent of heat is in the very nature of things destined to be the foundation for the edifice of a scientific physiology."[30] So while the doctrine's widespread influence included physics and the understanding of mechanical systems, it grew to encompass the understanding of human activity in social and institutional life, including physical education settings.[31] As a result, scientific studies of the human body in motion were part of a general scientific world view premised on the first law of thermodynamics.

While the term "training" existed and was used prior to the mid-twentieth century, it was essentially a synonym for "drill" – the repetitive practice of skills or movements designed to refine technique, improve coordination, and enhance precision and execution. Coaches and athletes did not know they could systematically enhance physical power, speed, endurance, and agility through specific, targeted programs.[32] The scientific research community and the sport world believed those attributes were fixed capacities in each individual. Thus, even though the legend of the fifth century BC six-time Olympic champion Milo of Crotona – the ancient Greek wrestler who built his strength by carrying a calf on his shoulders until it grew into a bull – was well known, the socio-cultural conditions and scientific paradigm that would develop the basic principles of modern training (working against progressive resistance, over short intervals, for a long period of time) did not exist prior to World War II.[33]

Just before the turn of the twentieth century, training manuals counselled that the principles of training "differ but slightly from those of judicious living." Both, it was argued, "require the same close study and proper interpretation of the laws of health, and such an application of them as will produce temperate habits and a high degree of mental and bodily vigour."[34] Interest in human physiology would, however, soon begin to develop a knowledge base that would ultimately have far reaching effects on the world of sport.

Working with cadavers, C. Hirsch (1899) noted a relationship between heart size and body musculature. Three years later Schieffer (1902), and then H. Dietlen and F. Moritz (1908) corroborated Hirsch's observations by reporting that habitual cyclists had greater heart size than occasional and non-cyclists.[35] In 1905, W. Roux reported that increases in muscle size, strength and endurance were a chronic effect of exertion leading to his theory of "Aktivitätshypertrophie [hypertrophy through activity]" and "Inaktivitätsatrophie [atrophy through inactivity]."[36]

It is not surprising that German researchers played a leading role in these early studies of human physiology.[37] First, until the 1910 publication of Abraham Flexner's "Medical Education in the United States and Canada," medical education in North America lagged well behind Europe. During the nineteenth century and the early decades of the twentieth century many North American physicians studied abroad.[38] Second, within Europe, German leaders had consciously decided to make science one of the nation's focal points of success and pride.[39] Institutional investment in all areas of scientific research, including medicine and human physiology, was significant. As a result, following the world's first congress of sports physicians in 1912 at Oberhof, Thüringia, the Deutsche Reichskomitee für die wissenschaftliche Erforschung des Sports und der Leibesübungen [The German Empire's Committee for the Scientific Study of Sport and Physical Education] was founded. Although World War I interrupted the Committee's work, Arthur Mallwitz and August Bier quickly re-established German leadership by holding Europe's first lectures in sports medicine at the University of Berlin in 1919. Within a year, the Deutsche Hochschule für Leibesübungen [The German Academy for Physical Education] was established in the German capital and a few months later Das

Universitätsinstitut für Körperkultur [The University's Institute for Physical Culture] was opened in Gießen. In 1922, Germany held its first sports medicine conference in Berlin.[40]

However, interest in human physiology and the development of institutions where scientists and physicians could focus on human performance did not mean that sport science, as it is recognized today, began in the 1920s or 1930s. John Hoberman and Hildenbrant have emphasized that researchers at this time were preoccupied with discovering human potential rather than trying to modify it. "Performance-enhancement" Hoberman has emphasized, "meant tapping the hereditary potential of the human or animal organism rather than artificially manipulating the organism itself."[41] In the sport literature of the period, attention centred on "the biologically endowed, natural-born runner, jumper or thrower" and entire sections of books were dedicated to the suitability and significance of particular body types for specific athletic events.[42]

Based on the conservation of energy, training followed the "natural method" advocated by coaches such as France's Georges Hébert. Through drill and practice athletes became fully aware of their natural movements and focused on keeping a continuous pace and eliminating unnecessary movements. While "natural" in optimizing the natural talents of a given runner, the emphasis on pace, economy of movement, and clock time reflected something very unnatural, but the two were not at all contradictory.

The "natural method" was fully consistent with the first law of thermodynamics – a natural law. In addition, because the first law was a scientific law and applied to all movements, Hébert's technique was rooted in the same scientific principles that Frank and Lillian Gilbreth employed in their famous "time and motion studies" and Frederick Winslow Taylor's principles of scientific management.[43] Top results would be achieved on the basis of the same principles.

Taylor's science maximized workers' output by reducing their movements to individual components and then optimizing the execution of each one.[44] Performance improved through increased precision and better technique, not through an increased performance capacity. Similarly, time and motion studies, whether in the workplace or on the track, optimized a given output through efficiency; they did not try to develop an untapped "potential" capacity. Track and field coaches and industrial managers were working from the same set of assumptions about human performance, and sought increased efficiencies rather than expanded capacities.

Finnish distance runner Hannes Kolehmainen was one of the earliest beneficiaries of Hébert's technique. Kolehmainen trained at a specific tempo to determine the best running speed for his particular physique and style. At the 1912 Games, he won three gold medals and in the process defeated French world record holder Jean Bouin in the 5,000 meters. Kolehmainen initiated the era of the "Flying Finns," including Paavo Nurmi and Ville Ritola, who also focused on the style that best fitted their physiques, positioning on the track, and emphasized a continuous speed. Ritola and Nurmi, who ran with a stopwatch in his hand, dominated distance events throughout the 1920s.[45]

During the 1920s and 1930s, as European researchers began to build scientific knowledge about human physiology, they inevitably recorded observations related to exercise and human anatomy and physiology.[46] For example, Britain's Nobel Prize winning physiologist Archibald Hill's interest in muscle fatigue, lactic acid formation, and oxygen debt meant that his research required subjects who could withstand the rigors of his demanding protocols. As a result, he began to use athletes because they were among the few subjects who could complete his experiments.[47] Two outcomes emerged. First, Hill's findings were increasingly at odds with the conservation of energy thesis as it was understood by physiologists. Second, for those who knew about his work, there was an obvious application of Hill's research in muscle physiology to sport. Both of these would contribute to the development of a new paradigm in human performance and an emerging sport science.

Hill's work and his influence were not operating in isolation. Other researchers in basic physiology like S. Hoogerwert, W.W. Siebert, L. Pikhala, Arthur Steinhaus, A. Vannotti, H. Pfister, T. Petrén, T. Sjöstrand and B. Sylvén contributed to the development of an experimentally based body of knowledge concerning physiological responses to exercise.[48] For example, in 1930 Pikhala noted that athletic success required different physical "properties" – physical power, strength, and speed – and he argued that they could be realized if, in practice, there was a variation between activity and rest, there was a focus upon intensity rather than volume of practice sessions, and work was narrowed to specific goals. In the interwar period, Pikhala had begun to articulate the essential components of progressive resistance training for athletic development.[49]

Complementing Pikhala's work, E.H. Christensen found that regular training with a standard workload resulted in lowering the heart rate required to work at a fixed load. Further training, however, did not modify the response unless the load was increased in the subsequent training. When that was done, the original workload could be performed at an even lower heart rate than before. Christensen also established that physiological adaptation took place at a given load: to gain further improvements, training intensity had to be increased.[50]

In North America, leading edge research in human performance was centered in the Harvard Fatigue Lab, which was established in 1927 and operated until shortly after World War II. The relationship between the Fatigue Lab and sport is interesting because the Lab's primary inspiration, which was overseen by the Harvard School of Business, arose out of the "human factors" approach to industrial relations that stemmed directly from the Gilbreths' time and motion studies, and Taylor's principles of scientific management. As noted earlier, time–motion studies and scientific management had begun to exert an indirect influence on athletic training in the 1920s.[51]

The Fatigue Lab's genuinely collaborative research program involved physiologists, biochemists, psychologists, biologists, physicians, sociologists and anthropologists. The collaborative focus allowed investigators to study the effects and interrelation of the human body's many systems. Most important, research centered on "man's adaptation to his environment ... not only his normal, everyday, and working environments, but his adaptation to unusual stresses, such as athletic competition, exposure to strange environments and war."[52] The Fatigue Lab focused research on the physiochemical properties and behavior of blood – at rest, work and altitude – and pioneered many aspects of exercise physiology and the study of physiological responses to altitude.[53]

Although the Lab's researchers used athletes in many of their protocols, their inclusion was fortuitous. The researchers carried out most of their exploratory research on the Lab workers themselves; because a number happened to be athletes of various levels and abilities they discovered, by chance, significant differences among normal, trained, and well-trained subjects. Nevertheless, despite the differences they discovered and the Lab's particular interest in fitness, none of the research was directed toward enhancing athletic performance, even though the discoveries made in the areas of blood chemistry in exercise, aerobic and anaerobic work capacity, diet, and physiological adaptation to physical work at altitude would later all be used to enhance world-class athletic performance.[54]

Discoveries in Europe and North America during the first quarter of the twentieth century provided information that was increasingly difficult to explain on the basis of the first law of thermodynamics and the dominant paradigm of fixed capacities. Rather than reinforcing the idea of the body as a vessel with fixed, inherited traits and capacities, research began to suggest that the body adapted and responded to its environment. In *The Wisdom of the Body* (1932), Walter Cannon presented one of the early, full-length statements of the conception that the body seeks physiological stability and when that stability is upset "then the various physiological arrangements which serve to restore the normal state when it has been disturbed" are brought into play.[55] The notion that the body could use a complex set of physiological processes to maintain its homeostatic condition in the face of significant, external changes and pressures suggested that it might be possible to develop its physiological work capacity.

Despite the research findings in human physiology in the 1930s and 1940s, there was a significant lag between the development of new knowledge in universities and institutes and its application in the field of sport. Part of the reason was the inevitable and perpetual gulf that exists between theory and practice. A second major impediment was the philosophical approach that dominated sport at the time. This was the era of nascent commercialism and the apogee of amateur sport's emphasis on character development and education through athletic competition. As a result, outcome and performance enhancement were of secondary importance. Finally, there was an irrefutable reality within the realm of sport: "Lord Kelvin's dictum," Jokl chided as late as 1958 in "The Future of Athletics,"

> unequivocally accepted by the natural sciences as long ago as during the last quarter of the nineteenth century, viz. "that no science can flourish without theory," *has made no impression whatever on physical training.* The latter remains one of the few disciplines of education whose affairs are still conducted without the benefit of theoretical concepts [emphasis added].[56]

A random survey of training books in the late 1940s and early 1950s substantiates Jokl's critique of physical education in general, and athletic training in particular. *Physical Conditioning: Exercises for Sports and Healthful Living*, a 1942 publication in the Barnes Sports Library, is a good example of how even though the basic principles of an emerging physiology of exercise were recognized by proponents of athletic training, they were applied in a highly limited manner.[57] Like Pikhala, George Stafford and Ray Duncan defined fitness as those "qualities best represented by strength, power, speed, skill and endurance for the task, plus proper enthusiasm (mental equilibrium, morale, and mind-set)."[58] But Stafford and Duncan include no discussion of intensity in training sessions and variations between activity and rest although there is some attention to specificity (a concept understood through the study of Olympic athletes as early as 1929).[59] The authors' main guiding principle for athletic training is "you learn to do anything whatsoever by *doing it* [emphasis in original]."[60] Thus athletes who ran the 440 yards should train at distances of 350 to 500 yards. In other sports, practices should last about the duration of an actual competition "and accomplish about the same amount of work at the same speed."[61]

Chapter Four, "Sports Conditioning," presents conditioning activities for a number of sports ranging alphabetically from basketball and boxing, through football and gymnastics, to track and weightlifting. The most striking feature of these "conditioning" exercises is that even high school athletes today would regard them as warm up callisthenics. *Physical Conditioning* recommends athletes follow these exercises throughout a four-week period, reducing their duration from 15 minutes in week one to only five minutes in week four.[62] Stafford and Duncan never draw upon Pikhala, Christensen, Steinhaus or the Fatigue Lab's insights; their recommendations do not remotely approach contemporary regimes of training and conditioning.

Physical Conditioning does not direct athletes to long-term development through progressive resistance and varied intervals of work and rest. It does not indicate that a regime of exercises as sport specific as possible, carefully designed to build power, strength, speed, agility, coordination, quickness, flexibility, local muscular endurance, and cardiovascular aerobic capacity is the most proficient and useful approach to enhancing athletic performance.[63] In fact, Stafford and Duncan's text does not suggest, or even imply, the two most basic principles of contemporary training and conditioning – the "overload principle" and the "principle of specificity."[64] Moreover, there is no discussion that would either suggest that such a program might be possible and desirable, or that the authors had the knowledge base from which they might formulate those principles or develop more elaborate training programs.

Texts such as *Track and Field Athletics* (1947), *Championship Technique in Track and Field* (1949), and the United States Naval Institute's *Track and Field* (1950) demonstrate approaches to training and conditioning that also lack a sophisticated knowledge base in exercise physiology. As a result, the general guidelines for training and conditioning do not contain the sophistication of today's texts or the type of intensity that would soon characterize athletic training from the mid- to late-1960s onwards.[65] The principles that guide training in *Track and Field Athletics* stem directly from the first law of thermodynamics by focusing on drill to refine technique, improve coordination, and enhance execution. "At the present time," George Bresnahan and W.W. Tuttle note,

> the study of the techniques involved in these sports has become a science worthy of the thought and attention of a profession which is trying, through scientific investigation, to improve technique and skill for all, as well as to cut tenths of a second from running times and to increase jumping and throwing distances by fractions of an inch for the expert performer.[66]

The main chapter on conditioning focuses on the variables that "build and maintain physical and mental states which are most conducive to acceptable performance." The variables discussed are diet, elimination, exercise, weight, rest, sleep, staleness, stimulants and the use of tobacco.[67] The discussion of exercise is confined to two paragraphs – about half a page – where the authors indicate that the exercise in an athlete's regular daily routine is usually sufficient to maintain health. In cases where an athlete must carry out manual labor, "there exists the danger of over exercise." Ideally, the "athlete has no responsibilities requiring strenuous exercise other than the prescribed work in the event."[68] The only discussion of physiological principles occurs in the chapter "Preliminary Season Preparations," but these focus mainly on the importance of warming up and the development of muscle coordination.[69] While the workouts outlined in the text demonstrate a progressive workload, the principles involved in the development of the workouts are not discussed at all.

Championship Technique in Track and Field begins by associating success in track and field with race and national histories before moving into principles of training. The "key word in what we miscall training for track and field" Dean Cromwell and Al Wesson note, "is moderation."[70] The vital principle for training in track and field is training muscles for "special duties. No elaborate system of exercise is necessary if one will just remember that the aim is to develop muscular coordination rather than just muscle." For Cromwell and Wesson, "the two basic exercises that everyone should take are walking and chinning the bar." The latter develops the body from the waist up and the former from the waist down. Cromwell and Wesson maintain that people enjoy sports most when they win; this is why athletes train "and do without a few little things like pie crust and tobacco," which is so easy to do "that we don't need to call it training at all. It is just living a normal, moderate, regular life. It is also the secret of how to live to be a hundred."[71] Sharing more in common with training manuals from the late nineteenth century, *Championship Technique* does not demonstrate any of the insight into the physiological discoveries that researchers had uncovered in the 1920s and 1930s.

The Naval Institute's *Track and Field* was "prepared and published during World War II to provide the best standardized instruction in the sports selected to give the youth, training to be combat Naval pilots, the maximum physical and psychological benefits." The text emphasizes that "the modern coach is a college graduate, versed in kinesiology, physiology, anatomy, hygiene and physics. ... [H]e keeps abreast of physiological studies relating to fatigue and exercise."[72] The information presented, however, is very basic. Like the other work cited above, *Track and Field* distinguishes between "core material" which focuses on "circulatory-respiratory functions related to exercise" and "supplementary drills and races" in which drills of short duration or "acts of pure skill" are proposed to improve coordination and help athletes "meet sudden, emergency physical demands."[73]

The cold war divide

World War II and the beginning of the cold war transformed international, world-class, high-performance sport as approaches to training, the use of scientific knowledge to enhance performance, and the resources directed towards the pursuit of the linear record changed dramatically. Stalwart proponents of the educative value of Olympic sport, even by the late 1950s, were yearning for an age that never was and certainly would not exist in the remainder of the twentieth century. "The last decade [1950s] has covered a strange period in the history of sport," Sir Roger Bannister argued, "a far cry from what was envisaged by Baron Coubertin."

> It has seen the emergence of the new professionalism not only in the sense of direct and indirect payment for sport, but also in devoting unlimited time and energy to sport, to the total exclusion of any other career – which has been rightly deplored. Every country seeks to enhance national prestige by physical achievements. ... Too few questions seem to be asked about the means and the motives, provided the end of national glory is achieved.[74]

But, Bannister maintained, sport would "survive the ethical and administrative problems" because, in the last analysis, sport is an individual affair with an individual meaning and "not a national or moral affair. We run not because our country needs fame, nor yet because we think it is doing us good, but because we enjoy it and cannot help ourselves." For Bannister, "sportsmen" compete because they seek "the deep satisfaction, the sense of personal dignity which comes when body and mind are fully coordinated and they have achieved mastery over themselves."[75]

The actual record of post-war sport demonstrates that the focus in Olympic and world-class sport was elsewhere. Frucht and Jokl's statistical analysis of records in world-class sport from 1948 to 1960 revealed continual improvement at an accelerating pace.[76] The features of world-class, high-performance sport that Bannister regarded as part of "a strange period in the history of sport" were firmly entrenched by the 1960s and would simply expand their influence rather than retreat into the background. Two of the central reasons were the strategic political objectives of particular national leaders and the increased allocation of resources directed to world-class sport. Scientifically assisted, high-performance *sport systems*, and not individuals, became the main agents in world-class, high-performance sport in the post-war period.

Although those changes were instrumental in changing the nature of world-class sport in the post-World War II era, their full impact rested on a significant paradigm shift in the ontology of human performance. Two sports – weightlifting and track and field – were at the centre of the paradigm shift and, ironically, Bannister may have played a central role in the emergence of the new performance enhancement paradigm.

Calvin Schulman notes that by 1954 the public at large was obsessed with the pursuit of the four-minute mile. John Landy had shaved the time to 4:02. "Two little seconds are not much" Landy said. "But when you are on the track those 15 yards seem solid and impenetrable – like a cement wall." According to Schulman

> It would take a miler of steel and imagination to break down decades of disbelief. It would take that special someone to summon the perfect blend of stamina and speed, with inner strength and supreme awareness of his own body, to batter down the cement wall and let the future of athletics charge into the promised land.[77]

It would actually take more – it would require a change in the approach to training which would, indeed, lead the "charge into the promised land" and fundamentally change athletes' orientation to performance and performance enhancement.

Efficiency alone would not make the barrier fall. In the pursuit of the four-minute barrier, Bannister, Wes Santee, and Landy began unwittingly to remove a more fundamental one – the performance paradigm rooted in the conservation of energy. In pursuit of the four-minute mile, Bannister, Landy, Santee and other athletes and coaches began to use training techniques that went beyond perfecting technique through drill; they aimed to build their performance capacities. As a result, rather than reflecting the apogee of amateurism, the "miracle mile" is better thought of as a dramatic, 3:59.4 turning point in the rise of the new paradigm in high-performance sport in the post-war era.

With bachelor's and master's degrees in physiology, and medical degrees, Bannister was uniquely situated in the track world of his time; he was familiar with the experimental literature in physiology and could have known Pikhala, Christensen, Steinhaus, Hill and others' work. Irrespective of the exact literature he drew upon, Bannister experimented on himself – including treadmill runs with oxygen enriched air – to enhance his performances. Neal Bascomb argues Bannister possessed unique expertise "for your average miler." He "was aswim in a sea of lactate counts, carbon dioxide readings, and oxygen consumption levels from his experiments."[78] Bannister used the new Swedish "fartlek" and "interval training" techniques which involved carefully planned work bouts alongside periods of rest and he used the most advanced technology available to enhance his performances.[79] Without necessarily subscribing to the emerging ontology of human performance, Bannister's use of physiological knowledge and newly developing training techniques were significant steps towards the replacement of the old conservation of energy paradigm.

Bob Hoffman, one of the most influential people in US weightlifting throughout the 1940s and 1950s, had at that time assembled America's most successful weightlifting team by recruiting widely and offering work at the York Oil Burner company. Not an innovator, Hoffman firmly believed that when athletes with talent worked hard, kept high moral standards and lived in a congenial atmosphere, they would succeed. His team's success was firmly rooted in the pre-World War II paradigm of human performance. However, as John Fair notes, by the mid-fifties "the course and character of American weightlifting" was changing as weightlifters began "a deeper search for ways to alter the body's chemistry to induce more efficient muscular growth."[80] The Soviets' use of testosterone in the 1952 Games, and John Ziegler's introduction of Dianabol to American weightlifters[81] reflected an understanding of the newly emerging paradigm of human performance.

While research results partly undermined the conservation of energy paradigm, a more important factor was the fundamental shift in some scientists' perception of the world based on their World War II life experiences. Donna Haraway argues that in the west, at the end of World War II, the discourse in biochemistry shifted from the mechanistic view of the first law of thermodynamics to one based in information theory.[82] The discovery of DNA and the way its properties were understood could only be explained within the discourse of information theory – the body was coded, with instructions, messages, controls and feedback mechanisms that could be decoded, manipulated and maximized. Part of the reason for the paradigm shift was the number of biologists who had been engaged in operations research during World War II which made the discourse of communications, codes, and cybernetic systems seem familiar and natural. The ontology of human development and human potential shifted to the cellular level where information was stored and could now be located and decoded to enhance performance. There was, however, a time lag between these developments in microbiology and applied sport science.

The paradigm shift on the other side of the iron curtain was probably caused by a different set of circumstances. The USSR's scientifically based, instrumentally rational approach to sport, adopted early in the post-World War II period, was part of a centralized plan. As a result, the sport system was directly subject to Communist Party policy and ideology and Stalin had dictated that all scientific developments must stem from the tenets of Marxism–Leninism and dialectical materialism.[83] The key text was Friedrich Engels' *Dialectics of Nature* which argued that all entities – social and biological – were subject to the "law of dialectics" and underwent continuous dialectical development and transformation.[84]

Throughout the 1920s and 1930s, Soviet biologists argued about natural selection, species development and genetics. Within that debate, in defence of his theory of "vernalization," the agronomist Trofim Denisovich Lysenko offered a theory about the plasticity of the life cycle. The crucial factor determining the length of the vegetation period was not its genetic constitution but its interaction with its environment. Because the theory was consistent with the *Dialectics of Nature* and, more important, Stalin's *Dialectical and Historical Materialism*, and "refuted" rival bourgeois and Menshevik theories, Lysenko's theory gained Stalin's support and approval. Lysenko rose to become the chief theoretician in Soviet biology.

Lysenko's chief argument was that heredity was not determined by genes. The growth and development of all organisms depended on the laws of dialectics. Genetic endowment or heredity was largely irrelevant because organisms developed through the dialectical interaction of organism and environment – through the internalization of external conditions. Although a disaster for Soviet agriculture, Lysenko's basic assumptions may well have opened the way to a new paradigm regarding the ontology of human performance.[85] Human performance capacity, within Lysenko's theory, could be altered and enhanced through the interaction of the organism with its environment. With state support, Lysenko's insights may have had a revolutionary impact on the concept of training and how the ontological foundation of human performance would be understood in the eastern bloc during the post-World War II period. Irrespective of the motivation, the Soviet Union (and later, East Germany and other eastern bloc countries) invested heavily in the development of well-funded sport systems and put particular emphasis on the development of applied sport science.

Sport science began to be firmly entrenched in the immediate post-World War II period. Thus, for example, as early as 1947, sports medicine clinics were opened in the Soviet Occupied Sector of Germany and, with the founding of the Deutsche Hochschule für Körperkultur [German Academy for Physical Culture] in Leipzig in 1950, the East Germans developed a special section for sports medicine. The SED established the Arbeitsgemeinschaft für Sportmedizin [Working Group for Sport Medicine] in 1953 and it was fully institutionalized as the Gesellschaft für Sportmedizin der DDR [GDR Society for Sport Medicine] by 1956.[86]

In North America, interest in the scientific study of sport and exercise grew with the "coming of age" of programs in physical and health education within Canadian and American universities. While primarily oriented to the preparation of high school physical education teachers, there was growing pressure on physical education programs to engage in scientific research, and it was in the study of applied physiology that departments of physical education could make the best connection between the scholarly community and their pedagogical mandate in universities.

A careful review of Åstrand and Rodahl's *Textbook of Work Physiology*, one of the most influential texts in exercise physiology, and Bert Taylor's 1975 *The Scientific Aspects of Sports Training*, indicates that during the late 1950s, exponentially increasing through the 1960s, the new paradigm of performance enhancement was firmly entrenched in Europe and North America.[87] More important than the movement to extend the use of physiological principles to understand and enhance physical performance in athletics, was the growth of institutional support for that undertaking.

In Canada, for example, institutional support for sport science grew out of, and along with, the emerging emphases on applied physiology. The Canadian

Medical Association in conjunction with the Canadian Association for Health, Physical Education and Recreation, established the Canadian Association of Sports Sciences at the 1967 Pan American Games held in Winnipeg. Renamed the Canadian Society for Exercise Physiology (CSEP), its goals were to "promote and foster the growth of the highest quality research and education in exercise physiology" and "to apply the knowledge derived from research in exercise physiology." CSEP holds annual meetings and publishes its own journal, the *Canadian Journal of Applied Physiology*, while also funding research in sport.[88] In 1970, the more exclusive Canadian Academy of Sports Medicine (CASM), open only to medical doctors, postgraduate medical trainees (residents or fellows) and medical students, was also established. CASM also hosts annual meetings, publishes a newsletter, has a fellowship program in sports medicine and produces the *Clinical Journal of Sports Medicine*.[89]

While much slower to invest in high-performance sport research than the GDR, the FRG established the Deutsche Vereinigung für Sportwissenschaft [German Union of Sport Science – DVS] in Munich in 1976.[90] The DVS was given the mandate to support, promote and develop sport science in the FRG. The DVS has held congresses, meetings and symposia, and in 1981 began disseminating the results of those events in the *Schriften der Deutschen Vereinigung für Sportwissenschaft* [Publications of the German Union of Sport Science]. Consistent with the strong humanist traditions in German scholarship, the *Schriften* are very broad in scope and include a number of works that are historical, philosophical, or socio-cultural in focus. It was not until 2002 that the DVS discussed the use of a periodical to disseminate its ideas; by November 2004, it had become an editorial partner with the DSB and the Bundesinstitut für Sportwissenschaft in the publication of *Sportwissenschaft: The German Journal of Sports Science* [Sport Science: The German Journal of Sports Science].[91] This journal reflects the same wide range of approaches to sport science as the DVS's *Schriften*. Following its commitment to the regular journal format, DVS also began to produce an electronic journal *Bewegung und Training* [Movement and Training] which focuses more narrowly on biomechanics, sport motor theory and training science.[92]

Training and performance enhancement today

While the decisions individual athletes make concerning their training regimens or the use of a banned substance appear to be isolated and voluntary, in reality they take place within the context of a large, complex set of historically created and socially situated actions and relationships. Most important, and most often overlooked, is the fact that at the root of those systems and decisions is an image of the ontology of human performance. Over the course of the mid-twentieth century, for a variety of reasons (scientific, political, performance-related, and accidental), a fundamentally important paradigm shift occurred in sport. Breaking away from the first law of thermodynamics over the middle years of the twentieth century, modern world-class sport now locates human performance within an ontological conception that permits and indeed promotes the continuous, scientifically assisted enhancement of athletes' performance capacities. Cycling can serve as an example of the impact this change has had upon the world of high-performance sport.

Mignon notes that during the first century of cycling (1850 to 1950), riders used stimulants and pain killers to maximize their performance.[93] These substances and their intended effects were consistent with the ontology of human performance dominant at that time; they were not intended to help riders develop or expand their performance capacities, merely to allow them to use their existing capacities fully. The substances were "home-made" and the knowledge surrounding them was passed, "like kitchen recipes," "from rider to rider and from *soigneur* to rider." After the 1960s, however, systematic programs were developed and success in cycling, as in other high-performance sports, required highly organized, scientifically based, large, well-funded, programs of development. "The 1960s" Mignon argues,

> saw the emergence of a new type of individual, "the trained athlete," different psychologically and physiologically from the man in the street. There also developed medical routines specific to the sports person, with specific treatments for specific injuries, but also specific care for preparation. This went hand in hand with the development of medical staff as a necessary condition of sports preparation: bio-mechanics for exercises and massages; nutritional scientists for vitamins and complements; psychologists for personal discipline and meditation; pharmacologists for the use of different medicines on the market. This rationale could also come to encompass non-medical uses of medicine such as steroids, analgesics, stimulants or tranquillisers.[94]

The paradigm shift in the ontology of human performance meant more than a new way of thinking about human capacities, important as that was. It focused attention upon performance enhancement – the scientifically informed enhancement of human athletic performance. This led to the growth of tremendous institutional support as expert knowledge, specialized materials, and innovative technologies needed to push human physical performance to its outer limits.

Throughout the twentieth century, the scientific community's understanding of human physiology has changed and deepened dramatically. The human body is no longer viewed as an organism with fixed capacities that can only be improved through better coordination and synchronization. Medical and sport science researchers now regard human physiological work capacity as a potential that can be expanded and tailored through specific, scientifically researched techniques and supplements. The new paradigm in sport science is dominated by an instrumental, technological rationality where the results of experimental research from around the globe concerning performance enhancement are placed directly at the fingertips of applied sport scientists, coaches, and athletes as they explore and experiment with training techniques and methods to enhance athletic performance. Athletes, professionals in sports medicine, and coaches now find themselves at the centre of a well-funded, high stakes drive to push human performance to its outer limits.

Sport, as an abstraction, is still tied in the vernacular to its etymological roots in disport as a diversion from serious duties, relaxation, recreation, entertainment and amusement. In the real world of world-class, high-performance sport in the twenty-first century, however, none of those traits apply any longer. On the contrary, world-class, high-performance sport is an intensive, exhausting occupation in which the athletes are fully committed to scientifically regulated training regimes and performance technologies that create long-term physiological and personality changes as they progress through the high stakes, winner-takes-all road to the pinnacle of world-class sport. Anything less is simply sport–tourism.[95]

4 From Stalingrad to Helsinki
The development of German sport systems

Chapter One presented, in outline, how sport at the international level changed from the 1950s through to the 1980s. The development of contemporary world-class, high-performance sport merits much more detailed attention. It is impossible to understand the world of international sport at its highest levels today without examining, in detail, the social and historical forces and pressures that built the high-performance sport systems on both sides of the iron curtain. The next two chapters focus on the political, social and material events that shaped the development of the high-performance sport systems in the GDR and the FRG. These systems have been chosen for very specific reasons.

First, as part of a unified Empire that extended from 1871 to 1945, Germans on both sides of the post-World War II east–west divide shared an identical sport history and sport culture. Despite that common heritage, the unique political dynamics among the Allied occupational forces in the immediate post-war period, along with the wider dynamics of the cold war in the 1950s and 1960s, led to two substantially different high-performance sport systems.

Second, the system established in the GDR reflects many of the major features that characterized high-performance sport systems within the eastern bloc. Similarly, the FRG's sport system shares the fundamental features of those established in the west.[1] The study of both provides detailed insight into how high-performance sport developed on both sides of the iron curtain.

Third, both systems clearly demonstrate the trajectory and momentum of the world of high-performance sport away from Coubertin's original vision as well as the quantum differences that now exist between the experiences of contemporary high-performance athletes and those at the turn of the nineteenth century. More important, the ensuing material establishes that despite the apparently divergent developments in East and West Germany, the performance imperatives of contemporary, international sport and the domination of technical rationality on both sides of the east–west divide created a fundamental convergence of the two systems concerning the central features of high-performance sport systems in the modern era. This convergence and the principles upon which it took place are central to any sociological understanding of the use of performance-enhancing substances in world-class, high-performance sport today.

Fourth, while television, the sporting goods industries and other commercial interests played significant roles in shaping contemporary world-class, high-performance sport and created the enormous impetus behind the quest for pushing human athletic performance to increasingly rarefied heights, it was the immediate and long-term political goals of nation states during the cold war that played the decisive role in shaping world-class sport today. The next two chapters indicate that the unprecedented investment of material resources, personnel, and research activity on the part of the GDR did more to shape the contours of high-performance sport today than any other factors in this complex and intriguing historical drama. For that reason, the use of banned, performance-enhancing substances in world-class, high-performance sport today cannot be understood without an analysis of the sport systems in the FRG and the GDR.

Finally, although the popular media, WADA, the IOC, judges, sport scholars, special interest advocates and others have attributed the GDR's phenomenal success in world-class sport to the use of anabolic–androgenic steroids, the explanation is too simplistic. It does not withstand the weight of evidence brought to light in a thorough analysis of the history and nature of the high-performance sport systems in East Germany. While making this point, the ensuing material also demonstrates that the dominant imperatives of world-class, high-performance sport today, including the use of performance-enhancing substances in some sports, stem directly from the internal logic of the comprehensive sport systems that nation-states developed over the last half century.

To fully understand the energy and resources the GDR directed toward high-performance sport, one must situate them within a complex array of social forces. One must understand, for example, the particular vision Walter Ulbricht, the first General Secretary of the Central Committee of the SED, held for East Germany and how he wanted to approach the "German Question" in general in the post-war period. Furthermore, the political differences, conflicts and struggles that existed between East and West Germany, as well as those between the GDR and the USSR, played an important role in shaping the GDR's high-performance sport system in particular, and high-performance sport systems more generally.[2] Although a history of the political, military, economic, and diplomatic conflicts and negotiations among the USSR, the USA, Great Britain, France, the GDR and the FRG can be written without mentioning sport, an understanding of the conflicts among those nations in the realm of sport must be written within the context of that larger history. The desire simply to win gold medals or push athletic performance to the outer limits of human possibility does not fully or adequately explain the GDR's and the FRG's commitment to, and investment in, high-performance sport. The reasons are deeply rooted in their social, political and diplomatic history, and it is from there that the full history of high-performance sport in the later, post-World War II era unfolds.

"Erobern und vernichten [conquer and annihilate]"

Adolf Hitler envisioned the war in the Soviet Union as his crowning achievement. Operation Barbarossa would result in the vast geographical expansion of the German Empire and total control over the abundant natural resources and rich agricultural land that the Thousand Year Reich would require. Most important, it would end in the total annihilation of "Jewish Bolshevism" and the complete "racial purification" of Eastern Europe and the USSR, realizing two of *Mein Kampf*'s most important objectives.[3]

German High Command shared the view that the war in the east was a campaign like no other. It was a "war of world historical decision," a "war of ideologies" in which there could be no compromise. "This war," Panzer Group 3 commander General Hermann Hoth wrote in a general order of November 1941, "can only end with the annihilation of one or the other; there will be no conciliation." General Field Marshal Erich von Manstein, the 56th Panzer Corps commander, noted much the same in a general order for the eastern front:

> The German soldier is obliged to not only destroy the means of military power of this [Jewish-Bolshevik] system. He marches forth as the standard bearer of [Nazi Germany's] racially pure idea and as an avenger of all the atrocities that have been committed against him and the German Volk. The solider must demonstrate an understanding of the harsh atonement to be brought down upon Judaism, the spiritual bearer of the Bolshevik terror.[4]

The eastern campaign began on June 22, 1941 with the same devastating, modern, mechanized Blitzkrieg tactics the Nazis had used in Poland and western Europe. By October 14, the 10th Panzer Division and the SS Das Reich Division had matched Napoleon's advance to within 100 kilometres of Moscow. Soviet leadership was in crisis and Moscow was under siege by October 19.[5] But the vast steppes of the Soviet Union soon swallowed up German supply lines; Panzer divisions were slowed to a crawl in the October rains; and the early November winter brought snow, bitter winds, and bone-numbing temperatures. Exhausted, ill-equipped infantrymen shed their close fitting, steel-shod jackboots, which hastened frostbite, and wrapped their feet in paper, rags, clothing, or pieces of felt stolen from the dead, Soviet prisoners, or unfortunate civilians. The war in the east was quickly reduced, at unprecedented human cost, to the brutal, demoralizing battle of attrition that had characterized the Great War 24 years earlier.[6]

The major turning point of World War II came on January 31, 1943. The war turned irrevocably when Field Marshal Friedrich Paulus surrendered the Wehrmacht's 6th Army to General Mikhail Shumilov of the 64th Army at Stalingrad. Two days earlier, on the eve of Hitler's tenth anniversary as German Chancellor, Paulus had put forth the bravest face possible in his army's desperate situation. "The swastika still flies over Stalingrad" Paulus noted in his congratulations to the Führer on his rise to power. "May our struggle" he continued, "be an example to present and future generations never to surrender in hopeless situations so that Germany will be victorious in the end."[7]

Luftwaffe Commander-in-Chief, Reich Marshal Hermann Goering, in his own tribute to Hitler, brought Paulus and his troops back to reality when he compared the fate of the 6th Army to the Spartans at Thermopylae.[8] Worse yet, Hitler's own anniversary speech included only one single sentence about the troops at Stalingrad. "The heroic struggle of our soldiers on the Volga should be an exhortation to everyone to do his maximum in the struggle for Germany's freedom and our nation's future." It was Hitler's first, tacit admission that the Wehrmacht was fighting to stave off defeat – not just in Stalingrad but across the entire front.[9] One day later, Paulus surrendered and World War II changed irrevocably.

The war in the east was the most destructive, brutal, and desperate conflict in human history. Its impact upon survivors never faded and its horrific legacy hung over the USSR and Germany throughout the entire cold war period. Twenty million Soviet citizens, more than half of them civilians, died along with 2.5 million German soldiers. The Germans took 5.7 million prisoners and executed more than 600,000 immediately, while another 2.1 million died as prisoners of war. In the siege of Stalingrad alone, the Red Army suffered 1.1 million casualties, almost half a million of whom died.[10] Worse yet, none of these figures begins to capture the true extent of the moral depravity, sadistic brutality, capricious, grisly violence, unbridled terror, and systematic, mechanized genocide that the Nazi state carried out in the occupied territories of the east.

By the end of January 1943, not all of the seeds of German–Soviet fear and loathing had been sown. Within two weeks of Paulus's surrender, Goebbels launched a new propaganda offensive before more than 14,000 frenzied supporters in the Berlin Sports Palace. "The English" Goebbels began, "maintain that the German people no longer believe in victory" to which the crowd responded loudly and derisively. "I ask you, do you believe in the Führer and with us *in the absolute final victory of the German Volk?*" As the crowd responded, Goebbels continued, "I ask you – are you committed to following the Führer and *to struggle for victory through thick and thin – under conditions that will require the most difficult personal sacrifice?*" Following another question of support, Goebbels said: "Third, the English maintain that the German people have lost their passion to take on the sacrifices for the war effort that its government asks." Building again, he continued: "I ask you – soldiers, and all workers – are you and is the German people committed, if the Führer orders it, *to work ten, twelve and – if necessary – fourteen and sixteen hours a day in order to bring victory?*" to which the crowd gave its roaring commitment. This led to Goebbels' key questions:

Fourth, the English maintain that the German Volk opposes the measures of total war required by the government [derisive crowd reaction]. The people will not fight a total war but would rather surrender. I ask you – *do you want total war* [overwhelming support from the crowd]! *Do you want, if necessary, an even more total and radical war than we can even imagine!* [Unconditional roars of approval.] Fifth, the English maintain that the German Volk has lost its faith in the Führer [lengthy, derisive reaction]. I ask you, *do you believe in the Führer* [tumultuous support]!

As the throng gave thundering support to the Reich Minister for Propaganda, Goebbels continued: "I have asked and you have given me your answer. You are a part of the people who, with your voices, have made manifest the views of the German Volk. You have told our enemies what they must know."[11] Goebbels' final comment – "From here on our slogan is 'The people rise and the storm breaks loose'" – was drowned out by the crowd's tumultuous roar of approval.

The total war Goebbels and Hitler undertook – an acceleration of mechanized murder in the extermination camps, the use of slave labor in the construction of the secret, self-propelled V2 rockets, forced death marches, and a vicious scorched earth policy as the Germans retreated from the USSR and Eastern Europe – left Germans with no option but to resist the Soviet Army with every means possible.[12] German atrocities, the sieges of Moscow, Leningrad and Stalingrad, and Stalin's propaganda had made an indelible mark on the Soviet troops whose hatred of anything German was truly visceral. As the Soviet Army advanced, more than two years of Nazi barbarism were repaid in full as the Germans were driven back to the confines of the bunker under the Reich Chancellery in Berlin. The German soldiers, terrified of the consequences that the Soviet advance meant for their families, resisted unrelentingly.[13]

The depersonalized, primordial revulsion that now existed on both sides of the German–Soviet conflict is vividly captured in an incident recounted by Beevor. A column of British prisoners of war passed a large group of Soviet prisoners in the bleak, snow-covered landscape of East Prussia.

"Their white starved faces," wrote Robert Kee, "contrasted horribly with the black unshaven growth of beard which covered them. Only their eyes shone out as something human, distressed and furtive but human all the same, flashing out a last desperate SOS from the person trapped inside." The British took what they had in their pockets, whether soap or cigarettes, and threw it across. One packet of cigarettes fell short. As a Russian prisoner bent to pick it up, a Volkssturm guard ran up to stamp on his outstretched fingers. He then kicked the man and began to strike him with his rifle butt. This provoked "a wild roar of rage" from the British column. "The guard stopped beating the Russian and looked up astonished. He had obviously become so hardened to brutality that it no longer occurred to him that human beings had any right to protest." He began to bellow and wave his gun threateningly, but they roared and jeered all the more. Their own guards came pounding up to restore order and push the Volkssturm man back towards his own prisoners. "My God!" said one of Kee's companions. "I'll forgive the Russians absolutely anything they do to this country when they arrive. Absolutely anything."[14]

As the Germans retreated, they laid waste to everything they had taken in the invasion of the USSR.[15] Most of the destruction was conducted under orders and in a disciplined manner but some of the troops did not wait for formal direction. Since the war in the east had already provided German troops with an array of rationalizations and incentives for brutal treatment of captured enemy soldiers and the occupied civilian population, these "wild actions" were not surprising. Moreover, the "scope of officially authorized murder, maltreatment, and destruction of property far outweighed 'wild' actions performed on the troops' own initiative." As Bartov argues,

> the troops' conduct can only be understood within the context of the Wehrmacht's far-reaching legalization of actions previously considered criminal, the organized manner of their execution, and the widespread agreement with the ideology which motivated them, all of which made for a situation whereby an army normally insistent on rigid obedience allowed its troops to get away with mass breaches of discipline regarding the treatment of enemy soldiers and civilians.[16]

Paradoxically, these "wild acts" of brutality allowed German officers to continue to inflict harsh combat discipline on their troops and maintain a fighting cohesion among the retreating German forces. Resistance to the Soviet advance was as determined as the young German conscripts could manage against the battle hardened Soviet veterans.

The brutality of war in the east and the holocaust of European Jewry left the German High Command with few options when faced with trying to end the war. Surrender to the Soviets was unthinkable but Churchill and Roosevelt would not negotiate a peace without Stalin.[17] Moreover, all three Allied leaders had agreed in January 1943 that the main Allied war objective was the unconditional surrender of the Axis enemy.

As Stalin's troops pushed the Germans back into Eastern Europe, he did not move directly on Berlin. Instead, following Soviet entry into Poland in 1944, Stalin began to lay the groundwork for the post-World War II world he wanted. Stalin's goal was "to outdo the founder of the Soviet Union, Vladimir Lenin, in spreading world revolution and the czars in establishing an empire."[18] His forces conquered all of Eastern Europe and the Balkans to ensure there was a significant Soviet-controlled buffer between the USSR and Germany. Stalin expanded the USSR westward into Poland while moving the Polish border deeper into former German territory, stopping at the Oder and Neisse Rivers. Stalin wanted to cripple Germany by exacting 20 billion dollars in reparations payments – half of which would go to the Soviets – and dismantle German industries and relocate them inside the USSR. Finally, Stalin opposed the permanent, territorial dismemberment of Germany because he believed that he could turn post-World War II Germany into a reliable ally and bring it into the Soviet sphere of influence. A Germany that was sympathetic to the Soviet Union would totally change the balance of global power.

Stalin's plan to annex Germany was not an idle dream. Following the armistice of World War I, a number of spontaneous, socialist revolutions had erupted in Germany; Stalin felt the same might occur as the Soviets liberated Germany from Nazism. Not leaving that outcome to chance, throughout World War II Stalin carefully groomed a unique, clandestine group of German communists, under Walter Ulbricht, which he transplanted into Berlin before the war's end. The "Ulbricht Group" actively infiltrated resistance groups inside Nazi Germany to rally them to the socialist cause. As the Soviets began to take control of Germany, the Ulbricht Group sought out administrators and local leaders who would be sympathetic to social democratic and communist objectives. Acting as a "fifth column" inside Berlin, the group undertook a wide variety of ideological activities to (re)shape post-war attitudes towards communism in general and the Soviet liberators in particular.[19]

Following the May 7, 1945 surrender of the Nazis' forces to the Allies, the USA, Britain, France and the USSR assumed supreme authority – including the powers of government at all levels – in Germany. They quickly divided the country into four Sectors of Occupation, with Berlin, in the midst of the Soviet Occupation Sector, also divided into four. The Potsdam conference of July 7 to August 1, 1945, signalled the end of the struggle against Germany but merely the beginning of the battle over Germany's future.

Stalin was not alone in seeking particular post-war objectives that would serve his national interests. France wanted to permanently divide Germany and place the Ruhr region under the control of the countries that used its rich industrial resources – France, Switzerland, Italy, the Netherlands, Belgium and Luxembourg. The Americans initially wanted to withdraw from Germany and Europe within two years of the war's end. But General Lucius D. Clay, General Dwight Eisenhower's successor as Military Governor of Germany, convinced President Truman that a continued American presence was necessary to keep the Soviets from eventually annexing Germany and depriving the west of its buffer from the USSR and its Eastern European satellites. The west would also lose access to important material resources while simultaneously surrendering an advanced industrial complex to the Soviet Union. Britain favored the partitioning of Germany but resisted reparations because it did not want the German economy to collapse as it had during the Weimar Republic. Britain would not support France's plan to gain control of the Ruhr or the Saar coalfields. Most of all, however, Churchill wanted a united, tripartite front against the USSR.[20]

The most decisive element in all the decisions the Allies made regarding the occupation of Germany and their plans for its future was the background of World War I and World War II, particularly the gruesome costs of liberating Europe from Nazi barbarism. Every decision that was made and every decision maker who put a plan into action took into account the Nazi atrocities. Diplomacy, in an ironic twist of Carl von Clausewitz's dictum, became "war by another means;" the gravity of every decision was colored by the new post-World War II reality.[21]

For two years, Ulbricht's fifth column worked inside Germany, and Stalin delayed all Allied decisions on the fate of Germany. By June 1947, however, Stalin had run out of time. The Americans were ready to launch their Marshall Plan which would rebuild the German economy and win massive support for the western Allies if it was expanded into the Soviet Occupied Sector of Germany. In addition, post-World War II German–Soviet loathing was too deep for even a master tactician like Ulbricht to overcome. Stalin was forced to abandon his plan for a united Germany within the Soviet sphere of influence.

It is at this point that the history of the Soviet Occupied Sector begins some of its most interesting, and ironic chapters. Rather than meekly following the Soviet Party line over the next several years, Ulbricht pursued his own objectives under the cover of Stalin's protection. Allowing Stalin to consolidate the Soviet Sector separately from the western Allied territories in Germany, Ulbricht also pursued his own plan to build on German–Soviet mistrust and develop a significant measure of freedom within the clutches of the Russian bear.

Throughout 1947, Ulbricht consolidated his control over the entire Soviet Sector and turned his attention to removing the western Allies from Berlin. In June 1948, Ulbricht, with the help of the Soviets, cut off the Allies' road access to Berlin. The Berlin Blockade lasted almost a year and drew Stalin into a confrontation he thought he could win – but he lost on two counts. First, the west maintained its link with the Allied Sectors of Berlin and second, resentment of the Soviets grew in Germany as a whole, but in the Soviet Occupied Sector in particular.

Ulbricht lost and won. Like Stalin, Ulbricht lost because the Allies remained in Berlin but he won because he realized that any actions he took to consolidate his control over the Soviet Sector had, ironically, to be supported by Stalin. Stalin could not afford to lose control of East Berlin and East Germany and Ulbricht, despite his treachery, was the only man who could deliver that control. As a result, Ulbricht could count on the Soviet protection he needed to consolidate his communist regime in East Germany, and could also carefully manipulate the deeply embedded prejudices and fears most Germans had of the Soviets, to secure his own position of power within the GDR.

During his entire tenure as the First Secretary of the Central Committee of the SED, Ulbricht played the risky game of using Soviet protection to build his own, particular, self-confident, communist German state. Ulbricht could never act with complete independence – the Soviets' embrace was too powerful. Ulbricht could, however, make the Soviet grip more bearable by skillfully rebuilding German pride via the subtle upstaging of the USSR in certain circumstances, while simultaneously confronting the west in ways that furthered East German and Soviet interests. Sport became one of the most high-profile vehicles used by Ulbricht's ruling SED party in the consolidation of a proud, self-confident German communist state which felt superior to its Soviet occupier while also operating under its protection.

From the ashes of defeat: sport's resurgence in post-war Germany

Despite their shared history and the experiences of war and total defeat, the high-performance sport systems that began to emerge in the GDR and the FRG could not have been more different. Germany was utterly destroyed by the Soviets, the western Allies, and the Nazis themselves. The unconditional surrender of Germany came on the verge of complete social breakdown. Nine days of fire bombing had, for example, destroyed more than 60 percent of Hamburg, leaving a million people homeless; the 700,000 phosphorus bombs dropped on 1.8 million people in Dresden created 1,600 degrees centigrade temperatures in the city centre, killing more than half a million non-combatants. In Düsseldorf, Allied bombing destroyed 93 percent of the buildings; from a pre-war population of 730,000, Cologne had 40,000 survivors eking out an existence in bombed out houses and cellars; Frankfurt, almost totally razed, retained only 80,000 of its pre-war 180,000 inhabitants. The conditions were the same in Essen, Dortmund, Hanover, and Mannheim. From the east, millions of refugees flooded into Germany ahead of the advancing Soviet troops. More than 3.5 million German soldiers were dead or missing in action; 6 million were prisoners of war; 3.3 million civilians had died. Nevertheless, despite the scale of the defeat, all of the Allies wanted to ensure that it was impossible for Germany ever to rise from the ashes of destruction and launch another war in Europe.

The western Allies' goals were simple; they would de-Nazify, demilitarize, decartelize, and democratize Germany.[22] The western Allies took a physically destroyed and psychologically traumatized Germany and sought to rebuild it from the ground up. Brick by brick the Allies would construct a nation that subscribed to the same pluralist, democratic principles that each of the western Allies advocated.

The Soviets had a similar objective but a very different image of the future German state. In all the areas they controlled, the Soviets sought to replace, as quickly and thoroughly as possible, all former Nazi leaders with individuals who had strong ties to democratic socialism or communism. The Soviets wanted to fill all positions of influence in Germany with individuals who were sympathetic to Soviet ideals, had an established, pre-war credibility as Nazi resistors or opponents, and would actively pursue the creation of a socialist state. This policy fitted the Ulbricht Group's mandate perfectly because the total removal of former Nazi sympathizers would enhance Soviet and communist credibility among the civilian population, and eliminate the greatest source of resistance to Ulbricht's ultimate plans.

Unlike the western Allies' reluctance to make full-scale changes, the Soviets had supreme confidence in the complete replacement of an entire cadre of leaders by inexperienced, yet politically reliable, communist supporters. Lenin and the Bolsheviks had removed all of the Tsar's political and economic leaders, successfully rebuilding the devastated post-World War I Soviet economy in 1917 and creating a new political system in the USSR. In a similar fashion, with no plans to institute a pluralist democracy, the Soviets sought to establish a strong centralized governing structure that would be directed by leaders whom Stalin or Ulbricht controlled. This difference was fundamental to the development of the contrasting sport systems in East and West Germany.

In the midst of the immediate post-war chaos, sport was not a priority for any-one and yet, despite the scale of the destruction, sporting activities sprang up extremely quickly. In the western Sectors, a mere two weeks after capitulation, there was a formal soccer game in Württemburg. A month later, there were games between teams from different cities and, incredibly, 32 teams took part in a tournament hosted in July 1945 by the Mayor of Stuttgart. By November 1945, a 16-team soccer league was established in the southern Sector of Germany occu-pied by the Americans.[23]

Eager to re-establish normal lives and seeking some respite from the heavy labor of clearing debris and beginning to rebuild Germany's economic infrastruc-ture, individuals wanted to bring back their old clubs and associations. At the same time, the Allies encouraged schools to return to their former curricula, which included physical activity and sport instruction.

Despite the directions established in the Allied Expeditionary Force's *Handbook for Military Government in Germany*, there was no uniform policy in the three western Sectors concerning sport. France was extremely restrictive regard-ing any athletic activities, the formation of athletic clubs, as well as interaction with sport associations outside the French Sector.[24] The British were less control-ling and encouraged the development of school sport to instil the British public school philosophy of character development through athletic experiences.[25] The Americans were the most laissez-faire, letting local leaders direct the earliest sport activities, although even they exerted their own cultural biases to shape emerging sport in Germany. Consistent with predominant academic thought at the time, sport was viewed as a positive way to deter youth from deviant activity, so the Americans encouraged the development of Youth Centers, and Boys and Girls Clubs. By 1947, more than 750,000 young Germans were registered in Boys and Girls Clubs in the American Sector.[26] Despite the subtle pressures exercised in the three Sectors, sport was extremely peripheral to the western Allies' fundamental objectives for the political reconstruction of Germany. As a result, sport develop-ment was largely *ad hoc* from 1945 until as late as the mid-1950s.[27]

In direct contrast to activity in the west, the Ulbricht Group, beginning first and foremost with Berlin, moved quickly and with purpose to assert its influence over sport in the Soviet Sector. Berlin held tremendous strategic and symbolic importance. Stalin had recognized the propaganda value of the Red Army's troops raising the Soviet Union's hammer and cycle flag high atop the German Reichstag in the midst of the street-to-street, building-to-building, battle for Berlin. In that single act, the Red Army – justifiably some would argue – took the lion's share of credit for the total defeat of Nazi Germany in May 1945. Berlin, the chief prize of the victory over fascism, belonged, for a short period of time at least, to the Red Army, the Soviet Union and Stalin.

Berlin, as the Ulbricht Group knew so well, was extremely valuable from the perspective of sport. Berlin had hosted the Games to which Coubertin had given his highest praise and it had always stood at the centre of sporting life in Germany.[28] Along with Leipzig, Berlin had been the center of Germany's vibrant Worker Sport Movement; it held, until 1933, the umbrella organizations for both the Worker and the Bourgeois Sport Movements – the Zentralkommission für Arbeitersport und Körperpflege [The Central Commission for Workers' Sport and Physical Hygiene] and the Deutscher Reichsausschuß für Leibesübungen [German Empire's Committee for Physical Education]. Finally, Berlin housed Germany's two main centers of physical education – the Deutsche Hochschule für Leibesübungen and the Prußische Hochschule für Leibesübungen [German and Prussian Academies for Physical Education].[29]

Under the Ulbricht Group's direction, the Soviet Sector of Berlin held the city's first post-war sports festival. The event was organized and led by a number of former leaders in the Worker Sport Movement who were recruited to the task by the Ulbricht Group and were eager to rebuild sport in the capital city. While the activities of former Worker Sport leaders were given the greatest support, Ulbricht also allowed sports leaders from the pre-war Bourgeois Sport Movement to re-establish some of the clubs they had run prior to their "coordination" into Hitler's Nazi sport associations.

By June 1945, the Ulbricht Group had established a structure and leadership group that would rebuild sport and physical education in Berlin in accordance with the principles of the "communal sport model" historically advocated by German communists. The Sportamt der Stadt Berlin [Sport Bureau for Berlin] was led by Franz Müller, a member of the German Communist Party and leader of the pre-1933 Worker Sport Club, Sport Cartel Berlin, and Max Preuß, a Social Democrat who was also a pre-1933 city sports official. The ten-member Central Sport Committee consisted of a mixture of people with backgrounds in the Worker and Bourgeois Sport Movements of pre-1933 Germany. By the end of June 1945, the Sport Bureau had already held sport competitions that attracted more than a thousand spectators, and the communal sport clubs had registered over 15,000 card-carrying members. Through the spring of 1945, local sport organizers throughout Berlin gave the Sports Bureau regular reports on developments in their areas; by July they had drafted a set of guidelines for the redevelopment of sport in Berlin. These guidelines, consistent with Ulbricht's and Stalin's vision of a unified, communist-oriented Berlin, proposed a single, city-wide sport structure. Symbolically and strategically these were all important and rapid gains for the Soviets.[30]

Occupied by the four victorious Allied powers, the overall coordination of activities in Berlin was rotated monthly among the Soviets, Americans, French and British. This also held for sport. In September 1945, while the British Military Authority was in command of activities in Berlin, members of the former Sport-Club Charlottenburg (SCC) – a traditional, multisport, bourgeois sport association – sought and received approval for reinstatement. This small act had far reaching consequences for the future development of sport in Germany. The reinstatement of SCC set off a struggle among Berlin sports leaders over what path could and should be followed in re-establishing sports clubs.

More importantly, the British decision was completely incompatible with the Soviet's plans for a unified, Communist/Social Democratic/Worker Sport oriented sport system in all of Berlin. The debate over communal sport associations versus traditional sport associations that the SCC approval instigated was, in essence, a struggle between the communists and the traditional middle-class interests over the control of sport in Berlin. The controversy put a sudden end to the momentum the Ulbricht Group had enjoyed in the field of sport and led to a formalized set of regulations that the western Allies would impose on the further development of sport in their Sectors of Berlin and all other Sectors under Western occupation.

"Directive 23" and sport development in the western occupied Sectors

Unlike the Soviets, beyond the key "4 Ds" (de-Nazify, demilitarize, decartelize, and democratize Germany), the western Allies did not have a comprehensive strategy for the occupation of Germany in the post-war period, and they certainly lacked specific plans for sport.[31] As sporting activity in the immediate aftermath of World War II arose more or less spontaneously, the western Allies used their educational policies for direction, but they had little else.[32] The struggle over the control of sport in Berlin was the major catalyst, which, along with the rapid emergence of sport in the other Allied Sectors of Germany as a whole, demonstrated the need for a formal policy. On December 17, 1945, the western Allies introduced Control Council Directive Number 23, "The Limitation and Demilitarization of Sport in Germany," as the overarching set of regulations for sport in their Sectors of Occupation.[33] Directive 23 became the foundation stone upon which the present day West German sport system was built.

The most high profile points in Directive 23 concerned the elimination and prohibition "of all military or paramilitary athletic organizations (clubs, associations, institutions, and other organizations) which existed in Germany prior to its capitulation." Similarly, Article 2 prohibited activities of "a military or paramilitary nature, including aviation, parachuting, gliding, fencing, military or paramilitary drill or display and shooting with firearms." Instruction of a military or paramilitary nature in "educational institutions, public or political organizations, in companies and factories and in all other organizations" was also forbidden. Directive 23 clearly stated that the emphasis in sporting activity and physical education for German youth "must be on health, hygiene and recreation which will exclude from this type of sport elements of assimilated military character."[34]

Important as those restrictions were, the less eye-catching restrictions in parts "a" through "c" of Article 4 had far greater long-term importance. Allied distrust of Germans in the immediate post-war period was extremely acute. To ensure there was absolutely no collaboration among German sportsmen and women over any extended geographical space – particularly in view of their long history of national military and paramilitary sport associations – the Allies restricted all emerging sport clubs to the local level. "These [non-military sport] organizations shall not be established above the Kreis [local] level, except with the permission of the Zone Commanders, which will be strictly limited to those sports that could not possibly have any military significance." Furthermore, "every newly established sport organization of a local character must have permission from the local Allied occupation authority [to be formed]" and its activities would be "subject to the supervision of this authority."[35] Finally, the western Allies did not permit the re-establishment of the nationalist Turner Sport Movement in the first two years following German capitulation, and heavily discouraged and deterred any efforts to revive the Worker Sport Movement in the western Sectors because they feared it would harbor sympathies for, or be co-opted by, the Soviets.[36]

Two additional principles guided the development of sport associations in the western Allies' Sectors of Occupation. First, the Allies ensured that the public administration of sport and the self-administration of sport in clubs were separate activities with the latter encouraged and the former heavily discouraged. This meant that whatever a sport club could do for itself, it would. Only when there was a genuine, obvious need for city, regional or state assistance could such support be offered.[37] Second, the leaders of sport clubs had to be democratically chosen and the affairs of the club run as independent, democratic entities.[38]

As a result, in accordance with Directive 23, the Allies allowed individuals who valued sport for its immediate rewards – the enjoyment of pure physical exercise, and as an end in itself rather than a means to some political goal or performance outcome – to create new, local sport clubs (Vereine). Although Directive 23 gave the Allies supreme control over which organizations could operate, they used informal discussions with local organizers and constructive facilitation to shape the environment in which acceptable sport organizations grew and developed.[39] Organized sport in the western Sectors began at the ground level in a variety of locally initiated, self-financed, organizationally independent clubs.

While the occupying powers felt they were allowing sport, freed from politics, to emerge, the restrictions they placed on sport and the differences that existed among the various districts, even in the same Sector of occupation, had a tremendous political impact on the long-term development of West German sport. The political structure of sport in the western Sectors was comprised of locally run, autonomous clubs that had their own constitutions, means of support, goals and objectives. There was no centralized body – other than the more or less watchful eye of different French, English, or American Zone commanders – which would, or could, coordinate them – and there was no body that would provide an overall direction to the many clubs' objectives.

Local sports clubs could develop only so far on their own; branching out and linking up with clubs outside their locale contravened the restrictions of Directive 23. Any activity above the local level required at least tacit approval of the Allied Zone Commander. The step from a number of independent clubs to an organized amalgamation of clubs – a sport association (Verband) – required negotiation and some creative manoeuvring by everyone involved.[40] Building a "system" from independent, relatively self-contained entities was not straightforward or easy. More important, the process through which independently organized and operated clubs were brought together into a formal association ultimately determined how the entire West German sport system would be "unified" and coordinated.

If tradition had held – and many who helped form local clubs and later played leadership roles in the formation of a sport system in the post-World War II period were very traditional in their outlook – then post-war sport in West Germany would probably have developed and grown as clubs joined, or were developed by, a relatively few, overarching sport associations that were based on a common worldview or a common religious perspective. Associations such as the Deutsche Turnerbund [German Federation of Turners], the Arbeiter Turn-und Sportbund [Worker Gymnastics and Sport Federation], the Catholic Church's Deutsche Jugendkraft [German Youth Movement], the Protestant CVJM Eichenkreuz [Young Men's Christian Association: Oak Cross], or the Jewish Makkabi Deutschland [Maccabi Germany] would undertake organized sport in West Germany. In fact, sports organizers developed unified, multisport associations at the regional level (Einheitsverbände) quite rapidly but they were dissolved as soon as Directive 23 came into force.[41] The Allies were reluctant to allow centralization of any sort: if it was not obviously and directly tied to vitally important functional requirements, it would never gain Allied approval.

To circumvent Allied regulations, and to promote the growth of sport beyond the local level, representatives of different sports clubs met informally and formed a remarkable variety of unofficial networks. While the Zone Commanders in the different Allied Sectors were differentially disposed to these interactions, it was not long – particularly in the American Occupied Sector – before informal "working committees" (Arbeitsausschüsse) or actual associations formed to develop an emerging organizational layer above the local sport club. These entities became – or ultimately formed into – area, city, or regional sport federations (Kreissportbünde, Stadtsportbünde, or Bezirkssportbünde), area-wide, single sport associations (Kreissportfachverbände), or regional, single sport associations (Bezirkssportfachverbände).[42] The Allies allowed these organizations because they were still largely localized in nature and required for athletic competitions to take place. In addition, individual, local sports leaders were skillful in their negotiations with different Zone Commanders, although this spawned a plethora of organizational forms. Most importantly, these organizations represented an amalgamation of clubs in a manner that broke from traditional sport arrangements in the German past.

Sportbünde, Kreissportfachverbände, and Bezirkssportfachverbände were still relatively local in nature: the organizational logic of sport competition led clubs and the representatives from larger sport associations to form working committees that encompassed larger geographical areas. These working committees were permitted to operate informally until the Zone Commander was comfortable with the creation of a formal regional or provincial level sport federation (Landessportbund). The Americans were most receptive to provincial level sport federations. In July 1945, for example, they approved the Bayerische Landessport-Verband [Bavarian Provincial Sport Association – BLSV] which oversaw the provincial level activities for associations in seven different districts. The Americans were open to the BLSV because it drew its leadership from four very different, previously existing, sport organizations ensuring the diversity of views and the democratic orientation valued so highly by the Allies.[43]

The British followed protocol more closely than the Americans but were less restrictive than the French.[44] When protocol was met, the British responded quickly. For example, in July 1945, the British Occupational Authority formally recognized the Hamburger Verband für Leibesübungen [The Hamburg Association for Physical Education – HVfL] – the precursor to the Hamburger Sportbund [Sport Federation of Hamburg]. A little more than a year after capitulation, in a city that had incurred massive war damage, 216 sport clubs with 49,000 members sought "a self governing organization for Hamburg sport" which would "link and oversee … sports clubs' activities."[45] In this instance permission was easy to grant because the clubs had been approved and the HVfL was comprised of representatives chosen directly from the clubs. The HVfL was set up as a diversified, democratically elected body that would coordinate an already significant volume of sporting activity in the Hamburg region. The HVfL did not, however, become the blueprint for later regional sport organizations in the British, French or American Sectors. Instead, the political dynamics within the re-emerging system charted the course towards a very different structure and form of representation for the future West German Sport System.

The 1946 debate that led to the formation of the Nordwestdeutschen Fußballverband [North West German Soccer Association] in the British Sector was crucial to the future overall structure of West German sport. Consistent with the pre-war past, Hugo Gömmer, a leading advocate of German sport interests in the British Sector, wanted to re-establish the Volkssportverband Westfalen [People's Sport Association, Westphalia]. He had been successful in the immediate post-war period but the association was quickly dissolved in the wake of Directive 23. At a Zone Sport Meeting held in Hannover in February 1946, Gömmer proposed guidelines for the formation of a single, multi sport Volkssportorganisation [People's Sport Organization] but many sport clubs in the British Zone resisted the proposal.

The debate carried over to a meeting in Detmold three months later and representatives from soccer became actively engaged because the formation of a single, multisport association might require soccer to divide its potentially significant resources among all the clubs within the association. The soccer leaders lobbied the British Military Command for the single sport association model, arguing that it would more accurately reflect the democratic desires of sport club members and also prevent the centralized control of a number of sports by a single association. Perhaps even more important, multisport organizations like Gömmer's proposed Volkssportorganisation could well be the thin edge of the wedge that would permit associations from the Workers' Sport Movement to reconstitute themselves in the western Sectors of Germany. Finally, a single sport association, like the one soccer was proposing, had already become common and had demonstrated the success of that particular arrangement. Following a vote by regional sport representatives, and with the support of the British Military Authority, the North West German Soccer Association was approved: the single sport association model became a viable option in the development of an overall regional system.

Over the next four years, working committees that had informally coordinated sports at the regional level received approval as official umbrella organizations in each of the provinces in the western Sectors. The dominant model became one in which Provincial Sport Organizations consisted of a central committee (Hauptausschuss) and a larger plenary of representatives – variously named as a Sportbundtag (Sport Federation Assembly), a Verbandstag (Association Assembly) or a Landessporttag (Provincial Sport Assembly). The representatives for the plenary body were drawn from sports clubs, local, city and regional sport federations, and local, regional, and provincial single sport associations. The federations' regular activities were usually conducted by a Praesidium [Executive Committee], which was run by the Federation President and other executive members.[46] By 1949 there were 15 provincial sport federations (Landessportbünde) including one for West Berlin.[47]

The Landessportbünde were umbrella organizations, which the clubs controlled through representative membership. The mandate for the provincial representatives encompassed the interests of all the sports clubs within the provincial federations, reflecting concerns that represented the full range of sporting activity from leisure and recreation to competitive sport. Working with the provincial government on behalf of the entire membership, the provincial sport federations responded to club initiatives and only initiated action when working on behalf of the clubs. The provincial federations pursued the construction of sport facilities and furthered broader sport and recreation-related social initiatives. But German sports leaders wanted to co-ordinate their emerging sport system beyond the provincial level; the debates that surrounded the development of the Deutscher Sportbund [German Sport Federation – DSB] determined the final characteristics of the sport system, in general, and the high-performance sport system in particular.

It took 11 inter sector conferences between May 6, 1946 and September 11, 1950 to work out the structure for a federally coordinated sport system. The Arbeitsgemeinschaft Deutscher Sport [The Working Association for German Sport – ADS] was established in October 1948, giving way to the DSB on December 10, 1950.[48] At stake was the question of which voices would be formally represented in a federal umbrella organization – the broad interests of the clubs through their provincial sport associations or the well-organized, high profile, single sport associations which placed competitive interests at the top of their priority lists. The debates, often heated, led to partial resolutions, but genuine progress was not forthcoming. On July 16–17, 1949 in Bad Homburg, the ADS executive members, who represented in relatively equal numbers the provincial sport federations and the single sport federations, along with representatives from the German soccer and gymnastics federations, met with administrators in the military government. At that conference, the military government put Directive

23 front and center. At the end of the meeting, the German sport representatives agreed to work towards the development of a new umbrella organization, which would be federalist in nature, of which both the elite, single sport associations and the provincial sport federations would be "full, equally legitimate" members.[49]

The final structure of the DSB was completely consistent with the western Allies' primary post-World War II objectives. The DSB was a federally constituted, national level umbrella organization that rested on a foundation of independent sports clubs. The essential sport groups, the provincial sport associations, the elite, single sport associations (Spitzenverbände), and associations with particular interests, were all represented within a constitutional structure that balanced competing interests while it could still pursue commonly held, national level goals.[50] Since the western Allies' goal was to develop the most democratic sport system possible in the western Sectors of post-war Germany, they had been extremely successful. As one that would have to quickly and effectively compete with the centralized sport system of the GDR, the DSB was far less of a success.

Sport in the GDR: the other side of the coin

The Ulbricht Group had worked quickly and effectively as it guided and shaped the re-emergence of sport in Berlin. Ulbricht's objectives were to establish some normality to everyday life, to raise the profile of the USSR as a supportive, fostering, caring power, to instil a sense of identity with Germany's socialist past and create optimism in the opportunity to build a glorious socialist–communist future, and to put in place an organizational structure he could control in the area of sport development. Ties to the Worker Sport Movement and leftist politics were facilitated while all traces of Nazi involvement were completely eradicated and the nationalist traditions of the Turner Sport Movement and the Western leaning Bourgeois Sport Movement were impeded.[51]

In his early actions related to sport in the Soviet Sector of Occupation, Ulbricht used all four of the main, national level Communist Party organizations – the Freie Deutsche Gewerkschaftsbund [Association of Free German Trade Unions], the Kulturbund zur demokratischen Erneuerung Deutschlands [The Cultural Association for the Democratic Renewal of Germany], the Freie Deutsche Jugend [Free German Youth – FDJ], and the Demokratische Frauenbund Deutschlands [The Democratic Women's Association of Germany] – to actively shape the re-emergence of sport, recreation and physical activity in East Germany. By 1948, however, the Executive Committee of the SED wanted to establish a single leadership group for sport.[52] Based on Ulbricht's recommendation, the FDJ, under Erich Honecker, was given the initial, sole responsibility for the development of sport in the Soviet Sector. Honecker quickly established the Deutscher Sportausschuss [Committee for German Sport – DS] in October of that year. Without delay, the DS consolidated its power over all the sport activities that were emerging in the Soviet Sector at that time.

By 1950, Ulbricht recognized that the assimilation of West Germany to the eastern bloc was not going to occur, so he turned his attention to consolidating his position within East Germany and asserting its influence wherever possible. To lay the foundation for the projection of East German excellence internationally, the SED founded the National Olympic Committee (NOC) of the GDR in April, 1951.

Although the rhetoric of the GDR's NOC was to work cooperatively with its West German counterpart, the intention was exactly the opposite.[53] At the all-German sport conference held at Oberhof in 1951, the East Germans claimed that although they approached the meetings "in a spirit of mutual respect and equality" they did not believe "the West German imperialists" had adopted the same approach. The East Germans argued that West Germany was only interested in the "annexation of the German Democratic Republic and with the expansion of imperialistic class rule throughout all Germany."[54] That claim was important because West Germany had applied to the western oriented IOC for the official recognition of the FRG's NOC.[55] At its 45th Congress in May 1951, the IOC admitted the NOCs of both the USSR and the FRG to the Olympic family. With that decision, the initial stage in the cold war confrontation of east and west was set and the groundwork for an identical, intra-German competition was falling into place. Within three years, East and West Germany would participate in the Olympic Games and Ulbricht's dream of a proud GDR would be brought that much closer to realization.

Sport systems in the FRG and the GDR: a study in contrasts

There is not a single aspect of post-World War II Germany one can separate from the legacy of its war on the eastern front or the conflicts, differences, and political ambitions that existed among the Allies that brought the Nazi war machine to heel. The Nazis' sadistic barbarism in Eastern Europe and the Soviet Union, the brutal, demoralizing battles of attrition under extreme conditions of cold, hunger, and fear, the mechanized murder of innocent people, and the retributions that were exacted as the Germans retreated to Berlin all hung over post-war Germany in every foreign and domestic relationship and decision. Post-war literature, art, music, business, education, and recreation were all influenced by the devastating, demoralizing, dehumanizing war unleashed by Hitler in Europe, North Africa, and the Soviet Union.

Though burdened by the war's legacy, political intrigue, and diplomatic conflict, Germans in the immediate post-war period showed a surprising – even incredible – resilience as the Germans and Allies began to rebuild the nation from its total defeat. Despite the devastation and the hardships they faced, the rebuilding process began immediately and gained momentum rapidly. Sport and recreation were just two areas where activity blossomed: within months of the war's end, clubs and competitions were springing up in all the Sectors of Allied occupation.

Although the Western Allies had some overall objectives for post-war Germany – de-Nazification, demilitarization, decartelization, and democratization – they had few specific plans and had certainly not made any preparations for the rapid re-emergence of sport in their Sectors. In response to the need for regulative control in the western Sectors, Control Council Directive Number 23, from December 17th, 1945, became the cornerstone of the re-emergence of sport in the FRG. The outcome was a national level umbrella organization that coordinated and facilitated the activities of numerous independent sports clubs, which in turn provided services, programs, and opportunities across the spectrum of sport and physical activity. As a federation of provincial sport associations, elite, single sport associations (Spitzenverbände), and selected associations with particular interests, the DSB balanced the competing interests of all those groups while establishing and pursuing commonly held, national level goals. Independent of local, provincial, or the federal government, the sport system of the FRG was pluralist and thoroughly democratic in its structure from the grass roots up.

Sport in the Soviet Sector of occupation developed in a totally different manner. Stalin had specific plans for post-war Germany, and began to implement them even before World War II had ended. Parachuting the Ulbricht Group into Berlin in the last months of the war, Stalin began to lay the groundwork for the rise of a communist oriented regime to power. Ulbricht used the opportunity not only to establish his own power base but also to instil a unique self-esteem within the population of East Germany. Sport, which was developed exclusively under the tight, centralized control of the SED, became one of the primary vehicles for establishing that nationalist pride. Beginning with the four main, national level Communist Party organizations, Ulbricht soon handed exclusive control of the sport portfolio to Erich Honecker and the FDJ. With the formation of the Committee for German Sport, Honecker indicated the importance and close direction he would confer upon sport. Centralized and responsive to the political goals of the SED and ranking among the government's highest priorities, the sport system of the GDR contrasted completely with the emerging system in the FRG.

By 1952, the trajectories of high-performance sport in the FRG and GDR were vastly different in virtually every aspect one could mention. Facing each other across the dividing line between east and west, the two Germanys represented the major differences between the two competing power blocs. The struggle for international supremacy was set to begin.

5 "Something had altered in the faces of the pigs ..."

Converging sport systems in the GDR and FRG

When Mr Jones and his wife and men were driven off Manor Farm in the revolution inspired by old Major's dream, the animals looked forward to that "golden future time" promised in the "Beasts of England."[1] Life on Animal Farm would be vastly different than under the tyrant and drunkard Jones.

Although only one of Stalin's lieutenants, Walter Ulbricht could guarantee a future for the Germans in the Soviet Sector of Occupation that must have seemed equally as golden as the one Napoleon promised his fellow beasts, especially in the wake of the immediate Nazi past. The dream Ulbricht held out centered on a totally new political system – the polar opposite of fascism – and the rekindling of a long tradition of German socialist thought, including the work of the favored sons Marx and Engels. Tied to Stalin's global ambitions, Ulbricht did not have complete independence in pursuing the dream but, as the Berlin blockade of 1948 had already demonstrated, he had more room to manoeuvre than the heads of other Soviet-controlled states. Cutting off the west's road access to Berlin proved three points.

First, the western Allies would not readily abandon their geo-politically important presence in the western Allied Sectors of Berlin or their other Sectors of Occupation in Germany. Second, Stalin and Ulbricht were dependent on one another: neither could realize his plans in Germany without the assistance of the other. Finally, the west's refusal to vacate Berlin demonstrated how important the politics of symbolism would become in the control of Germany.

The western Allies were determined to maintain West Berlin as a capitalist showcase right in the middle of the Soviet Sector of Occupation. Both sides would soon engage in a psychological warfare that swirled around images of strength and potential, on the one hand, and relative deprivation on the other. Ulbricht had always wanted to foster a cohesive force that would hold Germans in the Soviet Sector and serve as the basis for moving forward in its socialist project. Seeing the determination of the western Allies to remain in Germany, Ulbricht now knew he had to win the hearts and minds of the East German population.

Ulbricht drew upon three elements in particular to create the cohesion he needed to move forward. The first element was the stalwart pride Germans in the eastern regions of the Empire had always possessed when comparing themselves to their brothers and sisters in the industrially rich west. The second element was the historically well-developed, communal orientation workers and farmers shared as part of their immediate life experiences. Ulbricht nurtured and developed those sentiments through the education system and general party propaganda. Finally, Ulbricht drew upon the deeply engrained ideology of German superiority that Hitler had fostered and cultivated with respect to the Soviet Union. This, combined with the fear and loathing of the Soviet Occupational forces, created a powerful "us versus them" psychological bond among the East Germans. A strong East German Selbstbewußtsein (prideful self-consciousness) was crucial to Ulbricht's success as head of the Soviet Sector of Occupation.

Chapter Four presented the early history of the development of sport in postwar Germany. This chapter continues that history and documents the extent to which the sport systems on both sides of the East/West German divide changed over the next quarter of the century. The following material demonstrates, through an analysis of the sport systems in both Germanys, the degree to which, and the reasons why, world-class, high-performance sport moved further and further from the ideals Coubertin held for his Olympic project. Despite their differences, world-class, high-performance sport in East and West Germany required, by the late 1970s, an increasingly full-time commitment to sport, whereby professionalized athletes relied on ever more sophisticated scientific knowledge and cutting-edge expertise to reach the top of the Olympic podium. An instrumentally rational approach to winning progressively became the overriding concern of world-class sport.

A second theme this chapter develops is the impact that the GDR's unprecedented investment of material resources, personnel, and research activity in high-performance sport had in shaping the landscape of Olympic sport today. Although numerous commentators have tied East Germany's success to the use of performance-enhancing substances, that claim is too superficial and ideologically biased to stand the weight of historical evidence. For domestic and foreign political reasons, East Germany poured human, financial and material resources into a highly rational, instrumentally oriented high-performance sport system. Pursuing the logic of a scientifically advanced commitment to the pursuit of the linear record in human athletic performance, the GDR challenged other nations, including the USSR, to either adopt a similar strategy or fall behind. This chapter demonstrates that although television, the sporting goods industries and various other commercial interests significantly shaped world-class sport in the 1970s and 1980s, it was the immediate and long-term political goals of East Germany and other nation states that were decisive factors in shaping high-performance sport today.

The state-sponsored pursuit of Olympic gold

Ulbricht and Honecker could use the IOC's decision to recognize the FRG's NOC (while denying the GDR the same status because it was not recognized as a sovereign nation) as grist for their mill in two important respects. First, they could point to this as a further instance of the eastern region of Germany being undermined by the wealthy west, using the potential collective resentment in the east as the basis for an unprecedented state investment in world-class, high-performance sport. Second, the decision provided the opportunity for Ulbricht and Honecker to justify, within the SED, such a program of involvement. Building on the Nazis' successful use of sport for domestic and international propaganda purposes, the SED would pursue a similar path to consolidating its own regime in a very cost-effective manner.

Ulbricht and the SED portrayed the IOC's rebuff as an attack on the sovereignty of the GDR. Within a year, the Deutscher Sportausschuß [Committee for German Sport] was replaced by the Staatliche Komitee für Körperkultur und Sport [The State Committee for Physical Culture and Sport – STAKO] which was given the clear mandate to mobilize resources for the development of a centralized sport system.[2] STAKO'S mandate stated:

> There must be closer cooperation among the Free German Youth, the trade unions, the sport associations, and the People's Education Ministry so that there is a broad mobilization of youth and activities and that at least a million citizens of the German Democratic Republic take part in these activities creating an impressive testament to the defence of the German Democratic Republic.[3]

More important, STAKO's main responsibilities included the rapid improvement of the GDR's athletic performances. "In the most essential sports," the mandate directed, "top athletes should be concentrated in facilities where the requirements for the systematic improvement of performance are present or can be created."[4] Specific sports like track and field, swimming, gymnastics, boxing, cycling, wrestling, rowing, soccer, volleyball, basketball, and handball were singled out for particular emphasis. STAKO's creation also accelerated the implementation of an athlete classification system with twenty athletes awarded "Masters of Sport" designations so they could increase the profile of sport and draw young athletes into the system. Homegrown East German heroes were important to Ulbricht's overall political goals and served the developing sport system well.

To improve the development of East German athletes, STAKO began in a conventional manner by establishing a plan for appointing coaches and trainers to centralized training facilities, creating uniform regulations for athlete training, ensuring there were clear lines of responsibility which would ensure there was "a disciplined, systematic, and successful training regime," as well as the proper "political–moral education." To improve instruction and the quality of sport-related research, STAKO assumed the leadership of the work carried out at the Deutsche Hochschule für Körperkultur [German Academy for Physical Culture] as well as the other national and regional sport schools. STAKO also put more resources into the systematic study of sport performance, including an increase in the volume of Soviet research that was made available in translation, and increased the scale of sport research in the GDR.

The emphasis on the Soviet experience led the East Germans to open Kindersportschulen (sport schools for children aged 5–10) in the Straußberg district of East Berlin as well as in Brandenburg, Halberstadt, and Leipzig during the 1952–3 school year. Eight more followed a year later and the schools' facilities were expanded to include older boys and girls.[5] In addition to the regular school curriculum, students in all East German schools were to receive expanded sport instruction and weekend training.

Though only a partial victory, at its 50th Congress in June 1955, the IOC voted 27 to 7 to provisionally recognize the GDR's NOC. There was a catch, however. Although both NOCs would be recognized, the Germans could only enter a single, combined team.[6] Given the IOC's intransigence on separate teams, Ulbricht decided to make the best of a compromised situation. Despite the fact that East Germany had a weaker economy, could not take advantage of the capital investment available through the Marshall Plan, and was paying heavy war reparations to the Soviets through the relocation of industrial plants to the USSR, Ulbricht recognized that the spirit and commitment athletes and sport organizers were willing to make was a resource he could draw upon heavily. High-performance sport offered a unique opportunity to consolidate the position of the SED within East Germany, distinguishing and distancing East Germany from Stalin and the USSR, on the one hand, and the FRG, on the other, while allowing sport organizations to grow and flourish on the basis of their own energies and human resources, which the GDR sport organizations had in ample supply.

Rapid growth of the re-emerging sport system led to a further centralized restructuring: in 1957 the Deutscher Turn- und Sportbund [The German Gymnastics and Sport Federation – DTSB] replaced STAKO. With the DTSB's formation, sport was also incorporated into the state's seven-year plan. By 1959, the DTSB had integrated sport instruction into every grade level of all East German schools. The curriculum required five to seven hours of practical sport activity per week, centered on gymnastics, track and field, swimming and diving.[7]

Like the Soviets, the GDR made high-performance sport an intensive experience. Because it was so demanding and young athletes had difficulty balancing school and sport, there was increased pressure in the early 1960s to expand the "Special Schools for Athletically Talented Youth." The Kinder- und Jugendsportschulen [Children and Youth Sport Schools – KJSs] that emerged were developed, refined and guided by the Secretariat of the Central Committee of the SED to ensure that the state's political and athletic objectives were being met.[8]

The goals, character and structure of the KJSs were straightforward: "to take high ranking, high-performance athletes in Olympic sports and to develop them into the best in the world." To this end, "all the appropriate conditions and supporting measures" were developed so that talented athletes could top the international rankings while also gaining a general education. To optimize their development, KJSs and sport clubs were brought to the same location. Schools specialized in specific sports and enabled students to train longer while also completing the prescribed academic curriculum.

Sport schools allowed for the complete coordination of education, training, and free-time activity. Specialized staff worked with the children in school and sport, ensuring that there was full-time support for the athletes in the form of professional teachers, coaches and nutritionists, as well as medical support from sport physicians and physiotherapists. The KJSs allowed the GDR's government and sports leaders to increase the length of time child athletes – especially in sports such as gymnastics, diving, swimming, and figure skating – could take to meet particular educational objectives while engaged in the highly demanding training regimes required for ranking at the top of the world in international, high-performance sport. As the Olympic program expanded in the 1960s and 1970s, and more women's events were added, the KJSs grew in size and received increasing resources.

Some ten years after the installation of KJSs, so-called Trainingsstützpunkte and Trainingszentren [Training Centers] were established in different regions or districts so that the expectations of the KJSs could be met with greater certainty.[9] Resolutions supporting the systematic development of national training centers and regional training centers followed in 1969 and 1973. By 1969 almost half of the KJS athletes were in sport boarding schools. On the basis of these developments, the DTSB oversaw hundreds of training centers and training support centers within a few years.[10] While not a completely new approach to the organization of children's and youth sport and the development of athletic talent, the scale of the undertaking, especially in relative terms, separated the GDR's pursuit of high-performance excellence dramatically from even the USSR. When one adds in the East Germans' apparent penchant for detail and organizational efficiency, it becomes evident how high-performance sport was used to encourage and develop a more robust national pride within the GDR – especially with respect to the FRG and the USSR.

Despite the focus on talent identification and the development of young athletes through a system of sport schools, the sport system's overall success rested in the hands of Manfred Ewald, who was elected DTSB president in 1961, and controlled the sport system for the next 28 years. Ewald moved slowly at first, consolidating his position among the SED leadership before venturing any innovative changes. By 1966, however, he was handed the impetus needed to take some significant steps in the consolidation of high-performance sport as one of the central features of East German politics.

In May 1966, the IOC awarded the 1972 Games to Munich, and two years later it granted the GDR's longstanding wish to enter its own team into the Games. These decisions presented the GDR with a glorious opportunity; it could not have asked for a better Trojan horse with which to roll into Munich than its own independent team, although this time the recipients of the "gift" were well aware of the dangers hidden inside. Ewald recognized immediately an independent GDR team meant that its most significant political symbols – its flag and national anthem, which had never been officially recognized by Bonn – would, with every GDR victory in Munich, be paraded out, saluted, and celebrated before the world on West German soil.

Immediately after the IOC announced Munich was to host the Games, and not anticipating the IOC's 1968 decision on separate teams, the popular West German magazine, *Der Spiegel* [The Mirror], greeted the news with a measure of circumspection. "Rejected by half the world, respected but not loved by the other half, at loggerheads over the division of their own country, the Germans will try to bring a festival of reconciliation to the entire world" *Der Spiegel* observed.[11]

Two years later, without the slightest trace of any interest in global reconciliation, the Gesellschaft zur Förderung des olympischen Gedankens in der DDR [Society for the Promotion of the Olympic Idea in the GDR] was ecstatic over the prospects the IOC had handed the GDR. "Olympic history," the Society openly gloated in 1968,

> has stuck hard at the enemy of sport, the enemy of our Republic, and our socialist system. The anti-sport powers of the Federal Republic of Germany must now, in their own land, organize and prepare for the first fully sovereign Olympic team from the German Democratic Republic. They are the ones who, for the first time at the Olympic Summer Games, must raise the flag of the GDR, and rehearse and play our national anthem.[12]

In response to the IOC's decision on the Munich Games, Ewald established the Leistungssportkommission des DTSB [High Performance Sport Commission of the DTSB] in 1967, which soon became the Leistungssportkommission der DDR [High Performance Sport Commission of the GDR]. The Commission initiated a new structure for high-performance sport and implemented longer range planning based on Olympic quadrennials. Ewald's objectives, and those of the SED leadership, were clear. Sport was one of the most important battlegrounds upon which the west, in general, and West Germany in particular, could be joined and defeated. In language that characterized the East German regime, Ewald stated that:

> Class conflict in the realm of sport has reached such a level that, in principle, it is no different than any military conflict. Just as the GDR's soldiers guard the state's borders from the imperialist NATO enemies, so must the athletes of the GDR see the athletes of the FRG as their political enemies. Our battle is so difficult that it must be carried out in the same manner as the defence of our borders – it entails detesting imperialism and its agents, including the athletes of the FRG.[13]

With an East German team guaranteed, Ewald initiated a program in 1968 that would systematically use and develop "unterstützende Mittel (so-called uM – supplementary materials)."[14] In pursuing this program, Ewald was not a visionary.

Oral–Turinabol – one of East Germany's most well-known anabolic–androgenic steroids produced by the state-owned pharmaceutical firm VEB Jenapharm – had, for example, been widely used by male athletes in the GDR since 1966. Furthermore, as Werner Franke and Brigitte Berendonk have noted, anabolic–androgenic steroids were already in widespread use internationally by athletes in strength-dependent events.[15] Thus, it was not Ewald's decision to support the use of banned, performance-enhancing substances which made the GDR's high-performance sport system different.[16]

The sport system that Ewald oversaw was different and unique because it drew upon extensive, high-level, classified, laboratory research, substantial state resources, and detailed documentation of the system's research and implementation of uM.[17] Hundreds of documents provided comprehensive data on the types of substances used, the times of administration and pre-competition withdrawal, the annual and daily dosages, as well as the physiological impact the substances had upon the athletes. A study of male and female athletes taking Oral–Turinabol during the 1968–72 Olympic quadrennial, for example, showed that a particular "on–off" cycle produced optimal improvement among 40 world-class athletes in the shot-put and throwing events.[18] The East German records also contain the specific programs of performance-enhancing substances used by more than 400 athletes.[19]

Throughout the 1970s, numerous male and female athletes took oral anabolic–androgenic steroids as well as injections with anabolic–androgenic hormones, including nandrolone esters or, most frequently, testosterone esters. But in contrast to the impression created by many North American and west European journalists, there was tremendous support, on the part of athletes and their parents, for the East German system. Hoberman, for example, has cited Renate Neufeld's recollection, subsequent to her 1978 defection to the FRG, that parents expressed the same pride that North Americans and west Europeans would when their children were selected for the special sports schools. Moreover, Neufeld noted, parents had no reservations about the strict control exercised by authorities over their children.[20] In a similar vein, Franke and Berendonk have indicated that most female athletes accepted the strong virilizing side effects of injectable testosterone esters and those who could not accept the effects "refused to participate in this additional testosterone injection program."[21]

At the Munich Games the GDR more than doubled its Mexico City medal count: its 20 gold, 23 silver, and 23 bronze medals easily surpassed the FRG's 13, 11 and 16, propelling the GDR to third place behind only the USSR and the USA. Based on this success, sports leaders and government officials in the GDR were determined to continue researching and using banned, performance-enhancing substances. The introduction of tests for steroids in 1974, however, made this slightly more complicated. Indicative of the importance the SED attached to athletic success, its Central Committee passed a bill, classified as top secret, which set out the groundwork upon which the further use of performance-enhancing substances would be based. The Commission for High-Performance Sport (Leistungssportkommission) of the Central Committee agreed that performance-enhancing substances would remain an "integral part of the training process and of preparations for major international competitions." Their use would be "tightly controlled" and "regularly evaluated by sport physicians." The SED would continue to support research into performance-enhancing substances with a special emphasis on "the development of new substances and the most efficient patterns of administration" given the specific requirements of each sport, the timing of use and withdrawal, and the mechanisms used for detection. Finally, Central Committee members ensured that the program would "take place in absolute secrecy and be classified as an Official State Secret." [22] The Forschungsinstitut für Körperkultur und Sport [Research Institute for Physical Culture and Sport] was given sole responsibility for the well-funded "State Plan Research Theme 14.25."

Much can be made of the secrecy and cloak and dagger atmosphere that the East Germans created around their performance-enhancing substance program. Certainly part of the secrecy was aimed at keeping the IOC from learning about banned substance use by their athletes. Furthermore, the GDR did not want western media closely scrutinizing its preparation of world-class athletes. But equally – if not more – important was the SED's desire to keep ahead of the competition in all aspects of the scientific preparation of world-class, high-performance athletes.

East German research involved more than the administration of banned substances and the circumvention of IOC detection. World-class athletes – world champions in the case of the GDR – were precious commodities, so a considerable amount of research was directed towards the development of substances and training regimes that would minimize or eliminate any undesirable consequences those substances or regimes might have on the immediate or long-term health and performance of the GDR's athletes. In the world of scientifically directed, high-performance sport, the ultimate goal was to produce a continuous supply of athletes who could rise to the top and continue to hold a dominant position for as long as possible so that the GDR received full return on its investment in those athletes. As weapons in the war against "capitalist imperialism," and in the struggle to regain national pride and loosen the grip of the Soviet bear on the East German psyche, athlete preparation was a vital, expensive, closely guarded, official state secret. Preventing secrets from filtering out through "industrial espionage" was a highly predictable course of action, especially for a leader who was as Stalinist and obsessive as Erich Honecker.

By the late 1970s, at least some East Germans – particularly bureaucrats who profited politically as well as, one can imagine, financially, from the program – were consistent in their support of "uM." In a 1977 summary report to the Ministerium für Staatssicherheit [Ministry for State Security – the Stasi], Deputy Director of the Sports Medicine, Manfred Höppner, noted that:

> At present anabolic steroids are applied in all Olympic sporting events, with the exception of sailing and gymnastics (female) ... and by all national teams. The application takes place according to approved basic plans, in which special situations of individual athletes are also considered. The positive value of

anabolic steroids for the development of a top performance is undoubted. Here are a few examples. ... Performances could be improved with the support of these drugs within four years as follows: shot-put (men) 2.5–4 m; shot-put (women) 4.5–5 m; discus throw (men) 10–12 m; discus throw (women) 11–20 m; hammer throw 6–10 m; javelin throw (women) 8–15 m; 400 m (women) 4–5 sec; 800 m (women) 5–10 sec; 1500 m (women) 7–10 sec. ... Remarkable rates of increase in performances were also noted in the swimming events of women. ... From our experiences made so far it can be concluded that women have the greatest advantage from treatments with anabolic hormones with respect to their performance in sports. ... Especially high is the performance-supporting effect following the first administration of anabolic hormones, particularly with junior athletes.[23]

Within two years of this report, the East Germans extended the use of steroids to female gymnasts where many world-class competitors were minors. The decision was based on the availability of mestanolone, which was a more psychotropic steroid than Oral–Turinabol, and created a "positive aggressiveness" and allowed an athlete to withstand a heavier training load without much increase in muscle mass and body weight. Unfortunately, mestanolone was also thought to be a more androgenic steroid than Oral–Turinabol and posed a higher risk of virilization in the female gymnasts.[24]

There is no doubt that the system that supplied performance-enhancing substances to athletes in the GDR was extensive. Spitzer has indicated that the GDR's high-performance sport system employed 4,700 professional coaches and 1,000 doctors. It took almost 5,000 people to administer the entire system, with another 1,500 actively involved in research related to performance-enhancing substances. According to Spitzer, the top athletes in the GDR received what amounted to ten kilos of anabolic steroids – some two million tablets. Each year, he notes, the GDR added 2,000 new athletes to the list of those using artificial performance-enhancers.[25] One of the best indicators of the scale and sophistication of the GDR's system is the volume of research it generated, including some material that was important enough to publish even after the fall of the Berlin Wall and the unification of East and West Germany.[26]

DSB's response to GDR's high-performance sport system

The IOC's decision to hold the 1972 Games in Munich was as important to the development of the West German high-performance sport system as it was to the communist east, as numerous politicians in the FRG recognized. The symbolic cost of East German victories over West Germans at the Munich Games was not something they could easily accept. Political leaders in the FRG wanted to use the 1972 Games in the same way that Japan had used the 1964 Tokyo Games, to demonstrate West Germany's arrival among the most powerful, peaceful and successful nations in the world. Handed the opportunity to advance Germany's image as a peace loving, advanced industrial society, the

West Germans turned their unwieldy federalist sport system towards the systematic pursuit of Olympic gold.[27]

West German sport leaders began to coordinate their first High-Performance Sport Plan in 1965. Not surprisingly, the main reference point was East Germany, which was not only the object of FRG concern but had also already begun to indicate the political rewards a nation could gain through a systematic approach to the development of world-class athletes. Among the first changes in the FRG were the employment of national team coaches and the development of high-performance training centers (Stützpunkte).[28] These centers could allow athletes to remain with their local clubs while also creating opportunities for development with expert professional coaches who brought athletes together at appropriate times to train at either the provincial or federal level. The Stützpunkte were one of the only ways that the diffuse, localized nature of the West German sport system could be coordinated and harmonized with the emerging needs of world-class, high-performance sport.[29] From a modest beginning in the mid-1960s, there grew to be 180 Stützpunkte for national level athletes within 15 years.

The DSB introduced a sport and athlete classification system, promoted long term planning within the Fach- and Spitzensportverbände while seeking improvements to the pedagogical, medical and psychological development of athletes. Like the East Germans, the DSB promoted programs of early talent identification and, on the basis of the KJS experience in the GDR, introduced 35 elite sport schools. Following the 1968 Mexico Games the DSB expanded the program by promoting the development of sport boarding schools (Sport Internaten). Unfortunately for the West Germans, with few prospects for lengthy, well-paid careers in most high-performance sports, boarding schools were not embraced enthusiastically by many West German parents, and only played a significant role in those sports in which athletes competed at the world-class level at a relatively young age.[30]

On May 26, 1967, the DSB and the Deutsche Olympische Gesellschaft [German Olympic Association] made a critical decision in the development of a professionalized, high-performance sport system in the FRG. By founding the Stiftung Deutscher Sporthilfe [German Foundation for Sport Assistance – DSH] – a three-tiered body comprising a Board of Trustees (unspecified in number but containing almost 300 members in 2004), a 17-member Executive Board, and an "up to eight-person" Board of Experts – the FRG established a mechanism to bring funds into the top level of the national sport system rather than at the club level.[31] This development was crucial to the overall coordination and enhancement of the system. The DSH generated funds through tax-exempt donations, a surcharge on postage stamps, and a variety of entrepreneurial ventures, including sport exhibitions and, beginning in 1970, the spectacular "Sports Ball" which brings together national leaders in sport, business, politics, the media and high culture in an annual extravaganza.[32] In direct contrast to the SED's intimate involvement with high-performance sport in the GDR, the federal government in the FRG helped to establish the DSH and facilitated some of the revenue generating programs, but did not become directly involved in sport development, nor did it directly fund the high-performance sport system.

The DSH represented a significant change of direction for the post-World War II West German sport system. Until the mid-1960s, local sport clubs, which represented a broad spectrum of athletic and recreational activities, dominated decision making in the DSB. Consistent with the western Allies' goals concerning sport development in the post-war period, the West German system had been painstakingly built to emphasize the humanistic and educational qualities of the sporting experience. High-performance sport, as international combat, had been largely and successfully repressed throughout the 1950s and early 1960s. By the mid-1960s, however, a number of national level sport leaders in the FRG began to admit openly that West German athletes were at a serious disadvantage competing against state-supported athletes in the East and scholarship athletes of the USA. More important, they saw this as a significant cause for concern.

> The Olympic rules state that everyone should take part in Olympic competition under the same conditions. The equality of competitiveness is destroyed when sponsored athletes compete against pure amateurs whose social situation does not allow the necessary training expenditures to be covered and whose sport associations cannot supply the necessary assistance. Thus we are faced with the question: do we want to resign ourselves in international high-performance sport to a situation that contradicts the fundamental idea of sport? Or do we want, despite the unequal starting point, to give our young athletes at least a bit more of an equal opportunity to compete?[33]

The DSH was West Germany's first significant foray into the professionalized world of international, high-performance sport in the 1960s. Structured to meet the requirements of Rule 26 as it stood in 1967, the program was quickly broadened and liberalized with the 1974 changes to the Eligibility Code.[34] From the outset, the Foundation was established to insulate athletes from the pressures of the market by ensuring their basic material needs were supported so they could focus more exclusively on their athletic careers while they were national team members. The DSH provided a basic assistance package for athletes; there was a "lost-time payments" component for those who would miss time from work; and the program included an achievement-based incentive element. Athletes who were students received educational assistance. The Foundation also helped to cover travel and subsistence in connection with training at provincial or national training centers. From a modest beginning that supported 55 athletes at a cost of 77,000 West German Marks, more than 18,000 athletes had received DSH support by 1988. The DSH enabled West German athletes to be "fully integrated, socially secured and competitively eligible, paid members of the society."[35]

To parallel the GDR's Forschungsinstitut für Körperkultur und Sport [Research Institute for Physical Culture and Sport], the FRG established the Bundisinstitut für Sportwissenschaft [Federal Institute for Sport Science] in 1970 to promote applied research in sport. In response to the increased demands of world-class, high-performance sport in the contemporary period, the mandate of the Institute was refined in 2001 to focus more fully on high-performance sport, with particular emphases on talent identification, the development of potential athletes, the invention of better athletic equipment, and responsibility for doping control and prevention.

Due to the structure and orientation the western Allies had built into the West German sport system in the immediate post-war period, the FRG could not become a serious rival to the GDR without some major changes. DSB sport leaders recognized the need for change and did as much as they could to bring their system in line with the realities of Olympic sport in the late 1960s and 1970s. In a 1988 retrospective analysis of the work of the DSB, then president Hans Hansen noted that:

> The DSB's first high-performance sport plan [in 1965], in close association with the National Olympic Committee ... gave us an important stimulus and 1972 served as a genuinely successful transition point. After that we certainly made enough progress to be able to say that we were not standing still. In the meantime, international, high-performance sport took on new dimensions. High-performance sport was characterized by money and advertising, with media, marketing and agents, the marketing of sport in the entertainment business, the social uncertainty of contract-athletes, and open competition which required the DSB to make some very clear decisions.[36]

In its initial adjustments, the DSB prided itself on ensuring that West German athletes "remained people and were not sold out." The DSB claimed in its public pronouncements that the FRG would "remain in the lead for world standards" while balancing the demands of world-class, high-performance sport and the educational mission of elite sport in Germany. The DSB would find it extremely difficult to maintain this stance because high-performance sport in general was changing significantly in the late 1960s and early 1970s and, as indicated in Chapter One, would change irrevocably after 1974. At the same time, the major impetus behind the adjustment of the FRG's high-performance sport system was to keep abreast of the resource-intensive, gold medal-oriented system of the GDR. The West German government and sport leaders were equally as eager to use the Munich Games to present themselves as positively as possible to the world community as the East Germans were to use the Games to embarrass the host nation and promote the image of the GDR as a strong, independent, self-determined nation.

Aside from those obvious challenges, there were several major political obstacles that sport leaders and government officials in the FRG had to address if West Germany was really to compete with the GDR and the rest of the leading nations in international sport. First, as a direct result of Directive 23, the FRG's sport leaders had to work within a system that was cumbersome and had sufficient inertia to make change very difficult. The structure and expectations of West Germany's loosely federated, locally driven sport system was oriented to the delivery of sport and recreation opportunities across a wide spectrum of activities through a thoroughly democratic decision-making structure. It was far from ideal for the pursuit of Olympic gold in an international environment where resources had to be closely monitored and carefully allocated.

Second, another enduring legacy of the western Allies' control over the development of sport in post-World War II West Germany was the unique perspective that the DSB adopted for its fundamental conception of "sport." The official image of international, high-performance sport in West Germany included performance, competition, and peace. The image is strikingly different from any other nation's official statements of the overall goals of high-performance sport; despite the flaws it shares with all ahistorical conceptions of sport, it conveys the unique circumstances in which sport in the post-World War II, Federal Republic developed.

"Performance," an official DSB history notes,

> is one of the fundamental elements of sport. Without performance, human culture is inconceivable. ... Without their magnificent performances, the Olympic Games are unthinkable. Those are the salt of the Games. ... Perhaps it is utopian, what should be but is not yet, the genuine fascination of sport as a model for peace. ... In this sense sport today is from the ground up, political. With its principles it sets the political tasks of men and women, of nations and states in the proper light. The fundamental idea of sport is neither competition nor victory, but rather the peace which first reconciles victory and defeat; because both contribute to peace, they can bring fulfillment to victor and vanquished. No matter what the athletes' race, religion or ideology, through the fundamental principles of sport they come together in peaceful competition and put all divisive political conflicts aside.[37]

Third, sport leaders in West Germany could not withdraw their commitment to play, recreation and mass sport. As simply an umbrella organization, there were enough checks and balances for the grass roots level of the system to keep the DSB accountable to the broad interests of sport and recreational enthusiasts in Germany. The interests of elite sport in the FRG rarely moved ahead independently of the broader interests of recreational sport. The first important building block for the FRG's high-performance sport system is a good example of how sport was tied to broader recreational interests. The FRG's original "Golden Plan" directed 17.4 billion West German marks into the construction of play, recreation and sporting facilities between 1961 and 1975. Despite the changes that took place in the 1970s and 1980s, the tie between the grass roots interests in sport and recreation and high-performance sport have remained. As a result, in October 2000, the Federal Ministry for the Interior initiated a new "Golden Plan – East."[38] The new Plan will direct almost 52 million euros from the federal government and 152 million euros from municipal, city and provincial funds into the construction or renovation of more than 250 recreational facilities in the former East Berlin and the new eastern provinces.[39] Thus, despite pressures to direct precious resources to the more politically visible projects and undertakings of high-performance sport, the legacy of Directive 23 has ensured that the German sport system is responsive to the needs of a broad sporting public.

Despite the obstacles, the propaganda battle between the two Germanys meant that the DSB and the federal government had to support world-class, high-performance sport development. Deutsche Sporthilfe and the DSB strove to keep Germany's athletes among the best in the world as they invested more and more resources into the scientifically aided pursuit of the linear record. If there was a change, it was an increasingly closer and more explicit link between results and funding, consistent with other nationally sponsored high-performance sport systems in western Europe, North America and Australia.[40] While the Deutsche Sporthilfe was originally established as a program to aid and assist West German athletes in their endeavors to remain competitive with state-sponsored athletes from the east and scholarship or corporately subsidized athletes in the west, it has gradually, and now overtly, introduced performance-based incentives and made performance-based criteria among the most important for funding decisions. In 2001, the Executive Committee of the Deutsche Sporthilfe adopted a new principle for athlete support. "In the high-performance division," the Deutsche Sporthilfe homepage presently notes, "the performance principle has been neglected as the decisive criterion for overall support. Medals by A-Card athletes are now the declared goal."[41] The Deutsche Sporthilfe has made the same point in recent press releases. "The decisive criteria for admission into the sport program are, above all, athletic performance and the athlete's prospects."[42]

Recognizing the role that financial rewards play in keeping the best athletes involved in high-performance sport through their optimal performance years, the Deutsche Sporthilfe, prior to the 2002 Games in Salt Lake City, doubled to 15,000 euros the financial award given to FRG athletes for an Olympic gold medal victory.[43] In view of the increasing costs of funding world-class athletes, sport leaders like Hans-Georg Grüschow, the current DSH President, worry about how the FRG can continue to support high-performance athletes in the full spectrum of Olympic sports if Germany wants to continue its current level of success.

> In the next few years – I would say by Peking in 2008 – we have to seriously recognize that since high-performance sport, at the world-class level, has permanently changed, if we want to continue in the full breadth of high-performance sport, then we will have to look much more closely at [athletes'] individual needs.

His example is telling. Grüschow notes that if an athlete in, for example, one of the combat sports like wrestling, judo, or boxing, cannot find training partners of a sufficiently high calibre in Germany, then he or she must either travel to where they can be found or they must be brought to Germany.[44] That is an expensive proposition.

Finally, in 2000, the DSB, the national level, single sport associations (Sportfachverbände), and the provincial school boards engaged in a detailed study of how talent identification and development might be optimally pursued with education by developing and improving the current sport-school system.[45] The project was viewed as crucial to the continued success of world-class, high-performance sport in the FRG since the sport school system is a significant component to talent development in Germany. With more than 6,000 carded athletes in the school system – 745 at the federal level (40 of whom are international level athletes) and 5,567 at the provincial level – and a little more than 2,600 boarding full-time in sport schools and another 2,300 involved part-time in sport boarding schools, the system is one that is watched carefully by those who have interests in high-performance sport as well as those who have the long-term developmental interests of the young athletes in mind.

"The central objective behind the development of prospective athletes in a school–high-performance sport partnership is assurance of the optimal development of the children and youth from an athletic and academic as well as a social and personal perspective" the sport associations' report noted.[46] This objective can be met, it is argued, if nine particular features of the sport school system are followed. Among those noted were: the development of criteria to ensure the athletic, medical and academic suitability of student–athletes for the combined athletic–academic program of study they would begin, optimization of the physical arrangements for academic, athletic and general development, regularly scheduled athletic training, flexibility in the timing of a student's completion of the course of study, the use of highly qualified athletic instructors, scientific support personnel to ensure that the latest developments in sports science and sports medicine are being used with the young athletes, and a strong regional, coordinating committee that would optimally coordinate the sport school leaders, school board administrators, the provincial sport associations and committees, the federal sport associations, and the Olympic support centers.[47]

Two points, in particular, are striking about this list. First, while the early items stress the balance that is needed between educational and athletic development, the items progressively accentuate ways in which the athletic dimensions of the experience can be optimized. In and of itself, this should not be a problem, but it is symptomatic of the recognition by the DSB, the single sport associations, and the educators involved in sport, that the identification and development of young athletes has become an increasingly important area of research and activity in the pursuit of better and better high-performance sport athletes.[48]

Second, despite the fact that the West German high-performance sport system is not controlled by a state government with an extremely narrow conception of the political importance of high-performance sport, and there are still a number of competing and countervailing forces within the national sport system, high-performance sport in the FRG in the third millennium has not diverted its course all that far from that of the former GDR. In some key respects, it has moved closer to some of the main features that characterized the GDR's world-class, high-performance sport system.

The real strengths of the GDR's sport system

While it has been easy for the GDR's critics to claim that its success in international, high-performance sport rested solely, or even extensively, on the use of performance-enhancing substances, the allegation misses two fundamental realities. First, the athletes of the GDR were never alone in the use of performance-enhancing substances. The sophisticated use of substances and performance-enhancing practices was, and remains, widespread internationally. Second, the use of performance-enhancing substances was simply one part of an extremely resource intensive, systematically developed, state-sponsored high-performance sport system. It is this latter point that really explains the success of the GDR and, interestingly, the basis for some of the current pursuits of the DSB over the last few years.

Following unification, West German sport scholars studied the GDR's success and identified the four key ingredients to its tremendous accomplishments. The key factors identified were the systematic and scientifically organized selection of boys and girls, in their early childhood, for particular sport activities; immersion of those young athletes in the best possible facilities where a methodical, developmental approach to training and conditioning was followed; the development of extensive networks of support by well-qualified scientists from all areas of research relevant to the enhancement of human physical performance; and the concentration of their efforts into a very restricted range of sports (usually individual sports as well as those with some Germanic tradition).[49] These points merit elaboration.

The early identification and fostering of talent was crucial to East Germany's athletic success. As a result, it was an extremely thorough, comprehensive process. At the most basic level, the East Germans gathered anthropomorphic data, ran motor tests, and conducted interviews with prospective athletes' parents so they could see the physical characteristics of the parents and gain some insight into the future physical development of the potential athlete.[50] Arnd Krüger argues that the systematic identification of talent "based on genetic tests" was "the basis for the athletic success of the small German Democratic Republic after 1968" and was derived from the "same anthropometric procedures developed by the racial scientists [of Germany] prior to 1945."[51] Unlike the United States or England, for example, where athletes are filtered and selected largely on the basis of their results in age-class competitions as they approach their competitive prime, the East Germans relied on the extensive use of anthropometric measures to predict athletic potential and then invested heavily in the development of those athletes through to their athletic prime. This was not an East German innovation but, according to Krüger, part of a long, well-established tradition in German sport.[52]

Talent identification and development relied heavily on the school system: East Germany's 2,000 sport clubs, which offered programs to more than 70,000 young athletes, was closely coordinated with the GDR's education system. Compulsory physical education programs were established in the primary schools, and motor tests, conducted in kindergarten or grade one, and again in grades three and six, screened and identified potential athletes. Unlike so much of North American minor sport, the East Germans did not leave talent discovery to chance or to the impulsive or capricious sporting interests of children or their parents. The SED and GDR sports leaders also held a variety of sport competitions and festivals, such as the winter and summer Spartakiads, to provide additional venues and opportunities to assess promising high-performance athletes.

By the late 1980s, children with the potential to become world-class athletes were enrolled in local sport centers that fed into the GDR's 25 elite KJSs, which trained almost 10,000 young athletes. Because 97 percent of the GDR's schools (5,222 of 5,369) were linked to sport associations where qualified instructors, teachers, and parents taught physical skills in a narrow spectrum of sports, the East German sport system ensured that potential talent was fostered and developed from as early an age as possible and as systematically as possible.[53]

Two important points about talent identification and development in the GDR are particularly noteworthy. First, while anthropometric measurements might not be useful predictors of talent in all sports, there is a limited number of sports, with swimming ranking among the most significant, where they can serve a valuable role – especially when enough athletes are selected and developed.[54] Moreover, though shunned in the west as a pseudo-science in much of the postwar period, there has been an increasing interest in anthropometry among mainstream applied sport researchers in the last decade or more because of its proven utility in certain sports.[55]

Second, the GDR's success in track and field can be attributed to the overall approach taken by the sport system to developing athletic talent. The system has provided other nations with some important lessons concerning the nurturing of athletic talent. The young athletes of the GDR progressed through a series of "building phases" which led from one to another. The foundation phase – usually completed by age 11 or 12 – focused on different forms of training in a wide variety of sports and was usually completed in early childhood. The second phase, which began in the early teen years and lasted from four to six years, narrowed the spectrum of sports but kept athletes in a variety of activities at progressively more demanding levels of performance. This phase encouraged versatility and developed athletes' abilities to learn quickly and correct faults more easily.[56] It was only after this phase that athletes began to specialize.

Resources were crucial to the GDR's success and it was only in the process of unification that one could fully appreciate the extent of resource investment in the former East German high-performance sport system. In 1989, the GDR had a sport budget of almost 700 million US dollars; a year later, the sport budget for the combined FRG and GDR sport systems was well under half that amount (270 million US dollars).[57] More significant than the amount of money directed to sport was the human investment. Following unification, only 72 of the GDR's 600 track and field coaches, for example, could be absorbed by the new, unified system. The GDR had eight elite training centers for rowing with an annual budget of more than 25 million US dollars; there were 200 full-time coaches. After unification, five of those centers were closed as the new FRG increased its elite rowing centers from three to six. While the FRG had 10 national level speed skating coaches in 1989, the GDR had employed 200; following unification only seven of the GDR's 350 gymnastics coaches were kept on in the newly unified Germany. In total, of the 10,000 professional coaches employed in the GDR, 500 have remained in the eastern parts of the new Germany, 1,000 have relocated to the former FRG or found work abroad, 3,000 have changed jobs and 5,500 were left unemployed. Prior to 1989 the FRG had 115 full-time national level coaches in 50 sports plus 220 honorary or volunteer coaches; only 120 of the GDR's 10,000 coaches found work at the national level in the combined sport systems following unification.[58]

West meets East

Chapters Four and Five have shown that despite their identical historical and cultural roots within a unified Empire that extended from 1871 to 1945 and their shared experiences of early victories, followed by ominous setbacks, then total war and a final devastating defeat in World War II, the unique political dynamics of the post-war period led to the development of two very different high-performance sport systems in the FRG and GDR. Both systems were influenced by the overall social trends in the post-World War II period, which helped shape the Olympic Movement generally, but it was the specific influences in each part of post-war Germany that had the most important impact in the creation of the high-performance sport systems found in the two Germanys.

In the case of the GDR, the legacy of the brutalizing conflict in the east and a deep-seated animosity towards, and distrust of, Stalin and the occupying Soviet forces encouraged Walter Ulbricht and later, Erich Honecker, to shape a high-performance sport system that not only competed against the west, in general, and the FRG, in particular, but was also designed to foster East German pride and confidence by differentiating the GDR from the USSR and outperforming the USSR in one of its areas of global superiority. The desire to simply win gold medals and push athletic performance to the outer limits of human possibility do not fully, or even adequately, explain the nature, development, orientation and measures taken in the GDR with respect to high-performance sport. A set of very specific political dynamics played the leading role in the constitution of world-class sport in post-war East Germany.

In the FRG, conflicting views among the western Allies over the fate of post-World War II Germany led to differing degrees of freedom for sport leaders to build sporting and recreational opportunities for Germans living in the western Sectors of occupation. Despite those differences, the western Allies' common goals of de-Nazifying, decartelizing, demilitarizing and, above all, democratizing their Sectors of control had a profound impact on the sport system that developed in the FRG. But this chapter also demonstrates that the IOC's 1966 decision to award the 1972 Games to Munich and the ensuing IOC decision in 1968 to grant independent status to the GDR's Olympic team for the Munich

Games led to a dramatic refocusing of the FRG's high-performance sport system towards performance and gold medals.

Although the FRG's and GDR's high-performance sport systems initially followed very different paths of development, they both supported world-class sport in a form that differed tremendously from Coubertin's original vision of the Olympic Games. In this respect, both systems reflected a general trend that was common to high-performance sport systems in both the east and the west. Part of the reason for the movement away from Coubertin's ideal was the growing role that scientific, instrumental rationality had begun to play in all spheres of human life: high-performance sport was not an exception. Part of the reason was the increased commercialization of the Games and part of it arose from the general politics of the cold war. But this chapter has made a more salient argument with respect to the development of high-performance sport in the modern era. Even though the Soviet entry to the Olympic Games and the growing commercialization of the Olympic Movement through the 1960s and 1970s were major factors in constituting world-class, high-performance sport in the latter half of the twentieth century, it was the particular, focused, resource-intensive, scientifically directed and fully state-supported, high-performance sport system of the GDR that was the key force in constituting the brave new world of world-class, high-performance sport in the latter quarter of the twentieth century.

Berendonk's decision to call the GDR's "State Plan Subject 14.25" the "Manhattan Project of Sport" was a well-chosen metaphor.[59] The Manhattan Project – the USA's clandestine, war time pursuit of the first atomic bomb – involved the investment of massive state resources in the research work of a small group of theoretical, experimental, and applied scientists who were commissioned – and sometimes compelled – to work under FBI-enforced state secrecy, to deliver a result that would completely alter the existing balance of global power. State Plan Subject 14.25 – the GDR's clandestine, cold war pursuit (when diplomacy was still "war by other means") of world supremacy in high-performance sport – was the mirror image of the Manhattan Project. State Plan Subject 14.25 received substantial state resources to fund the research work of a small group of theoretical, experimental, and applied scientists who worked under the protection of the state security apparatus (the Stasi) to refine already existing and widely used performance-enhancing substances. Their goal was to determine the optimal implementation of those substances so the GDR could significantly alter the existing balance of power in world-class, high-performance sport and thereby change the ideological balance of power between the GDR and the FRG, on the one hand, and the GDR and the USSR on the other. Furthermore, while the explosion of atomic bombs in Hiroshima and Nagasaki sent shock waves around the world and changed the way men and women thought about the prospects of global confrontation in the future, the performance-enhancing results that emerged from State Plan Subject 14.25 also changed how men and women thought about world-class, high-performance sport. The Olympic Games were progressively turned into a commercial and political spectacle in which highly trained athletes, in specialized events, aggressively and relentlessly pushed the envelope of human performance.

For the people charged with producing gold medal results in their respective national, high-performance sport systems, it was not the ideologically driven sentiments of the media or the IOC upon which they focused their attention or actions as the GDR rose to athletic supremacy. They recognized that success in world-class, high-performance sport, in the latter quarter of the twentieth century, required a well-funded, carefully coordinated, long-term, experimental research program.

In Orwell's *Animal Farm*, the revolution at Manor Farm promised a complete break with the past and a glorious, prosperous future. As the story unfolds it becomes apparent that the interests of the pigs dictate the lives of everyone and, moreover, "some strange thing was happening." As the animals gathered outside the farm house to watch the first meeting of the pigs with the farmers in the region, they saw that "something had altered in the faces of the pigs." As farmer Pilkington and Napoleon both played an ace of spades simultaneously in their card game, a violent argument broke out.

> Twelve voices were shouting in anger, and they were all alike. No question, now, what had happened to the faces of the pigs. The creatures outside looked from pig to man, and from man to pig, and from pig to man again; but already it was impossible to say which was which. [60]

In the world of international, high-performance sport, the story has unfolded somewhat differently. Rather than the USSR, the GDR and other east bloc nations moving progressively towards the sport systems of the capitalist west, the GDR set the standard toward which others moved. Despite the tremendous differences that existed between the high-performance sport systems in the FRG and GDR in the 1970s and 1980s, the two converged on the GDR model as they competed head-to-head. The leading high-performance sport systems in the twenty-first century now all share the following characteristics: the systematic use of pure and applied sport research to enhance performance; a search for the optimal means of identifying and developing athletic talent from a young age; the provision of professional training teams comprised of coaches, nutritionists, biomechanicians, exercise physiologists and sport psychologists; the provision of the best possible training facilities even if only on the basis of intermittent, but carefully planned and scheduled visits or intervals; and the provision of financial rewards and incentives for athletes and sport associations. The divergence from Coubertin's original ideal is obvious. What may be less apparent is that even though the cold war incentives that led to the emergence of such an approach to sport have largely receded, the momentum behind such an approach to world-class, high-performance sport remains as strong as ever.

6 Ethics reconsidered
The spirit of sport, the level playing field, and harm to the athlete

Nike's current undertaking in Portland, Oregon, is the latest development in the total integration of commercial marketing interests, vast private sector resources, patriotism, cutting-edge science and technology, and world-class, high-performance sport. Originally inspired by Tom Clarke, an avid runner and head of Nike's "new ventures," the "Oregon Project" has brought some of the best American runners to the Portland area to train under the watchful eye of former US marathon great Alberto Salazar.[1] Nike plans to capitalize on the future success of the Portland group by developing the next generation of great marathoners in a hothouse setting that involves a tightly controlled, scientifically developed and technologically sophisticated training environment.

Dismayed by the lackluster record of American distance runners in international and Olympic competition, Clarke sought out the highly visible Salazar and gathered together a select handful of runners with proven success, future potential, and who were willing to move to Oregon and live in Nike's unique training facility. Part of the Project is standard fare in any world-class, high-performance training program: scientifically produced training schedules, complex diets, specialized and expert coaching, state-of-the-art oxygen and blood testing technology that monitors aerobic capacity (VO_{2max}) and lactate threshold, high-tech video–computer imaging software for conducting technique analysis, vibrating platforms to develop increased leg power, and even the latest, Russian-produced, "Omega Wave Sports Technology," computer software that provides "stress feedback" from a runner's heart, lungs, brain, liver and kidneys in order to determine optimal training intensities. In short, Nike has created a closely monitored, scientifically advanced, and technologically sophisticated training milieu that would make even sport scientists and administrators from the former East Germany or USSR envious.

On top of the standard fare, however, the Oregon Project offers much more. The Project's technological infrastructure includes a 3,000 square foot "hypobaric house" that Nike built for the runners' daily accommodation when they are not training. A central air-control system in the hermetically sealed house creates an artificially depressed oxygen concentration, similar to that found at high altitude, throughout the dwelling. Based on the latest applied sport research, the Oregon Project is the next step in optimizing oxygen concentrations when training distance runners. Recent scientific data indicate that living in a low-oxygen, hypobaric, state during non-training hours – which artificially increases the production of oxygen-carrying red blood cells – but training in a low altitude environment (Portland is near sea level), dramatically improves performance outcomes in aerobic sports. Therefore, runners in the Nike facility eat, sleep, watch TV, play video games, etc., in a hypobaric house, but each day they can simply take two steps out of the front door to train in Portland's low altitude, oxygen-rich environment.

Nike has taken the latest scientific data on human responses to oxygen concentration further still. In addition to the hypobaric house, each athlete has access to a couch-sized, pressurized hyperbaric chamber. When sealed around the athlete's body, the chamber saturates the muscles with an artificially elevated oxygen environment to accelerate recovery from tears, sprains, bruises and other injuries.[2] As a result, athletes in the Oregon Project can rehabilitate injuries within a hyperoxygenated environment, live and carry on normal everyday activities in an oxygen-reduced environment, and still train in one that has a normal or slightly above normal oxygen concentration in the air.

The Oregon Project puts into sharp, socio-historical relief some of the most pressing ethical questions regarding what is "fair" and what is "natural" in high-performance sport. While the Nike Project might appear as an extreme manifestation of corporate desire to win world championships and gain consumer attention, it is actually much more mundane. Project Oregon is simply the logical outcome of decades of applied sport research aimed at pushing back the limits of human athletic performance.[3]

Earlier chapters have demonstrated that although ethical principles may have been the basis for prohibiting selected performance-enhancing substances in the post-World War II era, those principles were constantly contested and violated in the pursuit of specific geo-political objectives and the rapidly changing reality of world-class, high-performance sport. The challenge performance-enhancing substances brought to the embattled amateur ideal in the post-World War II era, the intensified psychological fears of steroids in light of their reported use by Nazi troops, and the subsequent fears that athletes in communist countries were using them as part of a grand, totalitarian regime-building strategy, all combined and manifested themselves in subconscious fears of certain performance-enhancing substances. Additional fears of the alleged "gender bending" of the eastern bloc and the possibility that hyper-masculinized female athletes would become standard in both the east and west led to the formation of a list of prohibited substances and practices. Prohibition – even the name itself strikes an ominous chord – has crystallized the anxieties of more than half a century and, according to some commentators, has become the single most important problem in world-class sport today. Earlier chapters have focused on the historical circumstances in which performance-enhancing substances were banned; this chapter deals directly with the ethical arguments that proponents of prohibition have used to justify their decisions.

The discussion begins with a critique of the superficial manner in which the history of performance-enhancing substances is most often presented. A lack of good information is the first problem one encounters in too many discussions of the use of performance-enhancing substances in world-class, high-performance sport today. The bulk of the chapter examines the main ethical and philosophical arguments that pertain to any discussion of performance-enhancing substances. Although much of the preceding material has emphasized the importance of studying sport in its socio-historical reality, the main ethical claims against the use of performance-enhancing substances maintain that their use is contrary to "sport" or the "spirit of sport." This chapter critically assesses the three premises upon which those arguments are founded – that the use of performance-enhancing substances contravenes the "essence" of sport; that substances disrupt the "fair and level playing field" of sport; and finally that performance-enhancing substances undermine the healthy, ennobling, and virile nature of sport.

Within the discussion of the fair and level playing field, the question of "rules" is carefully examined. The significant difference between formal, codified rules and those that are deeply sedimented in everyday life as well as the social significance of those different types of rules is critically assessed with reference to the use of performance-enhancing substances. The issues of paternalism, protection and athletes' welfare are also examined in detail as is the question of coercion and its relevance to the arguments supporting the proscription of selected substances and practices in high-performance sport.

Attitudes towards performance-enhancing substances and practices

One of the most perplexing features of standard pieces concerning the use and prohibition of performance-enhancing substances is their superficial nature. Most accounts begin with a cursory history that leads to what is assumed to be the most important issue – the "problem of cheating" – or are politically motivated pieces that champion improved detection schemes and the effectiveness of testing. In the histories, "doping," as it is almost always labelled, is usually traced to the earliest recorded cases in ancient times where, it is argued, the Greeks and the Romans used dietary supplements, stimulants, hallucinogens, and even testicular extracts to gain a competitive advantage. The chronicle then quickly shifts to more recent periods, typically the late nineteenth century, when athletes used caffeine, opium, nitro-glycerine, or any number of creative concoctions to gain an advantage. These abbreviated histories then characteristically skip to the beginning of the 1950s or 1960s. It is at this time, the argument runs, that "doping" suddenly "became" an ethical problem. These adumbrated histories imply that although the contemporary problem is simply a continuation, though on a greater scale, of something athletes have done since ancient times, the crucial difference is that sports officials now have the scientific technology and moral resolve to catch the "cheats."

A typical example of this type of history may be found in *Athletes at Risk: Drugs and Sport*, an edited volume published in 1990. *Athletes at Risk* is, in itself, an important part of the history of the so-called "war on drugs" because it was one of the first English language texts to address, in a comprehensive manner, the full spectrum of issues – from the biophysical and psychological through to the historical and policy-related – associated with substance use in the 1980s – those "unsettling and worrisome times for intercollegiate athletics."[4]

Second, the book is the direct result of a key proposal from Kansas State Governor Mike Hayden's task force on drug education and strategies for intervention.[5] On the recommendation that "athletic departments should continue to stress the educational aspects of their programs for athletes" *Athletes at Risk,* the Kansas Board of Regents' Executive Director noted in his foreword, would "assist in educating those who believe a competitive edge in athletics is justification for any action, no matter how dangerous."[6] As a result, *Athletes at Risk* has served as the authoritative and formally authorized source of information for all state-sponsored programs at the secondary and post-secondary levels, related to performance-enhancing substances in Kansas.

Finally, *Athletes at Risk* is important because its publication came in the direct aftermath of Ben Johnson's positive test for stanozolol at the 1988 Games. As one of the text's authors states, "the 1988 Olympic Games in Seoul, Korea, presented more problems of drug abuse by athletes than at any previous competition, and the integrity of the Games is at an all time low."[7] Appearing in 1990, *Athletes at Risk* was frequently cited in discussions of performance-enhancing substances that ranged from the history of their use and the health dangers they posed to policy recommendations that would eliminate their presence in competitive sport.

In the chapter "History and Evolution of Drugs in Sport," Bruce Woolley, whose doctoral degree is in pharmacy, begins his account with the sweeping generalization that: "The use of substances for performance enhancement has existed since the dawn of man's history."[8] In one page of text, Woolley glosses over several examples from ancient Greece and Rome and then jumps directly into the nineteenth century, avoiding the question of why the use of performance-enhancing substances only became an ethical issue in the last 40 or 50 years given their long history of use. Instead, Woolley presents, in four pages of text, some prosaic descriptions of performance-enhancing substance use from the 1904, 1952, 1964, 1968, 1972, 1976, 1980 and 1984 Olympic Games. Two additional pages of text cover professional sport and "Other Problems and Action."[9]

In addition to being superficial, Woolley's history demonstrates another problem in numerous histories of performance-enhancing substances. In light of some of the first suspected uses of performance-enhancing substances at the 1952 Winter Games, Woolley writes, "no concerted action was taken to prevent or stop this type of *cheating* until years later [emphasis in the original]."[10] The construction of Woolley's statement is telling. By italicizing "cheating," Woolley wants to emphasize that the use of performance-enhancing substances is, in and of itself, even in the complete absence of formal prohibition, cheating. Woolley's account, and others like it, ignores the fact that steroid use did not contravene any rules in 1952 and therefore could not be cheating in the formal sense of the term. However, even in the absence of evidence to demonstrate that steroid use would have been informally regarded as cheating, Woolley makes the judgement anyway – and with emphasis.

More nuanced and informed historical evidence indicates that referring to cases of "cheating" in sport's distant past is more a reflection of transposing contemporary sensibilities onto history than it is of the reality of past practices and the sensibilities towards them at the time. For example, in one of the more complete and authoritative accounts of drug and substance use in the past, Charles Yesalis and Michael Bahrke correct Woolley's history. "Not until the 1920s" Yesalis and Bahrke write, "was there any widespread attempt to admonish doping in sport, much less designate it as a formal violation of rules or as cheating."[11] As difficult as it may be to accept today, sound historical studies have documented that the use of performance-enhancing substances has a long history of acceptance. During ultra-marathon cycling races lasting many days, and the late nineteenth century pedestrianism craze, the use of stimulants among contestants was commonplace. "[M]oreover," Yesalis and Bahrke write, "there was no attempt to conceal drug use with the possible exception of some trainers who guarded against the proprietary interest in their own special 'doping recipes'."[12]

The emergence of anabolic steroid use is one of the more important examples of not only their accepted use but, more importantly, the way sports officials and medical scientists used their specialized expertise to develop synthetic steroids and then openly promote their use among athletes. Chapter One detailed the events that followed the Soviets' performances at the 1952 Games and the 1954 World Weightlifting Championships when John Ziegler, the American weightlifting team's physician, recruited Ciba Pharmaceutical Company to develop the synthetic steroid methandieone (Dianabol). Ziegler gave Dianabol to weightlifters at the York Barbell Club in Pennsylvania and kick-started steroid use among American athletes.[13] Ziegler, and those around him, never considered the Soviets' use of anabolic steroids or the development and distribution of Dianabol to American weightlifters as cheating, nor was there anything illegal in their action since steroids were not a controlled substance at that time. Ziegler was simply a patriotic sport physician who recognized the rapidly accelerating importance of international sport in the cold war period. He saw it as his duty to find and develop the requisite performance-enhancing techniques and substances that would assure American victories in world-class competitions.[14]

Scientific support for performance enhancement did not always begin with performance improvement first and foremost in mind. When the IOC awarded the Olympic Games to Mexico City, exercise physiologists and sports physicians were concerned that athletes in distance events might harm themselves when competing to exhaustion at altitude. While researching the effects of exertion at altitude and trying to determine the best way to prepare athletes for distance events in Mexico City, researchers explored the notion that one's oxygen carrying capacity could be "boosted" so that a performance at altitude would be similar to one at sea level without the intervention. By withdrawing an athlete's blood, allowing his or her body to equilibrate its blood volume and then reinfusing the previously withdrawn blood into the athlete prior to exercise, physiologists found that there were indications that they could enhance an athlete's aerobic capacity through reinfusion.

There was a problem, however: the results of the reinfusion technique reported in the literature were inconsistent and even contradictory. Throughout the late 1960s and 1970s physiologists continued to study the effect of withdrawing and reinfusing blood into exercising subjects and, over the course of refining the technique to obtain consistent results, they perfected the technique for boosting athletic performance in aerobically based events.[15] Blood boosting would allow a runner arriving at altitude to compete with roughly the equivalent oxygen-carrying capacity that he or she would have had at sea level. In the process of developing a technique to assess the effectiveness of a particular practice, to ensure comparable, scientifically valid results, so that athletes' health could be safeguarded when competing at altitude, exercise physiologists developed an excellent means of enhancing performance in aerobic sports.

The procedure that would enhance performance to normal levels for competition at altitude was soon employed to enhance performance at sea level beyond normal levels and blood boosting became an openly used, widespread technique for aiding distance athletes in their quest for world records right up to and including the gold medal performances by the American cyclists at the 1984 Los Angeles Games. At no point was the procedure sanctioned or denoted as cheating prior to its proscription by the IOC in 1984. The technique arose from research in well-funded laboratories that were open to public scrutiny, where research scientists and medical experts sought to test and then refine a theoretical problem.[16]

The examples of steroid use in the 1950s, 1960s and 1970s, and blood boosting in the 1960s, 1970s and 1980s indicate that sports officials, medical personnel and athletes did not regard the use of these particular performance-enhancing substances and practices as cheating. Since no rules were broken it was not formally cheating, and since their use did not contrive any "unwritten" rules or codes of conduct shared by world-class, high-performance athletes, neither was it cheating in an informal sense. On the contrary, the unwritten code affirmed the use of all scientific expertise in the pursuit of victory on the world-class stage.

Yesalis and Bahrke's research substantiates the strength of the unwritten code for sports officials, athletes and coaches. Even after the IOC had formally proscribed certain performance-enhancing substances, "athletes and coaches did not debate the morality or propriety of taking drugs; the only debate was over which drugs were more effective."[17] There is substantial evidence to suggest that even as late as the early 1970s the use of various prohibited performance-enhancing substances and practices was openly, and sometimes publicly, advocated.[18]

Earlier chapters have already documented the importance of World War II and the emergence of the cold war for so many of the defining characteristics of high-performance sport today. This is also true of the development of the moral questions surrounding the use of performance-enhancing substances and the ethical issues that are, and are not, associated with them. Yet despite the complex, unique, socio-historical forces that led to the prohibition of selected substances and practices, the first policies proposed in the 1960s, and all the major policies since then, have used a transhistorical image of "pure sport," unfettered by social and political impediments, as their basic foundation. Policies that prohibit certain substances overwhelmingly base themselves on vague notions of sport's "purity," the so-called "level playing field," the "spirit of sport," and "fair play."

Owing to the status of the *Commission of Inquiry Into the Use of Drugs and Banned Practices Intended to Increase Athletic Performance* and the stature of the commissioner himself, Chief Justice Charles Dubin's prefatory comments have carried particular weight in discussions of performance-enhancing substances following the report's release. Dubin's position is paradigmatic of those who have written policies and regulations that are rooted in a transhistorical conception of the essential "spirit of sport." "The use of banned performance-enhancing drugs is cheating," Dubin admonished in his opening statements, "which is the antithesis of sport. The widespread use of such drugs" he continued,

> has threatened the essential integrity of sport and is destructive of its very objectives. It also erodes the ethical and moral values of athletes who use them, endangering their mental and physical welfare while demoralizing the entire sport community. I have endeavoured to define the true values of sport and restore its integrity so that it can continue to be an important part of our culture, unifying and giving pleasure to Canadians while promoting their health and vitality.[19]

WADA's most recent *World Anti-Doping Code* echoes Dubin's position. The section entitled "The Fundamental Rationale for the World Anti-Doping Code" begins, "Anti-doping programs seek to preserve what is intrinsically valuable about sport." The *Code* continues, "[t]he intrinsic value is often referred to as 'the spirit of sport'; it is the essence of Olympism; it is how we play true. The spirit of sport" the *Code* proceeds to claim, "is the celebration of the human spirit, body and mind."[20] This "spirit of sport" is, according to WADA, characterized by a long list of values: "ethics, fair play and honesty; health; excellence in performance; character and education; fun and joy; teamwork; dedication and commitment; respect for rules and laws; respect for self and other participants; courage; community and solidarity."[21] The section concludes, "Doping is fundamentally contrary to the spirit of sport."[22]

The assertion that the use of performance-enhancing substances is "contrary to the spirit of sport" rests on three fundamental premises. The first was addressed extensively in Chapter Three but needs to be re-examined in a different manner within the context of the ethical questions of performance-enhancing substances in sport. The premise is that a transhistorical entity "sport" exists – an ideal form of competitive activity that can be realized and enjoyed if everyone would simply subscribe to, and abide by, its essential qualities.

The second premise is one of the most universally acclaimed and enduring presuppositions about "sport." It is also the premise that is most frequently used to substantiate the claim that there is an "essence" to "sport." The premise is that "sport" and "the spirit of sport" rest on an unequivocally fair and level playing field. "True sport" is always a completely fair contest in which the unwritten rules of fair play and sportsmanship regulate the competition. The premise reflects the desire that the rules and conditions of athletic competition take place in a venue and environment that does not favor one competitor over others, and allows each athlete to fairly test her or his natural skills and prowess. Equally critical, though almost always overlooked, is the concomitant condition that an athletic contest, conducted within the genuine "spirit of sport," has exceedingly little to do with the immediate outcome of the competition and everything to do with the character-building, educational experience associated with the wholehearted, yet appropriately mature and reserved, participation in the competitive sport.[23]

The final premise behind the assertion that the use of performance-enhancing substances is "contrary to the spirit of sport" is that "sport" is a healthy, ennobling, and virile activity and any practices that endanger athletes' health should be prohibited. The "health" or "harm to the athlete" premise supports the prohibition of certain performance-enhancing substances because of the potential health risk they are alleged to pose. The "clean," naturally virile athlete is the enduring image in sport that stems from, and gives life to, this particular premise.

Each of these premises merits detailed examination. If Dubin is correct in asserting that the use of banned, performance-enhancing substances represents the single greatest moral crises in sport today, if "drugs" represent "the antithesis of sport" and violate its "essential integrity," then it is because each of these premises holds true. If they do not hold up to careful scrutiny, then his claim is nothing more than political rhetoric. No less than the very foundation of the ethical principles for the banning of performance-enhancing substances rests on these premises.[24]

The myth of "sport" – "sport" as myth

French cultural and literary critic Roland Barthes referred to myth as the confusion of history with nature. Myth, he wrote, "deprives the object of which it speaks of all history."[25] In contrast to the common perception that myths hide or falsify some aspect of the world, Barthes' argument is that the power of myth resides precisely in what it makes available, self-evident, and clear. What is historical and cultural is presented in mythology as self-evidently "natural." Myths do not hide and falsify as much as they expose and distort so that all one has to do "is enjoy this beautiful object without wondering where it comes from."[26]

To demonstrate the notion of total myth, Barthes turned to one of Europe's most venerable athletic contests, the Tour de France, although he could have also chosen the Olympic Games. "The Tour," Barthes noted, "is at once a myth of expression and a myth of projection, realistic and utopian at the same time." The Tour is a vehicle for the expression of genuine, concrete, physical athleticism that is, simultaneously, a projection of – gives a glimpse into – an implied supreme perfection of "athleticism." Like Plato's allegory of the cave, the riders are real but they are also the shadows on the wall that are simply the reflections of a perfect truth and supreme reality. The actions of the riders are the natural expression of universal, supreme athleticism.

"The Tour" Barthes emphasized, "expresses and liberates the French people through a unique fable" in which a distorted image of reality mingles with a utopian image of the world. The result is a spectacle which appears to provide a "total clarity of relations between man, men, and Nature." What the Tour, as myth, distorts is the real basis upon which it is run – "the economic motives, the ultimate profit of the ordeal" – which are the "material generator of the ideological image" that is viewed and admired by its spectators.[27] As myth, the Tour continually takes people back to a sense of eternal awe at the riders' genuine athleticism that is merely a glimpse into the "supreme athleticism" of "The Tour de France" writ large.

To fulfil his Olympic dream, Pierre Coubertin faced two tremendous, yet inseparable, obstacles. He could not realize his educational project and all of its ideals unless he could convince others to actually stage at least one Olympic Games. Sophisticated in public relations, propaganda, and the shaping of public opinion, Coubertin took full advantage of all the image-creating techniques he could use to garner support for the Movement.[28] To overcome the apathy of the British, American, German, and French officials and to prevent the host nation's organizers from directly usurping his efforts in the interests of Greek nationalism, Coubertin built an image of the Games that was larger and more universal than any single concrete nation or national delegation could claim as its own.[29] In exactly the same manner that Barthes describes the myth of the Tour de France, Coubertin sought to establish a mythology of the ancient Games and their continuity with the proposed modern Games, which would stand above the material concerns of his project. In stark contrast to the truth that "sport" is a socially and culturally located human activity, Coubertin used powerful images, symbols, and existing Greek mythology to construct the notion that "sport" in the Olympic Games was something universal and pure which would, in the revived format, return that "essential purity" to humankind.

In pursuit of his twin goals, Coubertin used elaborate ceremony, iconography, and the arts to lift Olympic sport from the material realm and imbue it with quasi-religious qualities. In contrast to the coarse materialism and vulgar inclinations of industrial capitalism, Coubertin put forth an image of lofty ideals and universal benefaction. Unlike the real world of "advertisement and bluff ... [in which] effort is generally applied to the quest for material gain, where athletic sports are likely to be commercially exploited," the Olympic Games embody beauty, purity, "and inspire reverence.[30] The grandeur and dignity of processions, the impressive splendor of ceremonies, the concurrence of all the arts, popular emotion, and generous sentiment, must all in some sort collaborate together" Coubertin wrote of his goals and the Games' potential.[31]

Coubertin's decision to link his project to the Games of ancient Greece was crucial to his own immediate success and has also been instrumental to the enduring mythology of "sport" as a transhistorical entity that contains, in its essence, certain universally exalted virtues. At a point in European history when ancient Greece was venerated, and the supreme ideals of the Classical period were being raised as the critical forces that could halt Europe's slide into materialistic decline, the Games of ancient Olympia directly met Coubertin's needs. "There [at Olympia]," Coubertin wrote, "for a thousand years states and cities met in the person of their young men, who, imbued with a sense of the moral grandeur of the Games, went to them in a spirit of almost religious reverence." It was at Olympia, Coubertin claimed, that sport was publicly displayed as "pure and magnificent."[32]

Coubertin's imagery was striking, powerful, and persuasive. But the Games at Olympia – only one of several sporting festivals in ancient Greece – were very different. The real Games were deeply embedded in the material history of their time and bore little resemblance to Coubertin's inspiring prose and imagery. The young men, "imbued with a sense of the moral grandeur of the Games" were really professional warriors fighting for city–state favors, privileges and a life of luxury. Far from the world of religion, or any universal ideal of "sport," the ancient Games were so closely tied to military training that the athletic contests were frequently brutal struggles where the difference between victory and defeat was one of self-preservation or death. Sport in ancient Greece may have been preparation for war but war was also preparation for the combat of the Olympic Games.[33]

Myth, however, often usurps history. Thus, even though historians have corrected much of the record of the ancient Games, many of Coubertin's claims endure. They persist owing to the magnificence of their appeal and because contemporary sports leaders have continued to promote them to buttress their own political goals. Key to those objectives is the idea that "sport," in general, and as embodied in the Olympic Games in particular, is a universal ideal that should and can be realized so long as the sport leaders of today are given the powers and privileges to make that happen.

Giving continued credence to the idea that "sport" is a transhistorical, noumenal reality, which the modern Olympic Games seek to actualize, is one of the furthest reaching political aspects of Coubertin's legacy.[34] More than any other idea, this part of the Olympic myth hinders, with the greatest effect, the recognition that the Olympic Games can only be genuinely understood in their concrete, historical reality. Thus, in the context of the immediate and often petty problems Coubertin faced in the late 1890s, his quest to find an appropriately inspiring image that would overcome those difficulties created a mythology that continues to distort a true understanding of the Olympic Games themselves, and the reality of world-class, high-performance sport more generally. In addition, proponents of numerous restrictions in Olympic history have used the myth of "sport" as a transhistorical, pure form, as an unassailable foundation upon which they base those prohibitions.

Chapters One, Three and Four have documented and demonstrated the fallacies of the myth that one can properly understand "sport" in general, or "Olympic sport" in particular, in anything but their concrete, historical context. The ancient Games, the modern Olympic Games, and the world of contemporary high-performance sport are socially, historically and politically shaped activities that are constituted by athletes, officials, politicians, spectators, and, in the case of the contemporary period, advertisers, manufacturers, media and others. The competitive events themselves are real social practices embedded in a broad and complex network of activities and ideas that constitute and reconstitute a highly competitive, increasingly commercialized and professionalized, and often exploitative international system. High-performance sport today is just one small part of some of the broader structures and practices of the industrialized economies, the nation-building and identity-creating strategies of different nation states, the activities of the international media complex, and the marketing schemes employed by transnational corporations to sell specific consumer goods and services throughout the world. For better or for worse, the use of banned substances and performance-enhancing practices in high-performance sport is an integral component of the human activities that currently constitute the entire international, high-performance sport system.

Although the IOC may want these practices eliminated from high-performance sport internationally, the reality at present is that they have been woven directly into the very fabric of this form of human activity and any reference to some mythical "pure" or "authentic" "sport" only serves to divorce the use of particular substances from the constitutive practices that have led to their use in the first place. Vague notions of sport based on the mythology of some "pure" or "universal" athleticism, which is violated by the use of performance-enhancing substances, only diverts attention away from the real constitutive practices in high-performance sport today. Only by recognizing the entire set of activities that continually constitute and reconstitute high-performance sport will athletes and sports leaders be able to consider the problems of world-class sport in an open, concrete, and useful manner. World-class, high-performance sport is a complex, multifaceted institution and its many forms, locations, contexts, and levels must be acknowledged, and the role that its participants play in defining, producing and reproducing it cannot be ignored. The true goals and objectives of specific, socially located, differentiated sport forms must be identified, and those sport forms must be shaped by legitimately constituted leadership groups to meet participants' needs. The true "rules of the game" in world-class, high-performance sport must be addressed – not their mythological counterparts.

The "spirit of sport" and the "fair and level playing field"

The second premise behind the claim that performance-enhancing substances are "contrary to the spirit of sport" is that "sport" and "the spirit of sport" rest on the principle of an unequivocally "fair and level playing field." This premise is one of the most critical in the prohibition of selected performance-enhancing substances because any threat to fairness strikes directly at the "essence of sport." If the fair and level playing field is lost, then "sport" itself can never be realized. In addition, the fair and level playing field argument has been at the heart of substance prohibition since the IOC's first policies were created. During its annual meeting in 1967, the IOC first defined "doping" as "the use of substances or techniques in any form or quantity alien or unnatural to the body with the exclusive aim of obtaining an artificial or unfair increase of performance in competition."[35]

Although appearing, at first glance at least, to be straightforward and sound, a closer examination shows that issues of fairness and equality are extremely complex. Upon careful review, the claim that the formal banning of certain substances creates, or even leads towards, fairness and equality is not at all convincing. To address this issue, an important distinction between fairness and equality must be considered.

Even when competition is fair in the sense that all competitors follow the same formal and informal rules, this does not mean that it is equal. Even in the total absence of all performance-enhancing substances, there is a tremendous inequality that pervades the competitive conditions in international high-performance sport. But even the concept of "inequality" is not as straightforward as often assumed.

Inequality is an involved concept in which one must distinguish between inequality of opportunity and inequality of condition. Inequality of opportunity concerns how equally opportunity for participation in a particular activity is spread throughout a society. Inequality of opportunity can be examined with almost any pursuit ranging from educational opportunity, to labor force participation, to taking part in sport or leisure activities. Even in countries as prosperous as the United States, Germany or Canada there is not an equality of opportunity in the realm of sport. Swimming pools and gymnastic and track and field facilities, for example, are not distributed equally throughout these countries and while proportionately many more young athletes in large, thriving, urban centres have abundant opportunities to pursue the sport(s) of their choice, those who live in smaller, less economically developed and robust or more rural settings do not. Even within large, prosperous, urban settings, there is not an equality of opportunity. Gender, ethnicity, location of residence, class and race still limit the opportunities of many potential athletes in cities that are the richest in facilities and opportunities. These same conditions apply to the United Kingdom, Russia, Hungary, China – the list goes on.

Inequality of condition refers to a more entrenched dimension of inequality. Even if all Americans, Germans or Canadians had the opportunity to take part in gymnastics, dressage, field hockey or luge racing, the conditions under which they would enter the activity would differ markedly. While introducing programmes that would ultimately lead to extensive federal government involvement in the Canadian sport system, the Honourable John Munro, Minister of Health and Welfare, illustrated inequality of condition very clearly. "It is only fair, just as in a dash in a track meet it's only fair," he noted in introducing Canada's first comprehensive program to increase the opportunity for, and participation in, athletic activities,

> that everyone has the same starting line, and the same distance to run. Unfortunately, in terms of facilities, coaching, promotion and programming, the sports scene today resembles a track on which some people have twenty-five yards to run, some fifty, some one hundred and some as much as a mile or more.[36]

Unfortunately little has changed in the time that separates Munro's comments from the present day regarding the inequality of condition which structures sport.[37] If anything, the latest scholarly literature on all aspects of social inequality indicates that the gap between rich and poor – indeed, between the upper middle and the lower middle class – is widening.

The above points concerning inequality of opportunity and inequality of condition are magnified when viewed on a world scale. There is no comparison concerning opportunity and condition for sport among, for example, Germany, Poland, the USA, Mexico, and Cameroon. The inequalities are overwhelming and none of them are related to, or even tempered by, the use of performance-enhancing substances by some athletes in any or all of those countries. Substance use is only one among many conditions of inequality. Unfortunately, in too many discussions of the "fair and level playing field," it is commonly assumed that the inequalities produced by performance-enhancing substances are substantially different than the inequalities that exist between nations and even within nations in world-class, international sport. But this is not the case.

The fair and level playing field argument also assumes that the use of banned substances contravenes established rules. It must be cheating. This appears straightforward. But rules, as Anthony Giddens has indicated, are extremely complex entities.[38] Rules can, for example, be classified as indications of habit (as a rule Martin Brodeur is a butterfly style goaltender in hockey), constitutive of action (sprinters should remember that the shortest distance between two points is a straight line), or regulative (it is a rule that practice begins at 9:00 am).[39] Giddens also establishes that although we have formalized rules to regulate behavior – one cannot tackle in soccer "in a manner considered by the referee to be careless, reckless or using excessive force" without penalty – these rules, as an ontological fact of social conduct, stem from human practice and must be interpreted in action.[40] In other words, once written down and codified, the real meaning of a formal rule is determined in and by social practice. The judiciary, for example, carries out the important task of interpreting a Civil Code, particular statutes in both the Civil and Common Law traditions, and its decisions constitute the cases which comprise Common Law.[41] Similarly, referees interpret and determine what constitutes an acceptable versus a careless or reckless tackle in soccer on the basis of the rule found in FIFA's *Laws of the Game*.

Giddens takes this point further.

> Let us regard the rules of social life ... as techniques or generalizable procedures applied in the enactment–reproduction of social practices. Formulated rules – those that are given verbal expression as canons of law, bureaucratic rules, rules of games and so on – are thus codified interpretations of rules rather than rules as such. They should not be taken as exemplifying rules in general but as specific types of formulated rule, which, by virtue of their overt formulation, take on various specific qualities.[42]

Two important points arise from Giddens' analysis.

First, when most students of social processes, let alone lay actors themselves, think about rules, they think in terms of codified rules and assume that codification determines or explains behavior. But, and this is the second point, Giddens argues that codified rules are only "interpretations of rules rather than rules as such." Thus it is not rules which have been "given verbal expression as canons of law," etc., that constitute social action, but the everyday rules of social conduct: these constitute social action and serve as the basis for formalized, codified rules. Human life is the reverse of our common sense understanding; formal, codified rules do not dictate our actions; our actions give rise to the codification of formal rules.

Giddens draws an important contrast between rules that are intensive, tacit, informal and weakly sanctioned, and those that are shallow, discursive, formalized and strongly sanctioned. With the former, he notes that intensive rules are constantly used in the course of our day-to-day activities. They, in fact, structure the texture of everyday life. The rules of language upon which we draw constantly but modify dependent upon context, the procedures we employ in taking turns in conversation or interaction are examples of these intensive, tacit, informal rules. They are, as noted above, the basis for those that are given "verbal expression as canons of law, bureaucratic rules, rules of games and so on."

Formalized, codified rules, by contrast, though wide in scope have only a superficial impact upon most of the texture of social life. While the sanctions for breaking a codified rule might be harsh, and they have been clearly articulated and formalized, their impact on daily life is actually very shallow. "I would propose," Giddens writes, "that many seemingly trivial procedures followed in daily life have a more profound influence upon the generality of social conduct [than formalized rules]."[43]

The "trivial procedures" to which Giddens refers have been discussed and analyzed by Charles Lemert who, in somewhat different terms, explains that people act by drawing upon their sociological "competence" which enables them to negotiate their way through the intricate – although usually unacknowledged – social rules encountered in everyday life. In this process of negotiation, the way to proceed or the ways to proceed are established.[44]

Giddens and Lemert's point regarding the way people live through and understand the rules of everyday life is directly relevant to notions of fairness in high-performance sport in three ways. First, the list of banned performance-enhancing substances was established well after athletes, coaches, administrators and medical personnel had already consistently used them and structured their use into not only their training programmes but also, and far more importantly, the way they thought about and accepted the work world of high-performance sport in their everyday lives. Although their use began in the mid-1950s, it was not until 1973 that an adequate test for anabolic steroids was discovered, 1975 that they were formally banned, and not until the 1976 Games that the IOC first tested for them.[45] Not surprisingly, as detailed in Chapters One and Five, steroid use on both sides of the iron curtain had become routine among numerous athletes in strength-related sports and events.[46] As a result, steroid use had become a deeply sedimented, intensive, constitutive element in the production of high-performance athletes for at least twenty years prior to its ban.

Equally important, not only was the formal rule as made by the IOC inconsistent with the established informal rules of everyday life in high-performance sport, but the IOC tried to reverse those rules completely. As a result, a strongly sanctioned, formalized rule was created to eliminate a set of intensive, tacit, informal rules that had become well entrenched in high-performance sport training by the 1970s. Unfortunately for the IOC, regulative rules do not trump deeply sedimented rules unless social practices change and the formalized rule is accepted as legitimate.

Second, the constitutive core practices and the dominant interpretation of the rationale behind high-performance sport are the tacit agreement that victory and the pursuit of the linear record are its primary goals. Though not formally codified in such terms – although the recent shift to performance criteria in the funding of high-performance athletes at the current point in time shows how this deeply sedimented reality is receiving formal, discursive recognition – the practices of high-performance sport have progressively, over the last half century, aimed at pushing back the limits of human athletic performance through the increasing use of an unabashed scientific, instrumental rationality.[47] Over the last 25 years a deluge of scientifically developed, innovative, performance-enhancing practices have become commonplace in the constitution of high-performance sport. In some instances, these practices have been formally proscribed after the fact; some have been prohibited for a specified moratorium; others have been unchallenged. Some performance enhancing practices have not even come to public attention. The point, however, is that both the logic and the real practices that constitute world-class, high-performance sport are unabashedly achievement dominated. Performance-enhancement is the core of the social system's logic and the core of its intensive, tacit, informal rule structure which is "constantly invoked in the course of day-to-day activities" by the athletes, coaches, performance scientists and administrators who make up that system.[48] As a result, what is fair, on the basis of following "the rules of the game," is more complex than simply referring to the IOC's codified rules. The less acknowledged, more profound, intensive rules of everyday conduct cast a much different light on the notion of "fairness."

The third point is that the actors themselves follow the intensive rules that constitute their particular life–worlds. When Charlie Francis was considering the possibility that Canadian sprinter Angella Issajenko would take steroids, he reflected on the question of "the fair and level playing field." "Fairness" he wrote,

> was not a practical issue for us. In Canada, Angella had already left the competition far behind; it wouldn't change the placing were she to move further in front. And on the international scene, our steroid program would make the playing field *more* level, not less [emphasis in original].[49]

In 2004, Francis reflected on his experiences as a coach at the world-class level and noted that "the playing field is level; it's just not the level playing field that you [the lay public] thought."[50]

On the constitutive rules of Angella Issajenko's life–world in high-performance sport, Francis wrote:

> Numbers define one's place in the track world. Now our place was receding – and I felt sure I knew why. Angella wasn't losing ground because of a talent gap. She was losing ground because of a drug gap, and it was widening by the day. As I tracked the steroid trail ... I arrived at a central premise which would guide my counsel for Angella, as well as for Ben and my other top male sprinters when they reached a similar crossroads: *An athlete could not expect to win in top international competition without using anabolic steroids* [emphasis in original].[51]

In her training diaries, Issajenko puts the intensive rules that constitute the deeply sedimented constitution of world-class, high-performance sport in poignant terms. "There is a lot of pain in the neat rows of figures that make up the diaries" she wrote.

> There are brief notes on the inside front cover, recording my best times and including times from 1977 that I must have thought worth noting. These are 25.5, meaning twenty-five and a half seconds for the 200-metres, and 12.2, meaning twelve and two-tenth seconds for the 100 metres. By 1982, the last year in this short list, the times are 22.25 and 11.00.[52]

In an ironic but accurate sense, Francis indicates that fair competition in international high-performance sport involves following the tacit, informal, weakly sanctioned rules that actually constitute that human endeavor. This means that numerous athletes in a host of sports, who are determined to win medals, circumvent the formal rules regarding selected, banned performance-enhancing substances and practices, while simultaneously entrenching themselves more and more deeply into the world of high-performance sport. Athletes seek a fair and level playing field in the real world of their everyday lives.

Even if the IOC wanted to dismiss the foundational nature of the tacit, intensive rules that are chronically employed in the constitution of high-performance sport, a careful consideration of the constitutive rule structure of sporting activities themselves reveals significant contradictions with respect to the use of performance-enhancing substances. The overriding assumption in popular accounts and the policies that prohibit performance-enhancing substances is that their use violates the essential or fundamental rules of sport. It is assumed that the use of performance-enhancing substances violates the very nature of the sporting competition; athletes who use them are, quite simply, no longer participating in sport itself because they are ignoring the very rules upon which a fair and level playing field would be possible.

However, just as Giddens and Lemert indicate the complexity of rules in social life, the formal rules of sport are also complex entities. While rules in general are essential to the constitution of sport, philosopher Bernard Suits distinguishes between two fundamentally different types of rules that are required in the constitution of sport. In *The Grasshopper: Games, Life and Utopia*, Suits reveals the nature of the formal rules which define sport and provide its foundation.[53]

When most people think about rules in sport they think of proscriptive rules. People think, for example, of rules that forbid actions such as tripping or slashing in hockey where penalties are imposed for their transgression. But Suits notes that there is a certain type of rule, which he terms "constitutive," without which the athletic activity itself could not take place. For an activity to take place that has, over recent history, become recognized as sport in a generalized form, there are four conditions that must be met. First, there must be rules that set out the specific objectives or goals of the contest. Second, rules positively establish how the goal(s) can be achieved – what techniques and means will constitute the contest. Third, the rules that constitute sport and establish how the goal will be achieved do not permit what is unquestionably the most efficient means to achieving the activity's goal. Finally, Suits notes, the limits to the most effective means to the activity's goal are accepted because they make the activity possible.[54]

In addition to constitutive rules, Suits indicates that sport is governed by regulative rules. Regulative rules govern the precise ways in which athletes may pursue the sport as it has been structurally defined by the constitutive rules. Constitutive rules are primary; they define the fundamental components of each sport. Regulative rules are secondary; they regulate behavior within the framework established by the constitutive rules.[55]

With respect to regulations that prohibit selected performance-enhancing substances, one of the central and most common mistakes is to assume that they are prohibited because their use violates one or more of the constitutive rules of sport – that they undermine the primary characteristics of high-performance sport. In fact, rules that prohibit some substances and permit others are simply regulative rules, as the late introduction of the steroid ban and the continual changes to the banned list demonstrate. If the use of performance-enhancing substances violated a constitutive rule, the contravention would be far reaching – it would alter the fundamental basis of the contest. But the rules prohibiting certain substances do not "define" sport any more than the regulative rule prohibiting aggressive tackling defines soccer. Both rules regulate behavior but at a fundamentally different level from the constitutive rules which actually establish sport as an activity.

In response to this distinction, an IOC member might argue that even if it is only a regulative rule that is broken and not a constitutive rule, the use of banned substances still violates a rule and should be punished. The problem with this response is that while true, it concedes that the use of performance-enhancing substances in no way undermines the constitutive, fundamental structure of sport. The real issue is the ultimate stature of the rule. Does the rule regulate a behavior that defines the very nature of high-performance sport or does it simply regulate behavior within the constitutive framework of sport? A regulative rule is an ancillary dimension of sport. As such it should be subject to continual review and adjusted, when necessary, in the best interests of the athletes and others who constitute sport at the world-class level.

"Sport," health, and harm to the athlete

During the 1998 Tour de France erythropoietin (EPO) scandal, the distinguished former professional cyclist Robert Millar – fourth place finisher in the 1984 Tour's "King of the Mountains" competition – described, in a widely distributed article published in the *Guardian*, the Tour's physical toll on a cyclist.[56] "The riders reckon that a good Tour takes one year off your life," he wrote, "and when you finish in a bad state, they reckon three years."

> You can't divide the mental and physical suffering; you tend to let go mentally before you crack physically. ... Riding up one of the mountains on the Tour if you're feeling bad is like being sick. ... The pain in your legs is not the kind of pain you get when you cut yourself, it's fatigue, and it's self-imposed. ... You can't describe to a normal person how tired you feel; how can you describe feeling so tired you can't sleep? ... I can understand guys being tempted to use drugs in the Tour. ... I don't think it's an isolated cycling thing, people just expect sport to be cleaner than real life.[57]

While Millar's description of the grueling physical hardships high-performance cyclists experience is important, it is his need to convey this information to the public that is most significant. Millar recognizes that someone with real insider's knowledge – someone who had endured a Tour – had to explain that world-class, high-performance cycling is far from a healthy ride in the park on a Sunday afternoon. Based on his own life experiences as a high-performance athlete, having interacted with many people from outside that life–world, he knew how little the public at large recognizes the semi-pathological character of high-performance sport. He knew how little the average fan understands athletes' actual experiences. The mythology that high-performance sport produces healthy, virile bodies is powerful despite all of the evidence of injury and the long-term ill effects of chronic training regimes on athletes' bodies.

The premise that sport and health are two sides to the same coin has an extremely long history, is deeply embedded in the notion of "sport," and serves as a powerful ideological weapon in attempts to legitimate the proscription of particular performance-enhancing substances. The relation is so entrenched that Dubin claimed that one of the "true values of sport" was its ability to give pleasure while promoting "health and vitality."[58]

Since sport is assumed to be healthy, a logical corollary is that possibly unhealthy substances and practices should be banned in the best interests of the athlete and of sport. The "best interests of the athlete" argument is, in fact, one of the longstanding justifications for the proscription of certain performance-enhancing substances, which, coupled with Knud Jensen's death in Rome, motivated the IOC to prohibit certain drugs and practices. The logic for the action is straightforward: if, in its extreme, win-at-all-costs form, some athletes engage in behaviors and practices that endanger their own personal health, then those practices should be eliminated by people who have a better understanding and perspective from which to make that judgement. Prohibition protects the athlete's health and the fundamental unity of sport and health.

Millar's description of riders' experiences on the Tour suggests that the sport–health premise is false. Health is not the other side of the high-performance sport coin; world-class sport is work and it entails a number of deeply embedded occupational hazards and health risks that are integral to the undertaking itself. Rather than supporting the assumption that certain substances represent health risks, Millar suggests that it is the activity itself that is unhealthy. Before looking at the material conditions of high-performance sport that support Millar's position, there are some logical inconsistencies to address.

When most people think of sport and injury – the counterfactual condition of sport and health – they think of sports that appear to be inherently violent or dangerous. It is useful to begin with those sports, because they point beyond themselves to the more salient fact that it is the social construction of contemporary high-performance sport itself that is dangerous to athletes' health, rather than just certain sports that can be easily and readily classified as violent or risky.

In his analysis of violence and aggression in sport, Kevin Wamsley has demonstrated that vicious and aggressive behavior is not just "part of the game." Consistent with a theme that has run through this book, Wamsley argues that a true understanding of violence in sport requires the location of historically specific sporting activities within a nation's social and cultural history. Violence in North American sport, Wamsley documents, has many of its historical and cultural roots in the nineteenth century when men in the upper and newly emerging middle classes wanted to establish their personal and professional entitlement through new men's sporting clubs. "Through sport," Wamsley writes, "masculinity was tested through an on-field, rule-bound aggression where participants and spectators came to associate the male body with power and authority, tempered by the values of Christianity and a code of fair play."[59] Two factors were most influential in the association of the male body with power, authority, masculinity, and apparently natural aggression.

First, the physical contests of nineteenth century sport appeared, to most, to rest on the natural, biologically determined, physical strengths of the competitors. As a result, the natural, physical aggression that was entailed in, and arose out of, those physical contests also appeared to be a natural part of the game. The social construction of the contests was lost from sight in the apparently basic, biologically natural, dimensions of the contests. As the physical nature of the competition was viewed as an inherent product, the physical violence also appeared to be a natural element to the games themselves. Very quickly "rule-bound aggression" was accepted as a "natural" component of sport. Second, the idea that aggression and violence were natural parts of athletic contests became more deeply entrenched as the sport forms were passed from one generation to the next. Over time, the historical and social roots of the games were completely ignored as the activities assumed an increasingly natural, transhistorical character.

Hockey in Canada serves as a good example of this process. Many Canadians view violence in hockey as a natural part of the game. Richard Gruneau and David Whitson, in their cultural history of hockey, have documented that violence in hockey – at the minor league, junior leagues, minor professional and NHL level – can be traced to nineteenth century traditions in which aggressive behavior was used as a means for boys and men to prove their masculinity and power in a world that was being increasingly regulated, "civilized," and, in the minds of some, made effeminate. Sport was a male preserve where the "natural need" to express male aggression was permitted. Over time, ritualized, masculine aggression became naturalized as a basic component of hockey, and the historical roots of the game's "unwritten code" fell out of the common cultural memory.[60]

Wamsley's work indicates another reason that physical aggression and violence are accepted as natural elements in contemporary sport. Media coverage of sport provides viewers with a daily diet of the most graphic images connecting sport and violence. "[F]alls, hits, and catastrophic injuries are the mainstays of highlight packages for specialized sport channels and even 'news' stories on network television" Wamsley notes. Bone-jarring helmet to helmet collisions, clothesline and blindside tackles in football, knockout punches on HBO fights, bean balls, concussion-causing body-checks and fights in hockey, "cart-wheeling, rag-doll spills in alpine skiing," along with spectacular crashes in cycling and auto racing are common images in televised highlight packages, advertising segments, leaders and trailers for regularly scheduled, prime time television. The more spectacular or the more violent, the more it is replayed.[61]

The work of Wamsley, Gruneau and Whitson indicates that certain sports are violent and extremely dangerous, but it is certain performance-enhancing substances that are singled out for concern rather than the nature of many sports themselves. W. M. Brown has documented that there have been only a handful of deaths from drug misuse among athletes – and many of those were due to recreational as opposed to performance-enhancing pharmaceuticals – while there have been countless cases of serious injury and hundreds of deaths in sports such as football, boxing, cycling, downhill skiing and other sports that involve either aggressive physical contact or require the propulsion of the body through space at extremely high speeds.[62]

As risky as some sports are, there is an even more salient point to note: it is not only the sports where risk, aggression and violence are seen as natural that are the counterfactual examples of the "sport as health" binary. High-performance sport in its current socially constructed form potentially undermines the health of athletes – a reality that is much more profound than simply the fact that some sports, due to their particular objectives, appear to be health risks for athletes.

Millar's description provides one instance of a sport which, even though there are some attendant risks to injury through crashes and other mishaps, is seen as a largely non-violent, non-aggressive sport. Cycling, like running, appears to be among the healthiest undertakings an athlete could choose. But Millar writes that is not the case at all; taking part in the incredibly demanding rigors of the Tour de France – even in a good Tour – compromises the health and well-being of an athlete. What is true of the Tour also holds for the central demands of almost all high-performance sports today. Terry Roberts and Dennis Hemphill make the point in their description of the general conditions that constitute world-class, high-performance sport:

> Whether essential, incidental or sought out, risks and dangers exist in progressive overload training and/or in confronting and attempting to surmount various sport specific, natural, human or mechanical obstacles and forces within the sport action itself. In an environment predicated on maximal effort and performance, risk and danger are essential and accepted elements.[63]

Risk and danger have become such central aspects of high-performance sport that the care and treatment of injuries is a taken-for-granted aspect of all world-class athletes' training environments. This was not always the case but, as Ivan Waddington's work demonstrates, sports medicine has, since the development of the first post-secondary sports medicine curriculum in Germany in the 1920s, become a well-established component of high-performance sport in the modern world.[64] In the wake of the intensification of the demands on athletes from the 1952 Games onwards, the idea "that athletes require routine medical supervision, not because they necessarily have a clearly defined pathology but, in this case, simply because they are athletes" has become firmly entrenched in high-performance sport.[65]

Given the manner in which athletes' medical needs for treatment have grown in both the scale of treatment required as well as the seriousness of the injuries treated, the claim that high-performance sport and health are two sides to the same coin can no longer be maintained. Along with that realization, the logical corollary that the proscription of certain performance-enhancing substances and practices will ensure the health and safety of world-class, high-performance athletes must also be abandoned. While performance-enhancing substances have been singled out for special scrutiny and prohibition under the "harm to the athlete" argument, it is the larger dangers and risks of high-performance sport itself that need to be examined if, indeed, one wants to try to legislate specific protections to ensure the health of high-performance athletes.[66] This conclusion leads directly to the issue of paternalism and the need for others, in "a better position than the athletes," to legislate protections since sport, in and of itself, can no longer be regarded as a healthy activity.

Paternalism, protection, and athletes' welfare

Paternalism is "the interference with a person's liberty of action justified by reasons referring exclusively to the welfare, good, happiness, needs, interests or values of the person being coerced."[67] Paternalistic protection is usually regarded as justified when a legislative body or persons in positions of legitimate power and authority take actions that ensure that persons who lack power and are vulnerable, or may be put in positions of potential risk, are protected. Labor standards legislation and bans on smoking in public buildings are examples of justifiable, paternalistic legislation. Rules that ensure order and good conduct in schools and other educational settings, or parents overseeing and guiding their children in their best interests are also instances that most people regard as justified paternalism.

With respect to performance-enhancing substances, the IOC used to include protection of the athlete within its rationale for the banned list. For example, in the *Olympic Movement: Anti-Doping Code*, which was put into effect in January 2000 and remained until it was replaced by WADA's *Anti-Doping Code*, the IOC clearly indicated that two of the reasons for adopting the code were the "Movement's duty to protect the health of athletes" and its obligation to "act in the best interests of athletes."[68]

WADA's *Anti-Doping Code* is more circumspect. The new code has formally eliminated protection of the athlete as the grounds for the banned list. The principle behind the *Code* is "[t]o protect the *Athletes'* fundamental right to participate in doping-free sport" while also intended to "promote health, fairness, and equality for *Athletes* worldwide."[69] As a result, the IOC has, through WADA, now moved away from its earlier commitment to paternalism. Nevertheless, because the principles of paternalism are discussed in so many ethical discussions of performance-enhancing substances, they remain important enough to fully explore why they were inappropriate grounds for justifying the list of banned performance-enhancing substances and practices.

The paternalistic "limitation of one's liberty is justified when one's behaviour or actions are not fully voluntary because they are not fully informed, or because one is not fully competent or is in some relevant way coerced."[70] Thus the paternalistic proscription of performance-enhancing substances would be justified in situations where a dangerous behavior is undertaken due to overt or covert coercion, or where athletes are not judged competent enough to make such a decision, or where they cannot gain access to information that the agents offering paternalistic protection have at their disposal. If none of these conditions hold, then the argument that athletes need to be protected from performance-enhancing substances on legitimate, paternalistic grounds, fails to make its burden of proof.

Consider knowledge and competence first. Policy makers have not argued that a ban on performance-enhancing substances is, or has been, justified because the IOC, the IOC's Medical Commission, WADA, any NOC, the medical community, or any other body has information that athletes, coaches, sport administrators or others do not have or cannot obtain. On the contrary, sport administrators in high-performance sport have a healthy respect for the information athletes possess. For example, the *Olympic Charter* and the WADA *Code* expect athletes to know all the substances that are proscribed and require them to avoid even the inadvertent consumption of any of those substances despite the myriad of ways they could be ingested. As a result, prior to the adoption of

WADA's *Code*, Articles Two and Three of the IOC's own *Anti-Doping Code*, which was based on paternalistic principles, indicated that knowledge was not an issue. The "Code applies to all Participants" and "it is the personal responsibility of any athlete subject to the provisions of this Code to ensure that he or she does not use or allow the use of any Prohibited Substance or any Prohibited Method."[71] Knowledge and competence on the part of the athlete was taken for granted in an IOC *Code* that was written within a framework of paternalistic principles.

WADA's *Code* adopts the same position on knowledge and competence. Article 2.1 states that an athlete has violated the *Code* simply through "[t]he presence of a *Prohibited Substance* or its *Metabolites* or *Markers* in an *Athlete's* bodily *Specimen*."[72] Article 2.1.1 states:

> It is each *Athlete's* personal duty to ensure that no *Prohibited Substance* enters his or her body. *Athletes* are responsible for any *Prohibited Substance* or its *Metabolites* or *Markers* found to be present in their bodily *Specimens*. Accordingly, it is not necessary that the intent, fault, negligence, or knowing *Use* on the *Athlete's* part be demonstrated in order to establish an anti-doping violation under Article 2.1.[73]

As a result, even though there are some sports in which minors compete at the Olympic Games, neither the IOC nor WADA make any provisions in the *Anti-Doping Code* to ensure that decisions affecting child athletes are made by competent guardians. All athletes are regarded as sufficiently knowledgeable and competent to be held responsible for any violations of the *Code*.

The next major point concerns paternalist protection in situations of overt or covert coercion. The most compelling case of the involvement of coercion in athletes' use of performance-enhancing substances is that of East Germany.

Before focusing on the GDR, it is important to note that any dispassionate, genuinely analytical discussion of its sport system is extremely difficult because it inescapably involves sensitive political, legal, moral, and emotional issues. Furthermore, there is considerable legal evidence documenting serious abuses of trust within the system. Court evidence shows that GDR politicians and sports leaders initiated or permitted practices that were, and remain, completely unacceptable by any standards. Most disturbing of all, much of the criminal activity in the system concerned young athletes who, as minors, were placed in positions of trust with their coaches and other sport leaders.[74] The discussion that follows is not, in any way, an apology for the GDR's political leadership or the criminal activity that took place within the East German sport system. The points made, as uncomfortable as some might be, are guided exclusively by the issues directly related to how appropriate the principles of paternalism are for the protection of high-performance athletes through the prohibition of selected performance-enhancing substances and practices.

The protection of minors for paternalistic reasons is not questioned in this argument. The most heinous criminal activity within the GDR's sport system was the coercion of minors. Child athletes in other countries have also lacked protection.

Unfortunately, the IOC and the banned list did not protect child athletes in the GDR (or elsewhere) and the new *Code* still does not – a major shortcoming in high-performance sport that too many policy makers continue to ignore.

What about athletes above the age of majority in the GDR – did they require paternalist protection from deceit or coercion? Were all (or even a majority or a significantly large number) of the GDR's mature athletes coerced or deceived into taking performance-enhancing substances by coaches, trainers, or sport administrators?

While, in retrospect, mature athletes might now indicate that they had no idea they were taking performance-enhancing substances, there is good reason for scepticism and thus bringing into question the relevant paternalistic principles for the prohibition of selected performance-enhancing substances. First, the claim of ignorance among athletes of majority age is not at all consistent with their phenomenological existence as extremely well-trained, sophisticated, finely tuned competitors. World-class, high-performance athletes are intimately aware of their bodies: the impact of steroids, for example, on an athlete's physiology cannot be missed by such well-attuned individuals. The point is further sustained by the on-again, off-again cycles that the GDR's athletes followed with respect to steroid use; the physiological changes between on and off cycles are too significant to miss even in low doses.[75] In addition, those athletes lived and thrived in a high-performance sport subculture where detailed knowledge about a vast array of complex, technically advanced, high-level, performance-enhancing techniques and substances circulated regularly and widely.[76] The counterfactual evidence against claims of ignorance among high-performance athletes in the GDR is too strong to accept deceit or lack of knowledge as general explanations for the widespread use of performance-enhancing substances in East Germany and as reasons for proscribing them on paternalistic grounds.

If the widespread use of performance-enhancing substances in Germany was not based on the deception or ignorance of the mature athletes in the system it might have stemmed from coercion. The power of the state and its security apparatus forcing athletes to comply with a state-run program might explain the widespread use of performance-enhancing substances in East Germany. There are three important points to recognize about this claim.

First, although the files exist which prove the extent to which the SED, through the Stasi, gathered and catalogued information on the citizens of the GDR, and although there have been claims that East Germans were passive, docile, automatons who never challenged state authority – in even the smallest acts of disobedience – the reality was that East Germans did make choices.[77] One did not have to be a high profile dissident like Wolf Biermann, Stefan Heym, or Christa Wolff to engage in everyday acts that created personal space and freedom. Citizens of the GDR did this on a regular basis at work and at home, in public and in private.

The fundamental, defining characteristic of a human being, Giddens has argued, is the ability to exercise agency even in the face of oppressive power and severe deprivation.[78] There is no credible evidence to suggest that East Germans were incapable of exercising that fundamental human property. Many may have chosen to acquiesce to the dominant power structure and to conform as much as possible but that was a decision nonetheless, even if largely by default.

Second, the claim that the SED and the Stasi successfully controlled the lives of all East Germans – including its athletes – not only denies Giddens' insights into the fundamental properties of human agency, it also gives far more credit to the Stasi and SED's Stalinist tactics than is deserved or is substantiated by empirical evidence. The celebrated acts of resistance are well known – the 1953 uprising in East Berlin, the exile of dissident figures like Biermann, the successful and failed attempts to cross the Berlin Wall – but these represent the high profile, visible manifestations of actions that took place at a personal level on a daily basis throughout the GDR. Countless East Germans made choices and exercised self-determination in numerous ways every day – from the schoolteacher who refused to join the SED and was therefore continually denied permission to take his school choir outside the GDR, to the medical doctor who collected Phil Ochs records and other books and CDs from the west, to the young woman who joined the SED, was as active as possible in the party, studied Marx and cited his work as often and fully as she could to broaden people's understandings of socialism, democracy and the shortcomings, without naming them precisely, of "Real Existing Socialism." The same is true of the family that read Rudolf Bahro's *The Alternative in Eastern Europe* and became activists in the ecological movement in East Berlin as well as the young teenager in stylish glasses who wrote glowingly of East Germany's achievements for his school project, celebrating 1989 as the 40th year of the GDR's existence, while simultaneously covering the walls of his room with posters of bands in the west, tuning in to "capitalist radio," and watching West German television.[79] The choices may not have always been appealing, but East Germans made them.

With respect to high-performance sport, two of the most careful, scholarly observers and critics of the East German system note that even within the confines of the GDR's ruthless pursuit of Olympic gold, high-performance athletes did, in fact, have choices: some chose to not take part in the "anabolics program."[80] Refusing to follow the fully prescribed training program set out for an athlete might have resulted in the termination of his or her career for political reasons rather than competitive ones but the choice to refuse existed. It would be almost impossible to determine exactly how many athletes refused to take performance-enhancing substances and, for political or performance-related reasons, fell out of the system but athletes certainly did opt out.

While some athletes were refusing to take performance-enhancing substances, Franke and Berendonk document that other athletes throughout the GDR were acting against the state by making a different choice. One of the SED's largest problems was the sale of performance-enhancing substances on the black market and their unregulated, unsupervised use by athletes outside the scientific and medical support community that oversaw their normal distribution.[81] Both the sale and the purchase of performance-enhancing substances on a black market indicate the ability of East Germans to create their own personal freedoms despite Stasi surveillance and state oppression. As a result, the claim that the SED and the Stasi completely controlled the lives of all East Germans fails on empirical grounds. As omnipresent as the Stasi and its informers were, they were never omnipotent. If they had been, the Berlin Wall would still stand today.

Third, the assumption that the SED, the Stasi, or even a coach who intimately knows a mature athlete can force him or her to take anything or do anything that the athlete has decided against fails to recognize the reality of high-performance sport and the athletes who make it up. An athlete who is forced, against her or his better judgement, to take a substance that she or he does not want to ingest will not, and cannot, be an enthusiastic participant in the remainder of his or her athletic commitments. A waning commitment is tantamount to the termination of a career in a world where thousandths of a second separate a gold medal winner from finishing off the podium. Furthermore, in a state that valued gold medals so highly and carefully recruited vast numbers of young athletes to win them, the opportunity costs involved in trying to persuade, or force, an intransigent athlete to conform would have been too great to bother. "No" had significant consequences for an individual athlete; for the system it merely meant focusing on the next athlete in line.

In view of the above, several things are clear. First, the claims that athletes of majority age in the GDR were forced to take steroids or they were unaware they took them do not stand up to close scrutiny. Second, and more important, even if those claims were true, given the manner and the resources the IOC used to monitor substance use prior to 1989, the paternalistic protection potentially created by the ban on specific performance-enhancing substances was totally ineffective in achieving that objective. The same would likely be true under WADA's monitoring today if the GDR still existed. Even with a ban on performance-enhancing substances in place, it would be difficult to provide paternalistic protection for athletes developing within high-performance sport systems inside totalitarian regimes.

Fortunately, coercion by totalitarian regimes is not the primary cause for athletes using banned substances and few would maintain that it is the type of compulsion that most athletes face. The strongest case for the claim that athletes are "forced" to take performance-enhancing substances is the allegation that they have no choice because other athletes are taking them. This argument fails on the claim that athletes have "no choice" or that they have "little choice," because athletes actually have abundant choice.

Even if one grants that a particular performance-enhancing substance seems to be required for athletes to rank among the best in the world, there are still a number of choices athletes may make. To not take the substance and settle for less than a top world ranking is one. This may not seem a particularly satisfactory choice given the life commitment athletes make to high-performance sport, but it still stands as one athletes can make freely of their own accord. Athletes may, and can, also make more nuanced choices.

Athletes may, and can, weigh and consider the potential impact a substance may have on their health and decide whether or not those effects can be sufficiently mitigated to permit its use. If that is not the case, athletes can still choose to assume the carefully considered risk, reducing it as much as possible through the manner in which the substance is used, and choose to try to rank among the best in the world. Or the athletes could take a more conservative position and, after a detailed review of the possibilities, feel that no risk is worth a top international ranking and yet still strive to improve their performances through other means.

When it is recognized that athletes do have a choice and can make choices, the point is often raised that it is a very difficult choice – one that athletes should not be expected to make. There are three fallacies with this argument. First, athletes not only make difficult choices but they make extremely far reaching ones all of the time. As Robert Simon argues, world-class athletes make choices about, and give consent to, any number of issues related to their health and well-being, including training regimens, high risk tactical decisions, and the fundamental choice to drive their bodies to the limits of their physical capacity in the pursuit of victory.[82]

Second, many of the choices athletes make outside of an athletic contest are not made alone. World-class, high-performance athletes who are of the age of majority do not require the protection of paternalistic legislation when it comes to training regimes, training techniques, or lifestyle. When they need counsel, they may find it.

Finally, numerous high-performance athletes are making decisions and choices over the use of substances under the current IOC regulations. The difference is that they are making two choices: the choice to use a proscribed substance and the choice to evade the IOC's regulations.

Ironically, except in the very specific case of minors – where the legislative protections that apply to all children should be applied to every aspect of high-performance sport but almost never are – the paternalistic justification for banning certain performance-enhancing substances is premised on the assumption that world-class athletes are not competent enough to determine their own best interests. The very virtues for which athletes are admired are denied them in this position. Athletes demonstrate throughout their careers the ability to take decisive action, to rapidly and accurately evaluate options, to set and, with determination, achieve their own goals. The paternalistic justification for banning selected performance-enhancing substances denies that athletes possess and exercise the key virtues of self-reliance, personal achievement, and autonomy that have long been admired in dedicated young athletes.[83] Well-established evidence from the real world of high-performance sport does not indicate that athletes lack those characteristics; it is quite the contrary.

The principal justification for the paternalistic regulation of behavior is the dangerous or risky nature of particular actions or activities. A justification on these grounds for the banning of selected performance-enhancing substances fails on four grounds. First, not all banned substances pose a health risk. The in-competition presence of wine, beer or spirits beyond certain levels is banned in archery, football, gymnastics, karate, modern pentathlon, skiing, triathlon, wrestling and other sports. Aside from the dangers of alcoholism or inebriation, those substances pose few immediate health dangers to athletes. Up until January 1, 2004, a number of over-the-counter medicines such as Benadryl-D, Codral, Coldrex, Nurofen Cold and Sudafed were banned. Even though the IOC will continue to monitor the levels of pseudoephedrine in athletes with the prospect of placing them back on the list, there is no claim that it or any of the medications in which it is contained are dangerous to athletes' health. Caffeine was on the banned list until March 2004 but not as a health risk.[84] Medicinal substances such as salbutamol, which is the beta-agonist in asthma medicines, and glucocorticosteroids, which are also used to treat asthma, are banned in specific concentrations or circumstances but the IOC has not identified any of them as major health risks to athletes.[85]

Second, with the exception of very specific categories of athletes – prepubescent boys and girls, and females who do not wish to experience the androgenizing effects that are associated with some anabolic-androgenic steroids – the dangers of performance-enhancing substances have been consistently overstated and misrepresented.[86] James Wright states:

> in adult males at least, androgen abuse is probably not as dangerous as most other forms of drug abuse. Discontinuation of AS [anabolic–androgenic steroid] intake by males generally results in a cessation or reversal of virtually all virilizing and feminizing effects. Life threatening hepatic effects are extremely unusual, and the long-term consequences of blood lipid alterations are unclear.[87]

Like all pharmaceuticals, it is the way in which performance-enhancing substances are used that may put athletes' health at risk.

Third, not only has the ban on performance-enhancing substances been unsuccessful in preventing their use, it may place athletes' health at risk far more than the substances themselves.[88] Despite an elaborate, sophisticated, expensive detection system, commissions of inquiry in Canada, Australia, the United States, and Germany, numerous independent studies, reports in the press, and detailed research reports in professional academic journals have documented the extensive use of performance-enhancing substances in every sport where particular substances or practices can aid performance.[89] The list has not served as a deterrent. But it has, at an increased risk to athletes' health, affected how substances are used and what substances are chosen.

In the case of anabolic–androgenic steroids, one of the potential dangers of their long-term use is kidney damage. Steroids are available in either an oil-based form that is injected or a water-based form that is taken orally. The injected form will circulate in an athlete's system for an extended period of time. Oil-based, injected steroids are not involved in the digestive system and do not pass immediately through an athlete's liver. Because they are not immediately filtered by the liver, oil-based steroids are much easier on the athlete's system and safer in terms of liver or kidney damage. The problem, of course, is that injected, oil-based steroids can be detected long after they have been taken. In terms of performance enhancement, oil-based steroids are very effective. With respect to athletes' health, they are much safer than water-based steroids. But because they can be detected long after injection, they are undesirable from a detection perspective.

Oral steroids enter the digestive system immediately and must pass, in a concentrated form, through the liver. As a result, water-based steroids are easily concentrated in the biliary and hepatic systems, creating greater potential for physiological damage. From a performance-enhancing perspective, many athletes find oral-based steroids to be more effective than oil-based. Because oral steroids clear the system quickly, they are much more desirable from the perspective of detection. However, from the health perspective, long-term oral steroid use has greater potential for liver and kidney damage.[90]

The properties of the two different media in which steroids are administered create an unfortunate dilemma for athletes who choose to use anabolic–androgenic steroids under the current IOC regulations. As Robert Voy, the former Chief Medical Officer for the US Olympic team has noted, if the IOC banned steroids because of potential health risks to athletes, they have exacerbated rather than eliminated the problem.

> The types of drug testing programs used by doping control authorities today have unintentionally created a greater health danger in that athletes are now using the shorter acting, more toxic forms of drugs to avoid detection. Athletes have stopped using nandrolone, which in relative terms is a safe AAS [anabolic–androgenic steroids], and are now using the more dangerous orally active forms of AAS, the C-17 alkyl derivatives. In addition, many have gone to using the third, and most dangerous, type of anabolic–androgenic steroids: the esters of testosterone.[91]

There is an important caveat about oral steroids and health that concerns women. Because the effect of oral steroids is more immediate, women will notice virilizing effects very quickly. If those effects are more than a particular athlete wishes to accept, she can immediately reduce the level of her intake or stop it completely and the drug, which is rapidly cleared from the system, will stop affecting her physiology. Oil-based steroids do not act upon the body as promptly and once they are in the athlete's system, they continue to have an impact. For women this can be a problem. First, there is not an immediate effect from oil-based steroids so that athletes must experiment with dosages to reach the levels that will allow the physiological changes they are seeking while not creating those they want to avoid. Second, if a woman experiences virilizing effects from oil-based steroids that go beyond what she is willing to accept, she cannot stop the drug immediately; it will continue to affect her body as it circulates through her system many times. Women must consider the trade off between the harsher impact of oral steroids upon their livers and kidneys and the opportunity to tailor dosage levels more promptly with oral steroids, immediately turning off an oral steroid's effect by cessation the day unwanted physiological effects arise.

The ban on performance-enhancing drugs also drives their use underground and can create desperate actions when things appear to go wrong. The tragic death of Birgit Dressel in April 1987 exemplifies this danger. Dressel, a West German heptathlete, died from an immune system breakdown that some attributed to steroid use, but the accounts published in *Der Spiegel* and by Berendonk as well as excerpts from Dressel's medical autopsy indicate that such an explanation is wrong.[92] Over the course of several years, Dressel had consumed more than 40 different chemical agents orally, and taken at least 400 injections (including cell preparations banned by the German Health Authority). When she began to experience chronic pain in her hip and buttocks, she sought relief from a number of medical specialists. In the two days leading up to her death, Dressel saw 24 different physicians, although none of them was ever given a complete medical history. Though no single cause of death could be determined, years of physiological reaction to injections of animal cell preparations (essentially foreign protein) seem to have had a devastating impact upon her immune system. The pursuit of performance enhancement was partially the cause of her death; the real cause, however, was the pursuit of performance enhancement through covert substance use – much of which was designed to evade IOC detection – in the absence of medical involvement and supervision. Wright's analysis, supported by Ryan, Strauss *et al.*, and Kopera, supports the argument that the responsible medical supervision of athletes taking performance-enhancing substances would significantly reduce any health risks associated with their use.[93]

The final way athletes' health is put at risk by the banned list is the growth of a black market for substances. In the same way that the prohibition of recreational drugs in the past – alcohol, cannabis, or heroin – spawned lucrative black markets, the ban on performance-enhancing substances and the criminalization of certain drugs like steroids and synthetic human growth hormone has given rise to a lucrative black market run by unscrupulous dealers.

There are two additional points on athletes' health that should be made. First, if athletes' health was a top priority for the IOC, it would ensure that the list made perfectly clear which substances were dangerous and the conditions under which that would be true. The current WADA list includes hundreds of substances, categorized as stimulants, narcotics, anabolic agents, peptide hormones, Beta-2 agonists and masking agents. Several "methods" for enhancing performance are also listed. The complex list makes no distinctions between substances and methods that are "natural" and those that are "unnatural." Potentially dangerous substances are listed alongside relatively mundane, safe ones. As a result, the banned list contains some relatively powerful biochemical agents, which, if misused, can have irreversible, undesired side effects along with substances like alcohol and blood doping where the demarcation between dangerous and safe or natural and artificial is not perfectly clear. The conflation of relatively innocuous substances with more physiologically active ones does not reduce the culture of risk within which athletes currently train; it makes it that much greater.[94]

The final point related to the ban of performance-enhancing substances on the grounds of health issues is the "slippery slope" argument frequently found in ethical argumentation. In this instance, however, it asks what lies at the bottom of the slope once one accepts a ban on substances to protect athletes' health that is of concern. Elite rowing coach Charles Erlich does not believe that performance-enhancing substances belong in high-performance sport. He opposes their use and counsels against them. But when his pairs crew was tested for banned substances at a "fun little Fall regatta" in Sursee, Switzerland in October 2000, he asked himself "where do we draw the line" in sport?

> If we ban elicit drugs because of health detriments, we then make the next step to banning drugs which merely enhance performance but do no known long-term damage to most people, and from there we can hit blood doping and other similar fool-the-body techniques. What next, though? Do we stop altitude training? Do we limit the number of hours anyone can train in a week? Do we limit the equipment people can use (should we say only hand-made equipment made from natural substances – wooden boats and oars, anyone?). I think it is a slippery slope.[95]

The contradictions, paradoxes and myths of "healthy" sport must be fully confronted before a truly rational analysis of performance-enhancing substances and practices – banned or otherwise – is made. The true nature of high performance sport as it has evolved throughout the twentieth century and into the twenty-first must be acknowledged. The specific events that have developed within the Olympic Movement's last hundred years have led to the unqualified zeal for victory and record breaking performances, conducted by full-time, professional athletes for whom training and competition form an all-encompassing, year-round vocation. Most important, victory and the conquest of the linear record have become the Movement's fundamental principles. The "ethics" of banned substance use must be placed fully within the context of that history and reconsidered in terms of the Movement's changed practices and principles.

Conclusion
The brave new world of high-performance sport

Sir Roger Bannister is a remarkable figure in the world of international sport. His claim that "sportsmen" compete for the deep satisfaction and personal dignity which they enjoy "when body and mind are fully co-ordinated and they have achieved mastery over themselves" directly mirrors Coubertin's ideal athlete who "enjoys his effort" and "likes the constraint that he imposes on his muscles and nerves, through which he comes close to victory even if he does not manage to achieve it."[1]

Nurtured on the ideals of the late nineteenth century English public schools, Bannister is best known as the man who broke sport's ultimate barrier – the four-minute mile. Ironically, rather than reflecting the apogee of amateurism, the Oxford-educated middle-distance runner's "miracle mile" may be most significant as a dramatic, 3:59.4 transition phase to the new paradigm of high-performance sport in the modern era. Bannister himself was somewhat aware of the transition he had lived through and to which he had, unwittingly perhaps, contributed. He reflected that the 1950s were "a strange period in the history of sport," and "a far cry from what was envisaged by Baron Coubertin."[2]

Three things are striking about Bannister's comments. First, they understate the pivotal changes that occurred in those years, transforming high-performance sport in ways that made the professionalism, national aggrandizement, and payments to athletes Bannister feared pale into insignificance. By the 1950s and early 1960s athletic records were broken at accelerated rates[3] as national sport systems shifted training dramatically and fundamentally beyond the "deep satisfaction" of individual athletic achievement and "sense of personal dignity" that Bannister's ideal, and increasingly mythological, athlete experienced.

Second, recent historical analysis has begun to demythologize the world of "pure sport" in the 1950s. Bannister integrated the latest medical, scientific and technological advancements into his training regimes in an attempt to gain an advantage over his two main rivals in the quest to be the first man to break the four-minute barrier – University of Kansas track star Wes Santee and the great Australian miler John Landy.[4] Bannister used pacemakers to help break the four-minute barrier – a performance-enhancing practice that many considered "strictly illegal."[5] He was also uniquely situated with a medical education that had followed bachelor's and master's degrees in physiology, giving him a working knowledge of the experimental literature in physiology and the ability to run oxygen-enriched treadmill experiments on himself and others to enhance his performances. Bannister also used new "fartlek" and "interval training" techniques that incorporated specified and very carefully planned work bouts alongside periods of rest. Whenever possible, Bannister used the most advanced technology available, including specially created, hand-made, lightweight (four ounce) shoes with sharpened spikes and graphite soles to quicken his stride on the cinder surface of Oxford University's Iffley Road track during the record breaking run.[6] In short, as Bale points out, "simple dualisms like 'amateur' and 'professional' are not all that helpful in looking at Roger Bannister who turns out, it seems, to have been a sort of professional amateur."[7]

Finally, and most importantly, his early training methods – appropriate to the true amateur who ran in his or her spare time amidst numerous other personal activities and obligations – could not produce the stamina and strength required to win an Olympic gold medal even in 1952. Instead of heats and a final with a day in between, the Olympic field had grown so large that in 1952 there were heats, a semi-final and a final on consecutive days. "It was crazy," Bannister would later reflect, "no man who trained as I did could possibly run three good races in three consecutive days." The mile at the Olympic Games had already become a race of power and endurance, not one of freshness and speed – the only race a true amateur's training could prepare him or her to win.[8]

Also, the popular obsession with the first man to break the four minute barrier had a direct and palpable impact on the world's best milers in the 1950s. Landy had run within two seconds of the magical barrier but, he lamented, "when you are on the track those 15 yards seem solid and impenetrable – like a cement wall." "The promised land" in sport, Calvin Shulman points out, was the magical barrier to which the runners aspired, but it was also the future of high-performance sport. It "would take a miler of steel and imagination to break down decades of disbelief. … [An athlete] who could summon the perfect blend of stamina and speed, with inner strength and supreme awareness of his own body, to batter down the cement wall."[9] "The promised land," in short, was the modern era of world-class, high-performance sport that began to unfold over the next 20 years and has been in full gear over the ensuing 30.

A central theme in this study is that "sport," as an abstraction, not only serves particular myth-making interests, but is also misleading in any serious discussion of world-class, high-performance sport today. The world of high-performance sport is a historically situated set of social practices which must be dealt with socio-historically and empirically. High-performance sport today inescapably involves the instrumentally rational, systematic, scientifically and technologically assisted enhancement of athletic performance in pursuit of victory and the ongoing assault on the linear record. As a result, the widespread use of performance-enhancing practices and substances has become a central fixture in the sport systems developed by nation states during the post-World War II period. Any efforts to control performance-enhancing substances and practices and to regulate athletes' lives that fail to address that reality are misguided. Policies based upon an abstract ideal of "the spirit of sport" will fail because they are completely inconsistent with the social, historical and political trajectory world-class sport has taken in the past 60 years.

The high-performance sport systems in the latter half of the twentieth century and now into the twenty-first are unlike any in human history. While they vary according to the particular nature of any one nation state's political structure, dominant cultural values, and civic or private bureaucratic structures, all systems share certain essential characteristics. World-class sport systems today include the systematic use of pure and applied scientific research to enhance physical performance; the early identification, streaming and specialization of athletic talent; professional coaching, the use of professional nutritionists, biomechanicians, exercise physiologists, and sport psychologists; carefully organized training facilities with state of the art equipment and instructional technologies; and financial reward systems and incentives for athletes and sport associations. While the general public may focus exclusively on performance results and the rewards of victory, high-performance sport in the contemporary era is a complex whole with performance enhancement as one of its most central features.

The work world of contemporary high-performance sport

Chapter Three began with Orwell's warning about surrendering to words and using them from the start when dealing with an abstraction like "sport." If one resists "the existing dialect" and "hunts about" to find "the exact words that seem to fit," what words would describe world-class, high-performance sport in the contemporary period? They would be numerous and would have to capture more than the sprint through the finish line or the goal that brings victory. But "victory," in the modern era of high-performance sport, might be the place to start.

The image of a gold medal presentation, which fuels young athletes' dreams, fulfills coaches' greatest aspirations, meets the cherished goals of sports leaders and politicians around the world, and epitomizes the central goal of modern sport, is a moment of exquisite glamor. The glitter of gold dominates, national pride soars as the victor's national anthem reaches its inspirational crescendos and the national flag rises above the pageant and ceremony below. The image seems to contemptuously defy Andy Warhol's claim that we all have just fifteen minutes of fame: Olympic gold is different. It seems like so much more – profoundly more, especially in a world looking for heroes. And it is more. The problem is that few know how much more lies behind the glamor. Very few know what a gold medal performance – enhanced performance – entails.

In *Ways of Seeing*, John Berger's classic account of art, advertising and the glamor of the fashion industry, he looks behind the superficial splendor of the Paris runways and the allure advertisers attach to products as exotic, yet also as banal, as perfume, lipstick, eye shadow, and silk blouses blowing in the breeze.[10] The medal ceremony is a similar façade that mythologizes the real world of high-performance sport.

To demystify the fashion industry, Berger focuses on the numbing work world of thousands of machine attendants who toil in monotonous assembly lines screwing tops on perfume bottles, using the same blouse pattern to stitch yet another pocket – pocket after pocket, hour after hour, day after day, month after month, and year after year to support and create fashion.[11] World-class, high-performance sport also rests on detailed labor whereby underpaid athletes train relentlessly to keep pace with others who are also single-mindedly pursuing their own assault on the limits of human athletic performance. For every athlete who wins a medal and enjoys the headlines, thousands live and train in obscurity. For every gold medal winner who becomes a millionaire, hundreds of other gold medal winners struggle to make a comfortable living despite being the very best in the world. And no matter whether an athlete is successful or continually striving for the Olympic standard, the working life of a world-class, high-performance competitor is comprised of an overwhelmingly demanding, repetitive, annual routine of practice after practice after practice interspersed with brief periods of intense, all-consuming, winner takes all competition.[12]

Oarsman David Calder, disqualified in a pairs semi-final in the 2004 Summer Games because the Canadian shell drifted into South Africa's lane at the end of the race, succinctly captured the reality of his life as a high-performance athlete. "To get to this level, I have made countless sacrifices," he began.

> I have spent years, rowing thousands of kilometres for this week of competition. I have put my life on hold. I have missed half my daughter's life by being on the road all summer and now to be disqualified is very difficult to swallow.[13]

Although sport sociologists have examined the socialization processes that lead boys and girls into sport, the majority of this work is superficial in nature. If there is a major omission in people's understanding of world-class, high-performance sport, it is a detailed expression of the experiences entailed in *becoming* a competitive, world-ranked athlete.[14] Within the real work world of high-performance sport, boys and girls and men and women become world-class, high-performance athletes over the course of a lengthy, physically and emotionally demanding period of time. Boys and girls become very specific types of performers who view and relate to the exceedingly high demands of their craft in ways that are almost unparalleled in any other vocation or occupation.[15] This has several consequences, the most significant of which is the practices that athletes internalize as normal – as simply part and parcel of becoming and being a world-class competitor.

In the high-performance sport world, an athlete's most essential tool is his or her body. Like all skilled crafts workers, athletes hone, tailor and specialize the instruments of their craft to produce optimal human performance. Athletes in weight-regulated sports – judo, wrestling, boxing, and weightlifting, for example – spend their entire international, competitive career controlling their weight so that it meets tolerance levels of fractions of a gram at the exact moment of a weigh-in while it may move upwards by several kilograms only hours later. Young female gymnasts and swimmers undertake progressively more demanding training obligations while eating from increasingly restrictive diets so they can maintain the optimal balance between body mass and strength.[16] Runners consume thousands of calories which they burn with equal speed as they log hundreds of kilometres per week training on the roads, athletic tracks, and countryside around the world. World-class athletes follow long-term, specialized weight training programmes driving themselves to produce the physique and optimal strengths specifically demanded by their sport. In short, athletes make and remake their bodies to meet the precise demands of their sport and just as a hockey player cuts and heats and shapes the blade of his or her hockey stick until it is just right, all high-performance athletes shape, contour, and compel their bodies to be the precision instruments that world-class performance demands.[17]

This is a very real and undeniable life experience that affects athletes' outlook on what is, in fact, the reality of sport. Furthermore, it is a reality in which the athletes take part from entry into the sport system and the reality with which they become more intimately involved throughout a 20- to 30-year career within the sport system. During this the stakes get higher, the demands more exacting, and the athletes' investment in the process develops apace. As a result, the central and paramount reality of sport for high-performance athletes – for the athletes who constitute the sport system through their human agency – is the perfection of a particular working instrument – their bodies – to perform at the outer limits of human potential and to attempt to excel beyond those limits.

World-class, high-performance sport is not for the uncommitted. Coubertin sought to establish a chivalric, international brotherhood-in-arms in his revival of the Olympic Games. Just over a century later, it is clear that the Olympic Games are contests among athletes who have fully dedicated a major portion of their entire being to the pursuit of Olympic gold. Diem's 1908 proclamation, "Fight [Kampf] – then you must win!" seems like a veritable truth of sport. But it is not. In pre-war Prussia the mantra had a specific meaning, as it would have in the world of sport that Brundage tried to enforce in the 1960s and 1970s. Under the specific conditions of today, where athletes from well-developed, resource intensive, high-performance sport systems that utilize carefully directed experimental research, the latest in high-performance technology, and years of investment, compete against one another, the notion of struggle (Kampf) is totally different. Hours and hours and hours of training, pushing the human body to perform at its physical limits is a modern phenomenon, unparalleled in human history. The drive to win has a different context from ever before. The conditions of today grew out of the cold war, the scientifically rational world view of post-war Europe and America, the consumer societies of the late twentieth century, and the geo-political goals of specific nation states. Any proposals for reform must begin with that reality.

The brave new world of high-performance sport: policy implications

This study has documented how the world of competitive, world-class, high-performance sport has dramatically changed – in kind as much as by degree – since

Coubertin's day. The twentieth century introduced a paradigm shift in sport in which the scientifically assisted, instrumentally rational pursuit of the linear record came to dominate international sport. Selected nation states like the USSR, the USA, the GDR and the FRG invested enormous resources to reap the political and ideological rewards that Olympic gold could bring to those countries. At the same time, strong commercial and media interests also invested heavily in, and reaped the benefits of, the shift to enhanced performance as the central ethos of the Olympic Games in particular and world-class sport more generally.

Within that shift, performance enhancement was pursued through numerous mechanisms – more demanding training regimes, the recruitment of professional specialists in biomechanics, exercise physiology, psychology, and numerous coaching and instructional experts. Among the variety of performance-enhancing substances and practices, a select few were proscribed. They were forbidden on the basis of specific ethical principles that were germane to the philosophical notion of "the spirit of sport" which the IOC chose to advocate even though it had no connection to the real world of sport that it governs. This study has charted the historical development of high-performance sport over the last century and, more importantly, challenged, on the basis of that historical development, the validity of the premises IOC leaders have used in proscribing certain performance-enhancing practices (while leaving others untouched).

In view of the failure of existing policies banning the use of selected performance-enhancing substances and practices, new criteria must be established to facilitate an open, socio-historically informed discussion of performance enhancement in sport. Owing to the unique historical trajectory high-performance sport has followed during the last century and the acceptance of performance enhancement as its central pillar, three general criteria should shape that discussion.

First, any and all policies concerned with performance enhancement must begin with the real world of high-performance sport itself. Reference to "the spirit of sport" is pointless. Only by acknowledging the full reality of modern high-performance sport can a truly productive discussion about performance enhancement take place. The main objective of this study has been to initiate an open and democratic debate about performance enhancement on the basis of the real social world in which athletes, administrators, policy makers, commercial interests and political leaders live. The social history of Olympic sport since 1896, integrated into the larger socio-historical forces of that period – especially between 1933 and 1974 – is the background upon which a discussion of performance enhancement must take place. It cannot productively begin with "the spirit of sport."

Second, given the reality of world-class, high-performance sport, its performance imperative, and the centrality of performance enhancement in the ethos and practice of Olympic sport, a frank discussion about the safeguards that are genuinely needed to protect athletes' health must be initiated. The focus on selected performance-enhancing substances has missed the mark in two fundamentally important respects and continues to thwart a well-reasoned discussion of the real issues that affect athletes' health and well-being.

The demonization of certain substances has, first of all, pushed their use underground where athletes may or may not be receiving sound medical advice and the quality of the substances they are using may be questionable. At the same time, sound, peer-reviewed, public, systematic research cannot be undertaken under the current conditions even though there are important questions that could be asked and should be answered about various performance-enhancing substances and practices. Part of the resistance to the use of, and research into, performance-enhancing substances is the fear that the information will be misused for nefarious ends. But the fear of misused technology always exists. It exists in research into, and the use of, stem cells, reproductive technologies, and genetic engineering, to choose only three examples. The single greatest danger to progress in any of those issues is the uninformed, arbitrary banning of practices, procedures and research in each of those areas. Research on, and the use of, performance-enhancing substances in sport are not even in the same ballpark as those three examples although, to individual athletes, the impediments to sound research could have long-term consequences. The steroid hobgoblin distracts attention from the real unknowns that can and should be investigated.

The arbitrary focus on selected banned performance-enhancing substances has a second consequence. It deflects attention from the wider question of high-performance sport as a set of social practices. As nation states, commercial interests, sport administrators, coaches, sport science experts, and individual athletes have engaged in the unrelenting pursuit of the linear record and pushed human athletic performance to its outer limits, the activities themselves have become questionable. How safe, how wholesome, how worthwhile are these pursuits?

There is a striking parallel between high-performance sport today and great art. There is a fine line, never easily placed and which can only be drawn for an instant on the basis of a particular event, between genius and insanity. While the public celebrates the accomplishments of high-performance sport, and sees most of its practices as healthy, wholesome and admirable, they are, in fact, directly associated with images and practices that the same public often deems pathological. For athletes, whose lives are spent right in the middle of the demands of high-performance sport, the distinction between health and pathology is even more difficult to make because tolerance for what is acceptable is increased imperceptibly each day and over the span of a career until it has changed dramatically.

For many high-performance athletes, there is nothing wrong with cutting an additional 100 calories from a 2500 calories a day diet when training four to six hours by itself is not producing the desired optimal lean body mass. For other athletes bulimic practices allow them to eat suppers on Friday and Sunday while still losing the extra 500 grams required to make a weight class. In pursuit of a world ranking, it becomes an obvious choice to log an additional 1200 km per month to build stamina, rather than meet with friends. The difference between earning minimum wage in a part-time job and going on welfare is clear: receiving welfare allows more freedom to train, thereby increasing the chance to meet the expectations of parents, school, community, provincial sport organization, NSO, political leaders, national media, and the national public. Both options leave athletes living well below the poverty line in any case. From within the system of high-performance sport, the longer one pursues a top three finish in the world and the closer one is to reaching the podium, the less and less easy it is to distinguish between health and pathology.[18] These issues are far more central to the health and welfare of athletes in world-class sport than the use of cold medicines, diuretics, marijuana, and anabolic substances. It is a focus on these questions that is a direct policy outcome of this study.

Finally, in Chapter One, we noted that leaders in positions of legitimate authority have the right to enact policies and impose sanctions on those who violate them. Leaders may even feel morally and ethically justified in their actions even though their policies widely diverge from an organization's actual principles and practices. But it may also be the case that the policy making process itself is flawed and lacks legitimacy not just because it is out of touch with the real world the policies govern but because the most important agents are excluded from the policy making process.

As the Olympic Games changed in the post-World War II period, and athletes were required to dedicate more and more of their lives to sport in pursuit of Olympic glory, the nature of their stake in the Games changed although their role in the decision and policy making process remained relatively constant. Despite the central role they play in the Olympic Movement, world-class athletes remain largely disenfranchised participants in a labor process that generates millions of dollars for the IOC, commercial interests and various media conglomerates. Unlike the immediate producers in other contexts, high-performance athletes have no mechanism through which they can meaningfully negotiate their working conditions. "Sport policy [in high-performance sport]," Barrie Houlihan has argued, "is generally made for, or on behalf of, athletes, rarely in consultation with athletes, and almost never in partnership with athletes." In the few governing bodies where athletes do have a voice, Houlihan's research shows that athletes have very limited membership or work through athlete commissions or committees that are "safely quarantined from any significant decision-making opportunities."[19] In short, Houlihan has argued that most athlete representation, if it exists at all, "is invariably paternalistic, tokenistic and fulfils purposes associated more with legitimation of NGB [National (Sport) Governing Bodies] decisions than with empowerment and involvement in decision-making processes."[20]

The very nature of high-performance sport in the twenty-first century, the sport systems that help constitute it, and the centrality of enhanced performance in the pursuit of the linear record have created a work world in which athletes and their advocates have genuine concerns. Thus the third major policy implication of this study is that given the significant transformation of the world of high-performance sport over the last century and the increased demands placed upon athletes in the present era, they must be centrally involved in any policies related to their training and working conditions.

World-class, high-performance sport today is, indeed, a brave new world in comparison to Coubertin's time and dream. It has emerged almost imperceptibly through changes that were often unrecognized or not fully acknowledged. However, the reference point for policies banning particular substances was the alleged "spirit of sport." These policies have failed because they have not recognized the socio-historical factors that shaped the development of high-performance sport today. This study seeks to make that socio-historical reality central to all discussions about the future of world-class sport. Without a sound grasp of the history of the Games, a full and genuine recognition of the forces that shape them, and a critical assessment of the real interests and needs of athletes, Olympic reform will simply repeat the follies of the past.

Notes

Introduction

1 The discovery occurred on January 8, 1998; see "Chinese Swimming Team Speaks Out on Drugs Controversy," (January 9, 1998), http://news.bbc.co.uk/1/hi/world/monitoring/46115.stm; Frank LItsky, "New Accusations Aimed at Chinese Swimmers," *New York Times* (January 9, 1998), C1–C2; "Swimmer in Hot Water," *Toronto Star* (January 9, 1998), B6; Derek Parr, "Suspicious Vials Confiscated from Chinese Swimmers' Bag," the *Globe and Mail* (January 9, 1998), S5; "Chinese Swimmers Bags Held Banned Hormone," *New York Times* (January 10, 1998), C2; Another Four Chinese Swimmers Banned after Failing Drug Test," (January 15, 1998) http://www.dispatch.co.za/1998/01/15/PAGE20.HTM; James Christie, "Chinese Swimmers' Scores Dive Down Under," the *Globe and Mail* (January 14, 1998), S2; "China's Fall from Grace," (July 18, 2000), http://news.bbc.co.uk/sport2/hi/other_sports/839040.stm.

2 See Craig Lord, "China Defiant Over Drugs," (January 10, 1998), http://www.times-olympics.co.uk/archive/newsdrug4.html and the FINA press release "Doping Inquiries – China," (February 19, 1998), http://www.fina.org/press_021998_china_doping.html.

3 See "Aujourd'hui: TVM-Profis nahmen Dopingmittel und Drogen [Today: TVM-professionals take doping substances and drugs]," (November 10, 1998), http://www.radsport-news.com/news/tvm-drog.htm and "TVM Trial Scheduled for May," (March 28, 2001), http://www.cyclingnews.com/results/2001/mar01/mar28news.shtml.

4 See "Chronology of 1998 Tour de France Drug Scandal," (September 22, 1998), http://sportsillustrated.cnn.com/cycling/1998/tourdefrance/news/1998/08/02/drug_chronology/ and John Hoberman, "A Pharmacy on Wheels: The Tour de France Doping Scandal," http://www.thinkmuscle.com/articles/hoberman/tour.htm.

5 See "Two More Charged with Tour Doping," (July 31, 1998), http://news.bbc.co.uk/2/hi/special_report/1998/07/98/tour_de_france/142958.stm.

6 Ten people associated with Festina, including French cycling star Richard Virenque, were brought before the bench on October 23, 2000; see "Cyclists in Spotlight as Tour Trail Begins," (October 23, 2000), http://news.bbc.co.uk/sport2/hi/other_sports/986272.stm. Virenque was acquitted by the courts while eight others were fined and given suspended sentences for their involvement in the distribution of restricted substances; see "Court Acquits Virenque in Tour de France Doping Trial," (December 22, 2000), http://sportsillustrated.cnn.com/cycling/news/2000/12/22/france_doping_trial_ap/. Three officials associated with TVM were given fines and suspended sentences by the court in Reims; see Nicholas Marrill, "Cycling Dope Cheats Sentenced," (October 24, 2001), https://lists.calyx.net/archives/urine-test/2001-October/000017.html.

7 "A Call for Doping Changes," *New York Times* (July 27, 1998), C2; see also "La polémica propuesta de Samaranch [Samaranch's Polemical Proposal]," *El Mundo* (July 27,

1998), 4; Jeremy Whittle, "Tour Trips Through Drugs Haze," *The Times* (July 27, 1998), 32; "Samaranch Seeks to Clarify Rules Governing Drug Use," The *Washington Post*, (July 27, 1998), C2; "Kürzung der Dopingliste [Reducing the Doping List]," *Süddeutsche Zeitung* (July 27, 1998), 23; "Zu viele Mittel verboten? – Samaranch fordert Kürzung der Dopingliste [Too Many Substances Banned? – Samaranch Proposes a Reduction of the Doping List]," *Frankfurter Allgemeine Zeitung*, (July 27, 1998), 20; "M. Samaranch veut réduire la liste des produits interdits [Samaranch Wants to Reduce the Banned List]," *Le Monde* (July 28, 1998), 18; "IOC President Denounced for Comments on Drug List," *Globe and Mail* (July 28, 1998), S3; Steve Keating, "Il Pirata Captures Tarnished Tour," *Globe and Mail* (August 3, 1998), S1; and Steve Rushin, "Throwing in the Towel: Beating a Hasty Retreat in the War on Drugs," *Sports Illustrated* (August 10, 1998), 17.

 8 The first public reactions to Samaranch's statements were incredulity and outrage; see, for example, "Drugs Stance Stirs Outrage," (July 27, 1998), http://news.bbc.co.uk/1/hi/sport/140315.stm.

 9 On the Lausanne conference see http://www.wada-ama.org/asiakas/003/wada_english.nsf/11b5c75053a82e11c225694c005450aa/97742b7ffe72c4e8c2256bb90037d408?OpenDocument. For the May 7–9, 1999 Duke conference, see http://www.law.duke.edu/sportscenter/conference.html. In August 2002, the World Anti-Doping Agency announced that there would be a second World Conference on Doping in Sport on March 3–5, 2003; see http://www.wada-ama.org/asiakas/003/wada_english.nsf/.

10 See John MacAloon, "Doping and Moral Authority: Sports Organizations Today," in Wayne Wilson and Edward Derse, eds, *Doping in Elite Sport: The Politics of Drugs in the Olympic Movement* (Champaign, Il.: Human Kinetics Press, 2001), 225–40; John Hoberman, "How Drug Testing Fails: The Politics of Doping Control," in *Doping in Elite Sport* and John Hoberman, "Learning from the Past: The Need for Independent Doping Control," presented at the Duke Conference on Doping, Durham, North Carolina (May 7, 1999), http://www.law.duke.edu/sportscenter/hoberman.pdf.

11 The Canadian *Commission of Inquiry Into the Use of Drugs and Banned Practices Intended to Increase Athletic Performance* still stands as one of the most thorough examinations of the world of high-performance sport but it too is seriously flawed in the approach Commissioner Charles Dubin took to understanding the Canadian sport system (see 3–65). The material Dubin relied upon was supplied by then Assistant Deputy Sports Minister Lyle Makosky. Makosky's presentation simply reiterated policy documents and provided Dubin with schematic charts of the Canadian system. His work paralleled Don Macintosh, Tom Bedecki, and C.E.S. Franks, *Sport and Politics in Canada: Federal Government Involvement Since 1961* (Kingston and Montreal: McGill–Queen's University Press, 1987) and David Hallett, *The History of Federal Government Involvement in the Development of Sport in Canada 1943–1979* (doctoral dissertation, University of Alberta, 1981). During the Dubin Commission hearings, there was no testimony that focused upon an athlete-centered, phenomenological analysis the Canadian high-performance sport system; see Rob Beamish and Bruce Kidd, "A Brief to Mr. Justice Charles Dubin," (January, 1990). See also Rob Beamish, "Major Omissions in the Dubin Commission of Inquiry," (a paper presented at the annual meeting of the Canadian Association of Sociology and Anthropology, Victoria B.C., May 26–30, 1990) or Rob Beamish, "Zur Professionalisierung des Hochleistungssports in Kanada [On the Professionalization of High-Performance Sport in Canada]," *Sportwissenschaft* [Sport Science] 21:1 (1991), 70–8.

12 See World Anti-Doping Agency website: http://www.wada-ama.org/en/t1.asp. For an account of the creation of WADA from the perspective of its first president Richard Pound, see Richard Pound, *Inside the Olympics: A Behind-the-scenes Look at the Politics, the Scandals, and the Glory of the Games* (Canada: John Wiley & Sons Canada Ltd, 2004), 49–86.

13 World Anti-Doping Agency, "World Anti-Doping Code", (March, 2003), http://www.wada-ama.org/docs/web/standards_harmonization/code/code_v3.pdf.

14 James Christie, "New Code Secures Control," The *Globe and Mail* (Thursday March 6, 2003).

15 See World Anti-Doping Agency, "Code Acceptance," (September 5, 2005), http://www.wada-ama.org/en/dynamic.ch2?pageCategory_id=161.

16 World Anti-Doping Agency, "The World Anti-Doping Code: The 2004 Prohibited List, International Standard" (updated March 17, 2004), http://www.wada-ama.org/docs/web/standards_harmonization/code/list_standard_2004.pdf. See also Fédération Internationale de Football, "Medical Matters," http://www.fifa.com/en/development/medical/index/0,1233,52502,00.html?articleid=52502.

17 See New Zealand Sports Drug Agency, "Summary of Key Changes to the WADA Prohibited List 2004," http://www.touchnz.co.nz/content/Policy/General/530/banned_list_summary.pdf; Paralympics New Zealand, "Explanation re: WADA Changes," http://paralympicsnz.org.nz/Default.aspx?instanceId=4138; Sports-drugs.com, "WADA Announces New (And Much Improved) Drugs List for 2004," http://www.sports-drugs.com/asp/ss_news29.asp.

18 See James Christie, "Some Stimulants May Be Allowed," The *Globe and Mail* (September 18, 2003), S5; "Caffeine, Sudafed Removed From Doping List," The *Toronto Star* (September 17, 2003).

19 The *Mercury News* "Doping Scandal" web page has considerable empirical information concerning the BALCO allegations; see http://www.mercurynews.com/mld/mercurynews/sports/special_packages/doping_scandal/. One of the key stories in the BALCO coverage was Elliott Almond, Mark Emmons and Pete Carey, "The Speed Demons of Balco: How Firm at Centre of U.S. Drug Scandal Built Tim Montgomery into the World's Fastest Man," *San Jose Mercury News*, reprinted by The *Toronto Star* (May 27, 2004).

20 Among the athletes subpoenaed before the grand jury were track athletes Marion Jones, Tim Montgomery, Chryste Gaines, Regina Jacobs, shot-putter Kevin Toth, quadruple gold medal swimmer Amy Van Dyken, professional baseball players Jason Giambi, Barry Bonds, A.J. Pierzynski, Bobby Estalella, Benito Santiago, and Armando Rios as well as National Football League players Tyrone Wheatley, Chris Hetherington, Dana Stubblefield, Chris Cooper and Johnnie Morton; see Richard Sandomir, "Stiff Penalties are Proposed to Rein in U.S. Drug Cheats," *New York Times* (October 23, 2003), D8; "U.S. Track Stars Testify in Supplements Lab Inquiry," *New York Times* (October 31, 2003), D3; "Tim Montgomery Testifies in Balco Case," *New York Times* (November 7, 2003), D4; "A Photographer Says Wheatley Hit Him Outside Courthouse," *New York Times* (November 14, 2003), D4; Jere Longman, "Drugs in Sports Creating Games of Illusion," *New York Times* (November 18, 2003), D1, D2; "Baseball Players Testify," *New York Times* (November 21, 2003), D3; Van Dyken Testifies in Balco Case," *New York Times* (November 28, 2003), D10; Jere Longman, "Inquiry on Steroid Use Gets Bonds Testimony," *New York Times* (December 5, 2003), D1, D3.

21 Sara Brunetti, "THG: The Hidden Steroid," (November 26, 2003), http://www.cbc.ca/news/background/steroids.

22 Gregory Strong, "Quebec League to Test for Drugs," The *Toronto Star* (January 22, 2004); reproduced as Gregory Strong, "Quebec Midget Hockey League to Begin Drug Testing in March," http://www.canoe.ca/Slam040121/hky_que-cp.html.

23 The main issue in hockey, as other commentators on junior hockey pointed out, was not steroids but the various stimulants the players use to overcome the long hours of bus rides, practices, and the demands of games over a lengthy season followed by alcohol consumption to bring players back down after a game. As player agent Gilles Lupien pointed out, "We can't blame the kids. You see the way they travel, how far they travel and how often they travel [in the QMJHL]. Going from Montreal to Cape Breton [by bus] is like going from Montreal to Winnipeg, or Florida." Cited in David Naylor, "Drug Use Rife in QMJHL: Report," (December 9, 2003), http://www.theglobeandmail.com/servlet/story/RTGAM.20031209.wjrhky9/BNStory/Sports.

24 See Naylor, "Drug Use Rife in QMJHL."
25 MLB press release, "MLB to Launch Dominican Republic Drug-Testing Program," (April 30, 2004), http://mlb.mlb.com/NASApp/mlb/mlb/news/mlb_press_release.jsp?ymd=20040430&content_id=732525&vkey=pr_mlb&fext=.jsp. See also, Steve Fainaru and Christine Haughney, "Pataki Urges MLB on Testing," *Washington Post* (July 16, 2003), D1 or The *Globe and Mail* (May 1, 2004), S6.
26 See "Millar dans la tourmente [Millar inside the storm]," *L'Équipe* (June 25, 2004), http://www.lequipe.fr/Cyclisme/20040625_091924Dev.html; Randy Starkman, "More Drug Bombshells Revealed," *Toronto Star* (June 25, 2004); William Fotheringham, "Millar's Tale of Life on the Edge Makes Sad Reading," The *Guardian* (July 21, 2004), http://sport.guardian.co.uk/cycling/story/0,,1265606,00.html.
27 See James Pope, ed., "Investigation Official Statement," on the David Millar website (July 2, 2004), http://www.itsmillartime.com/; Agence France Presse, "Millar Sacked, Likely to Lose World Title," *VeloNews* (July 20, 2004), http://www.velonews.com/news/fea/6619.0.html; and "Millar, Poised to Lose World Title, Opens Up," *VeloNews* (July 26, 2004), http://www.velonews.com/news/fea/6682.0.html.
28 Pierre Coubertin, *Olympism: Selected Writings*, ed. Norbert Müller (Lausanne: International Olympic Committee, 2000), 552.

Chapter 1

1 C. Wright Mills, *The Sociological Imagination* (New York: Oxford University Press, 1959), 6.
2 For detailed histories of the restriction of performance-enhancing substances in sport, see Wayne Wilson and Edward Derse, eds, *Doping in Elite Sport: The Politics of Drugs in the Olympic Movement* (Champaign, Il.: Human Kinetics Press, 2001) and Charles Yesalis, ed., *Anabolic Steroids in Sport and Exercise* (Champaign, Il.: Human Kinetics Publishers, 1993).
3 Pierre Coubertin, *Olympism: Selected Writings*, ed. Norbert Müller (Lausanne: International Olympic Committee, 2000), 571.
4 Ibid., 559.
5 Ibid., 294–5, 308, 531–2, 533–4, 543–6, 552, 564–5, 580–3, 592–3. See also John MacAloon, *This Great Symbol* (Chicago: University of Chicago Press, 1981), 43–112 and D. Brown, "Modern Sport, Modernism and the Cultural Manifesto: Coubertin's *Revue Olympique*," *International Journal of the History of Sport* 18:2 (2001), 79, 101.
6 Coubertin, *Olympism*, 532, see also 308. Interestingly, David Young has recently challenged the notion that the mind–body union later epitomized in the Latin adage *mens sana in corpore sano* was equally celebrated throughout Greek history. As ancient Greece progressed, there was growing support for privileging the mind over the body and athletes were increasingly denigrated as a result, a position that found strong support during the early Christian era. Nevertheless, Coubertin and others believed the ancients held to the notion that the body was important to character development. See David C. Young, "*Mens Sana in Corpore Sano?* Body and Mind in Ancient Greece," *The International Journal of the History of Sport* 22:1 (2005), 22–41.
7 Ibid., 534, 536.
8 Ibid., 536–7, 557, and 543. Reflecting in 1908 upon his revival of the ancient Games, Coubertin noted that he had "clearly perceived" the dangers associated with sports held "in an atmosphere of advertisement and bluff, ... in a society where effort is generally applied to the quest for material gain," and sport is "commercially exploited by the organizers of public exhibitions." He recognized that the Games could only achieve his educational goals if they were the "supreme consecration of the cult of athletics practiced in the purest spirit of true sport, proudly, joyfully, and loyally," 543–4.

9 Ibid., 552. Coubertin's interest in festival and grandeur for the Games was consistent with his tastes in music and aesthetics. "It is a small step from [Coubertin's taste for pageantry] to understanding Coubertin's taste for the music of Wagner, which brought him to the Bayreuth Festivals on many occasion," Norbert Müller writes. "However, Coubertin's artistic work is not called 'The Rings of Nibelungen,' it is entitled 'the Olympic Games'."

10 Ibid., 559.

11 Ibid., 654, 588. "The primary, fundamental characteristic of ancient Olympism, and of modern Olympism as well, is that it is a *religion,*" 580.

12 Ibid., 581; emphases in original.

13 Ibid., 593.

14 Barrington Moore, *The Social Origins of Dictatorship and Democracy* (Boston: Beacon Press, 1966), 488. Ironically, the French aristocrat Coubertin did not find the hereditary nature of the European aristocrats particularly appealing. Coubertin was in greater sympathy with classical Greece where, with the exception of the slaves, heredity played a less significant role in determining who was part of the ruling aristocracy.

15 Coubertin, *Olympism,* 545.

16 Ibid., 654.

17 Ibid., 546. The importance of honor in deciding who should participate in the Games and the role that an Olympic Oath would play were constant themes in Coubertin's various writings; see, for example, ibid., 557, 645, 647–8.

18 Allen Guttmann, *The Olympics: A History of the Modern Games* (Urbana and Chicago: University of Illinois Press, 2002), 16–17.

19 Richard Gruneau and Hart Cantelon, "Capitalism, Commercialism, and the Olympics," in Jeffrey O. Segrave and Donald Chu, eds, *The Olympic Games in Transition* (Champaign, Il.: Human Kinetics, 1988), 352.

20 Guttmann, *The Olympics,* 15–16.

21 Gruneau and Cantelon, "Capitalism, Commercialism," 353.

22 Robert K. Barney, Stephen R. Wenn, and Scott G. Martyn, *Selling the Five Rings: The International Olympic Committee and the Rise of Olympic Commercialism* (Salt Lake City: The University of Utah Press, 2002), 28–9.

23 Ibid., 31–49.

24 Alfred Senn, *Power, Politics and the Olympic Games* (Champaign, Il.: Human Kinetics Press, 1999), 9–11, 45–6.

25 See Eberhard Hildenbrandt, "Milon, Marx und Muskelpille – Anmerkungen zur Kulturgeschichte des sportlichen Trainings [Milon, Marx and Muscle Pills – Notes on the Social History of Training in Sport]," in Hartmut Gabler and Ulrich Göhner, eds, *Für einen besseren Sport…: Themen, Entwicklungen und Perspektiven aus Sport und Sportwissenschaft* [For a Better Sport…: Themes, Developments and Perspectives from Sport and Sport Science] (Schorndorf: Verlag Karl Hofmann, 1990), 270–3.

26 Cited in Senn, *Power, Politics and the Olympic Games,* 61.

27 It is interesting to note that Coubertin's three successors as IOC President – Henri Baillet-Latour (1925–42), Sigfrid Edström (1942–52) and Avery Brundage (1952–72) – all had backgrounds in track and field.

28 Coubertin, *Olympism,* 543.

29 See Lord Michael Killanin, "Eligibility and Amateurism," in Lord Michael Killanin and John Rodda, eds, *The Olympic Games: 80 Years of People, Events and Records* (Don Mills: Collier–Macmillan, 1976), 150.

30 Cited in ibid.

31 Ibid.

32 Cited in Allen Guttmann, *The Games Must Go On: Avery Brundage and the Olympic Movement* (New York: Columbia University Press, 1984), 116; see also Killanin, "Eligibility and Amateurism," 150. For detailed accounts of the amateur ethos, see Avery Brundage, "On Amateurism," a paper presented at the 68th session of the

International Olympic Committee (Warsaw, 1969) and Guttmann, *The Games Must Go On*, 110–13.

33 James Riordan, *Sport in Soviet Society* (Cambridge: Cambridge University Press, 1977), 161–2.

34 Ibid., 162–4; Senn, *Power, Politics and the Olympic Games*, 85.

35 From the Brundage Archive, University of Illinois; reproduced in annotated form in Senn, *Power, Politics and the Olympic Games*, 87.

36 Ibid., 84–90; Riordan, *Sport in Soviet Society*, 205–87, 336–47.

37 Guttmann, *The Games Must Go On*, 136–9; Riordan, *Sport in Soviet Society*, 162–82, 205–87, 336–47.

38 Cited in Guttmann, *The Games Must Go On*, 115–16.

39 Terry Todd, "Anabolic Steroids: The Gremlins of Sport," *Journal of Sport History* 14:1 (1987), 93.

40 John Ziegler, "Forward," in Bob Goldman, *Death in the Locker Room: Steroids and Sports* (South Bend, Indiana: Icarus Press, 1984), 1–3; see also Goldman, *Death in the Locker Room*, 73 and Todd, "Anabolic Steroids," 93–4.

41 John Ziegler, "Forward," in Goldman, Death in the Locker Room, 1; see also Todd, "Anabolic Steroids," 93–4; John Fair, "Bob Hoffman, the York Barbell Company, and the Golden Age of American Weightlifting, 1945–1960," *Journal of Sport History* 14:2 (1987), 164–88; John Fair, "Isometrics or Steroids? Exploring New Frontiers of Strength in the Early 1960s," *Journal of Sport History* 20:1 (1993), 1–24; Ivan Waddington, "The Development of Sports Medicine," *Sociology of Sport Journal* 13:2 (1996), 176–96.

42 Bob Goldman, *Death in the Locker Room*, 94; A.J. Ryan, "Athletics," in Charles Kochakian, ed., *Handbook of Experimental Pharmacology* (Vol. 43, *Anabolic–Androgenic Steroids*) (New York: Springer–Verlag, 1976), 516–17.

43 Goldman, *Death in the Locker Room*, 94.

44 Charles E. Yesalis and Michael S. Bahrke, "History of Doping in Sport," *International Sports Studies* 24:1 (2002), 53.

45 Bruce Woolley, "History and Evolution of Drugs in Sport," in Ray Tricker and David L. Cook, eds, *Athletes at Risk: Drugs and Sport* (Dubuque, IA.: WMC Brown Publishers, 1990), 18. For a comprehensive account of the issues surrounding Jensen's death, see Verner Mølher, "Knud Enemark Jensen's Death During the 1960 Rome Olympics: A Search for Truth?" *Sport in History* 25:3 (2005), 460–70.

46 Rule 26, the "Amateurism Code," was, in 1962, as follows:
An amateur is one who participates and always has participated in sport without material gain. To qualify as an amateur, it is necessary to comply with the following conditions:

1 Have a normal occupation destined to ensure his present and future livelihood.
2 Never have received any payment for taking part in any sports competitions.
3 Comply with the rules of the International Federation concerned.
4 Comply with the official interpretations of this regulation.

See Killanin, "Eligibility and Amateurism," 150.

47 Jan Todd and Terry Todd, "Significant Events in the History of Drug Testing and the Olympic Movement: 1960–1999," in Wilson and Derse, *Doping in Elite Sport*, 67.

48 Ibid., 68.

49 Cited in ibid.

50 The history and structure of the East German sport system is dealt with extensively in Chapters Four and Five.

51 Honecker would later capitalize on his position as head of the Free German Youth and the contacts he then established to become Ulbricht's successor as the General Secretary of the Central Committee of the SED in 1971.

52 Giselher Spitzer, Hans Joachim Teichler, and Klaus Reinartz, eds, "Das Staatliche Komitee für Körperkultur und Sport übernimmt die wesentliche Funktionen des Sportausschusses (1952) [The State Committee for Physical Culture and Sport Takes

Over the Essential Functions of the Sport Committee (1952)]," *Schlüsseldokumente zum DDR-Sport. Ein sporthistorischer Überblick in Originalquellen. Schriftenreihe: Sportentwicklungen in Deutschland* [Key Documents in GDR Sport. A Historical Overview of Sport through Original Sources: Sport Development in Germany], Vol. 4 (Aachen: Meyer & Meyer Verlag, 1998), 38–43.

53 Ewald maintained his position as head of East German sport until 1988. In 1985 IOC President Juan Antonio Samaranch honored Ewald with the Olympic Order, the highest award of distinction in the Movement. In 2000 the German courts found Ewald guilty for having inflicted bodily harm on 142 female athletes who used performance-enhancing substances under his direction. Ewald died in 2002; see James Christie, "Drug Lord of Cold War Olympics," The *Globe and Mail* (November 1, 2002), R17 and Peter Kühnst, Sportführer Manfred Ewald – Eine mentalitäsgeschichtliche Annärung zum Tod des ehemaligen DDR-Sportpraesidenten [An Attempt to Understand the Death of the Former DDR Sport President in Terms of the History of Mentalities], Das Sportgespräch [Sport Talk], DeutschlandRadio, Berlin [German Radio, Berlin] (February 27, 2002), http://www.dradio.de/cgi-bin/es/neu-sport/27.html.

54 See Doug Gilbert, *The Miracle Machine* (New York: Coward, McCann & Geoghegan, 1980) and John Hoberman, *Sport and Political Ideology* (Austin: University of Texas Press, 1984), 201–7.

55 Riordan, *Sport in Soviet Society*, 341, 211–12.

56 Klaus Lehnertz, *Berufliche Entwicklung der Amateurspitzensportler in der Bundesrepublik Deutschland* [Occupational Development of Elite Amateur Athletes in the Federal Republic of Germany] (Schorndorf: Karl Hofmann, 1979), 50.

57 Lehnertz, *Berufliche Entwicklung der Amateurspitzensportler*, 37–52; Karl-Heinrich Bette, *Strukturelle Aspekte des Hochleistungssports in der Bundesrepublik* [Structural Aspects of High-performance Sport in the Federal Republic] (St. Augustin: Verlag Hans Richarz, 1984), 25–8.

58 Rob Beamish, "Labor Relations in Sport: Central Issues in Their Emergence and Structure in High Performance Sport," in Alan Ingham and John Loy, eds, *Sport in Social Development: Traditions, Transitions, and Transformations*, (Champaign Il.: Human Kinetics Publishers, 1993), 187–201; Rob Beamish and Jan Borowy, *Q: What Do You Do For A Living? A: I'm An Athlete* (Kingston: Sport Research Group, 1989); Mick Green and Ben Oakley, "Elite Sport Development Systems and Playing to Win: Uniformity and Diversity in International Approaches," *Leisure Studies* 20 (2001), 247–67.

59 The Dassler brothers' history is a colorful one; see, for example, "Dassler Legacy" (2002), http://adidas.freehomepage.com/dassler_legacy.html. The name Adidas came from Adolf combining his nickname and his last name – Adi-Das (which soon became Adidas).

60 Killanin, "Eligibility and Amateurism," 151; Senn, *Power, Politics and the Olympic Games*, 136; Don Macintosh, Tom Bedecki and C.E.S. Franks, *Sport and Politics in Canada* (Montreal: McGill–Queen's University Press, 1987), 48–52.

61 J. Gould, "Nobody Was First," *New York Times* (December 9, 1959), Section 2, 15; Stephen Wenn, "Lights! Camera! Little Action: Television, Avery Brundage, and the 1956 Melbourne Olympics," *Sporting Traditions* 10:1 (1993), 38–53.

62 Barney, Wenn and Martyn, *Selling the Five Rings*, 69.

63 Ibid., 84.

64 Ibid., 153–273.

65 Killanin, "Eligibility and Amateurism," 151.

66 Ibid.; ellipsis in Killanin.

67 Ibid.

68 Cited in ibid., 152. It is worth noting that Coubertin dealt with many of these same issues in an identical fashion; see Coubertin, *Olympism*, 641–3, 646–7, 647–8. While Andrew Strenk's history of the amateurism question is factually correct, he suggests that the IOC had moved away from the encumbrances of amateurism in 1971. This was not the case even though the "Amateurism Code" was renamed the "Eligibility

Code." In fact, as Killanin demonstrates, Rule 26 in 1971 was more restrictive rather than less so and certainly at odds with the dominant trends in the Olympic Movement even as they were understood by members of the IOC's own board. See Andrew Strenk, "Amateurism: The Myth and the Reality," in Seagrave and Chu, *The Olympic Games in Transition*, 303–27.

69 Todd and Todd, "Significant Events," 68.

70 Todd, "Anabolic Steroids," 97; Todd and Todd, "Significant Events," 70–3.

71 See Pat Connolly, *Hearings on Steroids in Amateur and Professional Sports: The Medical and Social Costs of Steroid Abuse* (testimony before Committee on the Judiciary, United States Senate, One Hundred First Congress, first session, April 3 and May 9, 1989); Charlie Francis, *Speed Trap: Inside the Biggest Scandal in Olympic History* (Toronto: Lester & Oppen Dennys, 1990); Charles Dubin, *Commission of Inquiry Into the Use of Drugs and Banned Practices Intended to Increase Athletic Performance* (Ottawa: Canadian Government Publishing Centre, 1990); Todd and Todd, "Significant Events"; Werner Franke and Brigitte Berendonk, "Hormonal Doping and Androgenization of Athletes: A Secret Program of the German Democratic Republic Government," *Clinical Chemistry* 43:7 (1997), 1264. Franke and Berendonk cite Wader and Hainline, *Drugs and the Athlete* (Philadelphia: FA Davis Co., 1989); Charles Yesalis, *Anabolic Steroids*; J.R. Biden, "Steroids in amateur and professional sports – the medical and social costs of steroid abuse," *US Senate Committee on the Judiciary Hearing*, J101–2 (Washington, DC: Government Printing Office, 1990); Breo, "Of MDs and muscles – lessons from two 'retired steroid doctors'," *Journal of the American Medical Association* 263 (1990), 1697–705; Dubin, *Commission of Inquiry*; and Robert Voy, *Drugs, Sport, and Politics* (Champaign, Il.: Leisure Press, 1991). Furthermore, John Hoberman, *Mortal Engines: The Science of Performance and the Dehumanization of Sport* (Don Mills: Maxwell Macmillan Canada, 1992), 229–65, John Hoberman, "Sports Physicians and the Doping Crisis in Elite Sport," *Clinical Journal of Sport Medicine* 12 (2002), 203–8 and Ivan Waddington, *Sport, Health and Drugs* (New York: E & F Spon, 2000), 135–52 also document the widespread use of steroids in the west.

72 Todd and Todd, "Significant Events," 69; see also Yesalis and Bahrke, "History of Doping in Sport," 53–4.

73 Franke and Berendonk, "Hormonal Doping and Androgenization of Athletes."

74 Frank Pfetsch, Peter Beutel, Hans-Martin Stork, and Gerhard Treutlein, *Leistungssport und Gesellschaftssystem: Sozio-politische Faktoren im Leistungssport* [Performance Sport and the Social System: Socio-political Factors in Performance Sport] (Schorndorf: Karl Hofmann Verlag, 1975), 40–52.

75 Lehnertz, *Berufliche Entwicklung der Amateurspitzensportler*, 12–13.

76 L.P. Matwejew, "Periodisierung des Sportlichen Trainings [Periodization of Athletic Training]," *Trainerbibliothek* [Coaches' Library] 2 (Berlin: Bertels & Wernitz, 1972).

77 Tomasz Lempart, "Die XX. Olympischen Spiele München 1972 – Probleme des Hochleistungssports [The Twentieth Olympic Games of Munich 1972: Problems in High-performance Sport]," *Trainerbibliothek* [Coaches' Library] 5 (Berlin: Bertels & Wernitz, 1973); see also Lehnertz, *Berufliche Entwicklung der Amateurspitzensportler*, 14–18.

78 Avery Brundage, cited in Barney, Wenn and Martyn, *Selling the Five Rings*, 105.

79 Brundage also attempted to ban 40 other athletes from the Sapporo Games for "professionalism"; however, a majority IOC rule overrode his demands. See Barney, Wenn and Martyn, *Selling the Five Rings*, 105–6.

80 Ibid., 105; Strenk, "Amateurism: The Myth and the Reality," 315–17.

81 Cited in Killanin, "Eligibility and Amateurism," 143; see also International Olympic Committee, *The Olympic Charter: 1989* (Lausanne; International Olympic Committee, 1989), 18, 43–4.

82 Coubertin, *Olympism*, 581.

83 Richard Pound, "Never Give In, Never," The *Globe and Mail* (August 9, 2001).

Chapter 2

1 For the original German, see Karl Marx and Friedrich Engels, "Manifest der Kommunistischen Partei [Manifesto of the Communist Party]," in Karl Marx and Friedrich Engels, *Werke* [Collected Works] (Vol. 4) (Berlin: Dietz Verlag, 1972), 461; for Macfarlane's translation, see Karl Marx and Friedrich Engels, "Manifesto of the German Communist Party," *The Red Republican* 21 (November 1850) in Karl Marx and Friedrich Engels, *Gesamtausgabe* [Complete Works] (Pt. I, Vol. 10) (Berlin: Dietz Verlag, 1977), 605.

2 See John MacAloon, "Steroids and the State: Dubin, Melodrama and the Accomplishment of Innocence," *Public Culture* 2:2 (1990), 41–64.

3 Cited in John MacAloon, *This Great Symbol* (Chicago: University of Chicago Press, 1981), 171.

4 Ibid. See Alan Guttmann, *The Games Must Go On: Avery Brundage and the Olympic Movement* (New York: Columbia University Press, 1984), 14–15 and John Slater, "Modern Public Relations: Pierre Coubertin and the Birth of the Modern Olympic Games," in Kevin Wamsley, Robert Barney and Scott Martyn, eds, *The Global Nexus Engaged: Past, Present, Future Interdisciplinary Olympic Studies* (Proceedings for the Sixth International Symposium for Olympic Research, The University of Western Ontario, London, Ontario, 2002), 149–60 for the importance Coubertin attached to symbolism in the Olympic Movement.

5 On the effects of World War II on popular sensibilities, see Gabriel Kolko, *The Politics of War* (New York: Pantheon Books, 1990). Kolko writes that

> the impact of World War II on the rhythm of the daily experience of people throughout the world and on their consciousness was to shape its consequences for years to come even more than the visible immediate successes or failures of armies
> (xvii)

6 Recent scholarship clearly documents the extent to which the Nazis' ideology and Weltanschauung were adopted by many ordinary Germans from 1933 to 1945. See, in particular, Omer Bartov, "Jews as Germans: Victor Klemperer Bears Witness," in *Germany's War and the Holocaust: Disputed Histories* (Ithaca: Cornell University Press, 2003), 198–200, 206; Victor Klemperer, *The Language of the Third Reich. LTI – Lingua Tertii Imperii: A Philologist's Notebook* (London: Athone Press, 2000), and Victor Klemperer, *I Will Bear Witness: A Diary of the Nazi Years* (2 vols) (New York: The Modern Library, 1998, 1999). Even in the case of the Nazi's most gruesome objective – the annihilation of European Jewry – it was not, as Daniel Goldhagen contends, a pre-existing "eliminationist" anti-Semitism that spurred the Holocaust; see Daniel Goldhagen, *Hitler's Willing Executioners: Ordinary Germans and the Holocaust* (New York: Random Books, 1997), especially 14, 27–48. Rather, it was the almost unrelenting use of sophisticated propaganda, vast state resources and specific, situational–historical conditions and events that prepared "ordinary men" to commit those atrocities; see Christopher Browning, *Ordinary Men: Reserve Police Battalion 101 and the Final Solution in Poland* (New York: HarperCollins, 1992), especially 177–89; Omer Bartov, *Hitler's Army: Soldiers, Nazis, and War in the Third Reich* (New York: Oxford University Press, 1991), especially 4–11; Edward B. Westermann, "'Ordinary Men' or 'Ideological Soldiers'? Police Battalion 310 in Russia, 1942," *German Studies Review* 21:1 (1998), 41–68; Eric Johnson, *Nazi Terror: The Gestapo, Jews, and Ordinary Germans* (New York: Basic Books, 2001), 481–7 and passim; Omer Bartov, "Germans as Nazis: Goldhagen's Holocaust and the World," in *Germany's War and the Holocaust*, especially 147–8, 156–60; and Robert Shandley, ed., *Unwilling Germans? The Goldhagen Debate* (Minneapolis: University of Minnesota Press, 1998), especially 55–73.

7 Sigfried Kracauer, *From Caligari to Hitler: A Psychological History of the German Film* (Princeton: Princeton University Press, 1947), 6, 52–3. Kracauer argued that

through an analysis of the German films deep psychological dispositions predominant in Germany from 1918 to 1933 can be exposed – dispositions which influenced the course of events during that time and which will have to be reckoned with in the post-Hitler era

(v)

8 Ibid., 63–5.
9 Ibid., 66.
10 The inserted words are Karcauer's, ibid., 66.
11 Ibid., 67.
12 See Ian Kershaw, *Hitler, 1889–1936: Hubris* (New York: Norton Books, 1999); Brigitte Hamann, *Hitler's Vienna* (New York: Oxford University Press, 1999). Hamann, in particular, demonstrates how Hitler stole ideas from the pan-Germans, Teutonic supremacists and the Schonerians, from Nordic myths and old Germanic history, from Volkisch race theoreticians like Guido von List and Houston Stewart Chamberlain (with their ideas of Aryan supremacy) that circulated widely in Vienna in the six years he lived there. She also demonstrates how his experiences in World War I galvanized those ideologies into an apocalyptic vision of Germany's role in history.
13 See Adolf Hitler, *Mein Kampf* [My Struggle], trans. Alvin Johnson (New York: Reynal and Hitchcock, 1939), 243–69, 303–88, 389–455, 116–62. On the notions of the superiority of the German Volk and the need for a heroic leader extending deep into nineteenth century German thought and lore see also Ian Kershaw, *The Hitler Myth: Image and Reality in the Third Reich* (New York: Oxford University Press, 1987), 13–47 and Richard J. Evans, *The Coming of the Third Reich* (New York: The Penguin Press, 2004). On the role these themes played in Nazi propaganda during Hitler's rise to power, see David Welch, *The Third Reich: Politics and Propaganda* (New York: Routledge, 1993), 50–89.
14 See Mordis Eksteins, *Rites of Spring* (Toronto: Lester & Orpen Dennys, 1989), 316–17 and Klaus Fischer, *Nazi Germany* (New York: Continuum Books, 1996), 3–18, 356–8.
15 Eksteins, *Rites of Spring, 321.* See also Hitler, *Mein Kampf,* 107–8, 227–42, 696–716, 846–67.
16 See, for example, Peter Adam, *Art of the Third Reich* (New York: Harry N. Abrams, 1992) and Stephanie Barron, "1937: Modern Art and Politics in Prewar Germany" in Stephanie Barron, ed, *"Degenerate Art": The Fate of the Avant-Garde in Nazi Germany* (Los Angeles: Harry N. Abrams Publishers, 1991), 9–24. On the erotic treatment of women in Nazi fascism, see Klaus Theweleit, *Male Fantasies, Vol. I: Women, Floods, Bodies, History* (Minneapolis: University of Minnesota Press, 1987) and Maria-Antonietta Macchiocchi, "Female Sexuality in Fascist Ideology," *Feminist Review* 1 (1979), 67–82.
17 See Richard Mandell, *The Nazi Olympics* (Urbana and Chicago: University of Illinois Press, 1987) or Arnd Krüger, *Die Olympischen Spiele 1936 und die Weltmeinung: Ihre aussenpolitische Bedeutung unter besonderer Berücksichtigung der USA* [The 1936 Olympic Games and World Opinion: Their Importance in Foreign Politics with Special Reference to the USA] (Frankfurt: Bartels & Wernitz, 1972).
18 See Toby Clark, *Art and Propaganda in the Twentieth Century* (New York: Calmann and King, 1997), 49. See also Albert Speer, *Erinnerungen* [Memoirs] (Berlin: Verlag Ullstein, 1969), 103–11.
19 On Riefenstahl's role as a Nazi propagandist, see Susan Sontag, "Fascinating Fascism," *Under the Sign of Saturn* (New York: Farrar, Straus & Girous, 1980), 73–105.
20 We are indebted, in constructing this comparative commentary on the events in the two films, to Clark, *Art and Propaganda in the Twentieth Century,* 51, for the analysis of symbolism contained in *Triumph of the Will. Olympia* differed in key respects from the stern militarism of the Nuremberg Rally. To assuage international fears of a militaristic

Nazi regime, Hitler was shown as an engaged dignitary who was as keenly interested in the events as the typical spectator – a true man of his people. For a recent review of various theoretical perspectives on *Olympia*, see Maria Rodríguez, "Behind Leni's Outlook: A Perspective on the Film *Olympia*," *International Review for the Sociology of Sport* 38:1 (2003), 109–16.

21 Mandell, *The Nazi Olympics*, 277. See also Speer's almost identical description of the effect created at the 1934 Nuremberg Party rally; Speer, *Erinnerungen*, 96–7.

22 On the January 30, 1933 torch procession see Kershaw, *The Hitler Myth*, 48.

23 William Shirer, *The Rise and Fall of the Third Reich* (Greenwich, Conn.: Fawcett Crest Books, 1959), 322. Olympic historian Alfred Senn concurs. "Most contemporary observers tended to agree that the Nazi regime had produced a remarkable model for the political exploitation of international athletic competition in general and the Olympic Games in particular." Alfred Senn, *Power, Politics and the Olympic Games* (Champaign, Il.: Human Kinetics Press, 1999), 62.

24 See Speer, *Erinnerungen*, 363–79; Peter Padfield, *Himmler: Reichsführer-SS* (London: Papermac Books, 1990), passim; Anthony Beevor, *The Fall of Berlin, 1945* (New York: Viking Penguin, 2002). Gitta Sereny, *The Healing Wound: Experiences and Reflections on Germany, 1938–2001* (New York: W.W. Norton, 2001), 138–46 points out that the distinction between concentration camps and extermination camps is important; Holocaust deniers often use information from the concentration camps to "disprove" the mass murder of Jews. The conscious creation of extermination camps separate from the concentration camps underlines the calculation behind the mass murder. On Hiroshima and Nagasaki, see John Hersey, *Hiroshima* (New York: A.A. Knopf, 1946); Laurence Yep, *Hiroshima* (New York: Scholastic Books, 1995); Committee for the Compilation of Materials on Damage Caused by the Atomic Bombs, *Hiroshima and Nagasaki: The Physical, Medical and Social Effects of the Atomic Bombings* (New York: Basic Books, 1981).

25 Speer, *Erinnerungen*, 522. To view the apparent remorse Speer expressed in Nuremberg within a more total context, see Gita Sereny, *Albert Speer: His Battle with Truth* (New York: A. A. Knopf, 1995); Joachim Fest, *Speer: The Final Verdict*, trans. Ewald Osers and Alexandra Dring (London: Weidenfeld and Nicolson, 2001); Matthias Schmidt, *Albert Speer: The End of a Myth*, trans. Joachim Neugroschel (New York: Macmillan Publishing Company, 1984).

26 This fear was a continuation of the dystopian literature that had begun in the inter-war years. See, for example, Aldous Huxley, *Brave New World* (Markham, Ontario: Penguin Books, 1955) or Evgenii Zamiatin, *We*, trans. Gregory Zilboorg (New York: Dutton, 1952). The literature extended into the cold war; see, for example, Eugene Burdick, *Fail-Safe* (New York: Dell, 1963). See also note 5 above.

27 See Kolko, *The Politics of War*.

28 Cited in Senn, *Power, Politics and the Olympic Games*, 98.

29 By focusing on the USSR, we are in no way suggesting that the west was above the all out pursuit of Olympic gold. As noted in Chapter One, US weightlifters began to use synthetic steroids in the mid-1950s, and they spread quickly to other strength sports. But since our focus is on steroid anxiety in the west, it is only the rumors of Soviet use that are germane at this point in our discussion.

30 The similarities between the Nazis and the Soviets received its most celebrated academic support in Hannah Arendt, *The Origins of Totalitarianism* (New York: Harcourt, Brace, 1951) and Carl J. Friedrich, ed., *Totalitarianism* (Cambridge, Mass.: Harvard University Press, 1954). The theme stimulated more recent debate in the so-called "Historians Debate" in Germany. See *"Historikerstreit": Die Dokumentation der Kontroverse um die Einzigartigkeit der nationalsozialistischen Judenvernichtung* ["The Historians' Dispute": Documentation on the Controversy over the Uniqueness of the National Socialist's Destruction of the Jews] (Munich: Piper Verlag, 1987).

31 Nicholas Wade, "Anabolic Steroids: Doctors Denounce Them, But Athletes Aren't Listening," *Science* 176 (1972), 1400.

32 See Herbert Haupt and George Rovere, "Anabolic Steroids: A Review of the Literature," *The American Journal of Sports Medicine* 12:6 (1984), 469–84 and Robert Windsor and Daniel Dumitru, "Anabolic Steroids," *Postgraduate Medicine*, 84:4 (1988), 41. Terry Todd, "Anabolic Steroids: The Gremlins of Sport," *Journal of Sport History* 14:1 (1987), 93, note 25, cites Fred Silvermann, "Guaranteed Aggression: The Secret of Testosterone by Nazi Troops," *Journal of the American Medical Association* (1984), 129–31 although we have been unable to locate this reference despite a careful review of the *Journal*. Todd also writes that "William Taylor has speculated that since Hitler had used the drug [testosterone], it might have accounted for some of the mood swings and aggressiveness of the German fuhrer [sic]" (93) which is referenced in note 25 to William Taylor, "The Case Against the Administration of HGH to Normal Children," presented at the symposium *Ethical Issues in the Treatment of Children and Athletes with Human Growth Hormone*, University of Texas at Austin, April 26, 1986. Taylor, Todd writes, relied on Dennis Breo, "Hitler's Final Days Recalled by Physician," *American Medical News* (1985), 1, 34–43 (not 1, 58–69 as Todd notes) for his information, but Breo's interview with Ernst Gunther Schenck, the only surviving physician who was in the Berlin bunker when Hitler committed suicide and who studied Hitler's personal physician Dr. Theodor Morell's extensive diaries, does not support that claim. The article notes that Morell once "used the standard medication, belladonna drops, to quiet the tremors [of Parkinson's disease], and he also used a testosterone derivative, which was irrational" (40). There is no recollection of testosterone-based mood swings. The diaries show that Morell gave Hitler orchikrin, "a combination of all hormones of males," to combat fatigue and depression, and prostakrimum, "an extract of seminal vesicles and prostate" for a short period of time in 1943 to prevent depressive moods. See Theodor Morell, *The Secret Diaries of Hitler's Doctor*, ed. David Irving (New York: Macmillan Press, 1983), 162. Once again, there is no discussion of mood swings or aggression due to testosterone use in Morell's diaries.

33 Virginia Cowart, "Steroids and Sport: After 4 Decades Time to Return Genie to the Bottle," *Journal of the American Medical Association* 257 (1987), 423.

34 J. E. Wright, "Anabolic Steroids and Athletics," *Exercise and Sport Science Review* 8 (1980), 149–202.

35 Brigitte Berendonk, *Doping Dokumente: Von der Forschung zum Betrug* [Doping Documents: From Research to Deceit] (Berlin: Springer-Verlag, 1991), 227. The references to Butenandt and Hanisch, and David *et al.* refer to the chemical identification and synthesis of testosterone. They do not document the Nazis' use of the drugs. See A. Butenandt and G. Hanisch, "Über Testosterone. Umwandlung des Dehydro-Androsterons in Androstendiol und Testosteron; ein Weg zur Darstellungs des Testosterons aus Cholesterin [On Testosterone. Transformation of Dehydro-Androsterons in Androstendiol and Testosteron; a Means for the Separation of Testosterone from Cholesterin]," *Zeitschrift Physiologische Chemie* [Journal of Physiological Chemistry] 237 (1935), 87–9, and K. David, E. Dingemanse, J. Freud, and E. Lacqueur, "Über kristallines männliches Hormon aus Hoden (Testosteron), wirksamer als aus Harn oder aus Cholesterin bereitetes Androsteron [On the more Effective Preparation of the Crystalized Male Hormone Androsteron from Testicles (Testosterone) than from Urine or Cholesterin]," *Zeitschrift Physiologische Chemie* 233 (1935), 281–2.

36 See, for example, H. Haupt and G. Rovere, "Anabolic Steroids: A Review of the Literature," 469; Lawrence Surtees, "Paying the Price ... Later," The *Globe and Mail* (April 1, 1989), D1; Jorge Gomez, "Performance-Enhancing Substances in Adolescent Athletes," *Texas Medicine*, Symposium on Adolescent Health, (February 2002), www.texmed.org/ata/nrm/tme/texmedfeb02_performance_enhancers.asp; "Steroids," (2003), www.electronicreferences.com/view.php/English/Steroids.htm; "RAW REMARKS: Steroids – Wonder Drug of Wrestling," (May, 2003), http://www.wrestlingdotcom.com/columns/55482600.php concerning how widely these allegations are circulated.

37 Steven Ungerleider, *Faust's Gold: Inside the East German Doping Machine* (New York: St. Martin's Press, 2001), 45. Ungerleider does not supply any citations to substantiate his claims. See Bartov, *Hitler's Army*, Anthony Beevor, *Stalingrad* (London: Penguin Books, 1999), and Beevor, *The Fall of Berlin* for accurate, factually based, scholarly accounts of German troop behavior on the eastern front.

38 Hoberman has argued that there is no factual basis to the allegation. See John Hoberman, *Mortal Engines: The Science of Performance and the Dehumanization of Sport* (Don Mills: Maxwell Macmillan Canada, 1992), 214. On the basis of our own extensive search for any legitimate substantiation of the allegation and the documentation we have presented here, it is clear that we concur with Hoberman – the Nazi use of steroids is a myth.

39 See Berendonk, "DDR-Staatsplanthema 14.25 – Das Manhattan-Project des Sports [GDR-State Plan Research Theme 14.25 – the Manhattan Project of Sport]," *Doping Dokumente*, 91.

40 Bob Goldman, *Death in the Locker Room* (South Bend: Icarus Press, 1984), 2.

41 On both this point and the false accusations that men had been clandestinely entering women's events, see Ian Ritchie, "Sex Tested, Gender Verified: Controlling Female Sexuality in the Age of Containment," *Sport History Review* 34:1 (2003), 80–98.

42 Tomas Laqueur, *Making Sex: Body and Gender from the Greeks to Freud* (Cambridge and London: Harvard University Press, 1990). See also John Hood-Williams, "Goodbye to Sex and Gender," *The Sociological Review* 44:1 (1996), 1–16 and John Hood-Williams, "Sexing the Athletes," *Sociology of Sport Journal* 12 (1995), 290–305; and Ritchie, "Sex Tested, Gender Verified."

43 Cheryl Cole, "Resisting the Canon: Feminist Cultural Studies, Sport, and Technologies of the Body," in Susan Birrell and Cheryl Cole, eds, *Women, Sport, and Culture*, (Champaign, Il.: Human Kinetics, 1994), 15.

44 Cited in Ellen Gerber, "Chronicle of Participation," in Ellen Gerber, Jan Felshin, Pearl Berlin and Waneen Wyrick, eds, *The American Woman in Sport*, (Reading, MA: Addison-Wesley, 1974), 137. See also Pierre Coubertin, *Olympism: Selected Writings*, ed. Norbert Müller (Lausanne: International Olympic Committee, 2000), 447, 583, 711–13, 746. For a history of the naturalization of gender within emerging scientific disciplines during the same time period, see Cynthia Russett, *Sexual Science: The Victorian Construction of Womanhood* (Cambridge: Harvard University Press, 1989).

45 John Hoberman, "Toward a Theory of Olympic Internationalism," *Journal of Sport History* 22:1 (Spring 1995), 9–10.

46 For the Canadian, American, and British cases, respectively, see Helen Lenskyj, *Out of Bounds: Women, Sport and Sexuality* (Toronto: The Women's Press, 1986) and Margaret Ann Hall, *The Girl and the Game: A History of Women's Sport in Canada* (Peterborough, Ontario: Broadview Press, 2002); Susan Cahn, *Coming on Strong: Gender and Sexuality in Twentieth-Century Women's Sport* (New York: The Free Press, 1994); Jennifer Hargreaves, *Sporting Females: Critical Issues in the History and Sociology of Women's Sports* (London: Routledge, 1994).

47 Susan Cahn, "Crushes, Competition, and Closets: The Emergence of Homophobia in Women's Physical Education," in Birrell and Cole, *Women in Sport and Culture*, 329.

48 Ibid., 329–30.

49 Ibid., 327–39.

50 See Jennifer Terry, "Lesbians Under the Medical Gaze: Scientists Search for Remarkable Differences," *The Journal of Sex Research* 27:3 (1990), 317–39.

51 Cahn, *Coming on Strong*, 23–6.

52 Cited in Cahn, "Crushes, Competition, and Closets," 334.

53 On the historical construction of nationalism and nation building, see Benedict Anderson, *Imagined Communities: Reflections on the Origin and Spread of Nationalism* (New York: Verso, 1995). For examples of gendered and sexualized manifestations of cold war

ideology, see Elaine Tyler May, *Homeward Bound: American Families in the Cold War Era* (New York: Basic Books, 1988); Mary Louise Adams, *The Trouble With Normal: Postwar Youth and the Making of Heterosexuality* (Toronto: University of Toronto Press, 1997); Andrew Parker, Mary Russo, Doris Sommer and Patricia Yaeger, eds, *Nationalisms and Sexuality* (New York and London: Routledge, 1992); Susan Jeffords, *The Remasculinization of America: Gender and the Vietnam War* (Bloomington and Indianapolis: Indiana University Press, 1989) and Susan Jeffords, *Hard Bodies: Hollywood Masculinity in the Reagan Era* (New Brunswick: Rutgers University Press, 1994).

54 May, *Homeward Bound*, 11.

55 Ibid., 32.

56 Ibid., 16–19.

57 Ibid. Susan Gubar questions the idea that during World War II women's increased labor challenged popular sensibilities about gender. Both allied and axis powers initiated widespread "sexual propaganda" programs that played upon paternalistic and patriarchal fears of the enemy attacking homeland wives and daughters, reinforcing patriarchal ideals of men protecting "their" women. See Susan Gubar, "'This Is My Rifle, This Is My Gun': World War II and the Blitz on Women," in Margaret Randolph Higonnet, Jane Jenson, Sonya Michel and Margaret Weitz, eds, *Behind the Lines: Gender and the Two World Wars* (New Haven and London: Yale University Press, 1987), 227–59.

58 "Are Girl Athletes Really Girls?" *Life* (October 7, 1966), 63–6. See also Ritchie, "Sex Tested, Gender Verified," 87, and Lenskyj, *Out of Bounds*, 87–8.

59 Denise Grady, "Olympic Officials Struggle to Define What Should Be Obvious: Just Who is a Female Athlete," *Discover* 13:6 (1992), 80; Alison Carlson, "Chromosome Count," *Ms Magazine* 17:4 (1988), 42; Gail Vines, "Last Olympics for the Sex Test?" *New Scientist* 135:1828 (1992), 39.

60 M.A. Ferguson-Smith and Elizabeth Ferris, "Gender Verification in Sport: The Need for Change?" *British Journal of Sports Medicine* 25:1 (1991), 17.

61 Lenskyj, *Out of Bounds*, 87.

62 Ritchie, "Sex Tested, Gender Verified," 91.

63 Ibid.

64 Lenskyj, *Out of Bounds*, 89.

65 R.G. Bunge, "Sex and the Olympic Games," *Journal of the American Medical Association* 173:12 (1960), 196.

66 On the interrelationship between drug testing and sex testing, see Cheryl Cole, "Testing for Sex or Drugs?" *Journal of Sport & Social Issues* 24:4 (2000), 331–3; Ian Ritchie and Rob Beamish, "The Forgotten History of Drug Prohibition in High Performance Sport," presented at the annual meeting of the North American Society for the Sociology of Sport, Indianapolis (2002); Laurel R. Davis and Linda C. Delano, "Fixing the Boundaries of Physical Gender: Side Effects of Anti-Drug Campaigns on Athletics," *Sociology of Sport Journal* 9 (1992), 1–19 and Ian Ritchie, "'Gender Doping': Sex and Drug Tests in the Age of Containment," presented at the annual meeting of the North American Society for the Sociology of Sport, Tucson, Arizona (2004).

67 See Charles Dubin, *Commission of Inquiry Into the Use of Drugs and Banned Practices Intended to Increase Athletic Performance* (Ottawa: Canadian Government Publishing Centre, 1990), 341, 347; see also Michael Janofsky, "Doctor Says He Supplied Steroids to Medalists," *New York Times* (June 20, 1989), B12; Goldman, *Death in the Locker Room*, 80–1.

68 Cited in Goldman, *Death in the Locker Room*, 81; emphasis in the original.

69 On Hiroshima and Nagasaki, see note 24 above. Concerning the Cuban Missile Crisis, see Robert Beggs, *The Cuban Missile Crisis* (Harlow: Longman Press, 1971) or Mark J. White, *The Cuban Missile Crisis* (Basingstoke, Hampshire: Macmillan, 1996).

70 On the horrors of Mengele's and other physicians' activities during the Holocaust, see Gerald Posner and John Ware, *Mengele: The Complete Story* (New York: McGraw-Hill

Books, 1986) and Alexander Mitscherlich and Fred Mielke, *Doctors of Infamy: The Story of the Nazi Medical Crimes* (New York: H. Schuman, 1949). Concerning the Nuremberg Trials see Eugene Davidson, *The Trail of the Germans* (New York: Collier Books, 1966), Richard Overy, *Interrogations: The Nazi Elite in Allied Hands, 1945* (New York: Penguin Putnam Inc., 2001), Bradley Smith, *Reaching Judgment at Nuremberg* (New York: Basic Books, 1977), Robert Gellately, ed., *The Nuremberg Interviews Conducted by Leon Goldensohn* (New York: A. A. Knopf, 2005) and Gustav Gilbert, *Nuremberg Diary* (New York: Signet Books, 1947).

Chapter 3

1 Richard Pound, *Inside the Olympics: A Behind-the-Scenes Look at the Politics, the Scandals, and the Glory of the Games* (Toronto: Wiley Canada, 2004), 54.
2 George Orwell, "The Politics of the English Language," *Inside the Whale and Other Essays* (Markham Ontario: Penguin Books, 1962), 156.
3 *The Oxford English Dictionary* (Vol. XVI) (Oxford: Clarendon Press, 1989), 315–18.
4 Charles Dubin, *Commission of Inquiry Into the Use of Drugs and Banned Practices Intended to Increase Athletic Performance* (Ottawa: Canadian Government Publishing Centre, 1990), xxii.
5 World Anti-Doping Agency, *The World Anti-Doping Code* (Version 3.0, February 20, 2003), www.wada-ama.org/docs/web/standards_harmonization/code/code_v3.pdf, 7.
6 For example, in his contributions to the *Sportwissenschaftsliches Lexikon* [Sport Science Lexicon] from 1972 to 1977, Hajo Bernett sought to provide a precise definition for the key word "Sport;" see "Sport," *Sportwissenschaftliches Lexikon* [Sport Science Lexicon], first edition, ed. Peter Röthig, (Schorndorf: Hofmann Verlag, 1972), 212. By 1980, it was recognized that such an exercise not only had little meaning but was, in fact, impossible; see Peter Röthig, "Sport," *Sportwissenschaftliches Lexikon* [Sport Science Lexicon], 5th newly revised edition, ed. Peter Röthig (Schorndorf: HofmannVerlag, 1983), 338. See also Wissenschaftlicher Beirat des Deutschen Sportbund [Scientific Advisory Board of the German Sport Federation], "Zur Definition des Sports [Towards a Definition of Sport]," *Sportwissenschaft* 10:4 (1980), 437–9.
7 Bruce Kidd, *The Struggle for Canadian Sport* (Toronto: University of Toronto Press, 1996), 12. Kidd, as this work demonstrates, is too restrictive when limiting the fashioning and refashioning of sport to industrial capitalist societies alone – non-capitalist, eastern bloc societies have played a significant role in the shaping of world-class, high-performance sport in the modern era – a point which Kidd would quickly corroborate. See also Lois Bryson, "Sport, Drugs and the Development of Modern Capitalism," *Sporting Traditions* 6:2 (1990), 135–53.
8 There is nothing unique about these three examples; they are a selection from a potentially incredibly long list. The focus upon Germany is simply for consistency – other countries could have been chosen.
9 See Gerd Steins, *Wo das Turnen erfunden wurde… Friedrich Ludwig Jahn und die 175jährige Geschichte der Hasenheide* [Where the Turners were Founded: Friedrich Ludwig Jahn and the 175 Year History of the Rabbit's Heath], (Berlin: Kupijai & Prochnow, 1986).
10 Cited in Michael Krüger, "Ruhmsucht und Rekordfimmel – Zur Geschichte der Leistung im Sport [Thirst for Glory and Record Crazy – on the History of Performance in Sport]," in Hartmut Gabler and Ulrich Göhner, eds, *Für einen bessern Sport …* [For a Better Sport …] (Schorndorf: Verlag Hofmann, 1990), 346.
11 Krüger, "Ruhmsucht und Rekordfimmel," 345–7.
12 See, for example, Arnd Krüger and James Riordan, eds, *The Story of Worker Sport* (Windsor, On.: Human Kinetics Press, 1996); Herbert Dierker, *Arbeitersport im*

Spannungsfeld der Zwanziger Jahre [Worker Sport in the Cross Currents of the Twenties] (Essen: Klartext Publishers, 1990); Herbert Dierker and Gertrud Pfister, eds, *"Frisch heran! Brüder, hört ihr das Klingen!" Zur Altagsgeschichte des Berliner Arbeitersportvereins Fichte* ["This way Brothers! Hear the Call!" Towards a History of Everyday Life in Berlin's Fichte Worker Sport Association] (Duderstadt: Mecke Printers and Publishers, 1991); Helmut Wagner, *Sport und Arbeitersport* [Sport and Workers' Sport] (Cologne: Pahl–Rugenstein Publishers, 1973) and Pierre Arnaud, ed., *Les origins du sport ouvrier en Europe* [The Origins of Worker Sport in Europe] (Paris: Harmattan, 1994).

13 Hajo Bernett, "Sport zwischen Kampf, Spiel und Arbeit – Zum Perspektivwechsel in der Theorie des Sports [Sport Among Struggle, Play and Work – On the Perspective Changes in the Theory of Sport]," in Gabler and Göhner, *Für einen bessern Sport,* 163–85.

14 Ibid., 166.

15 In 1919, Anton Sickinger, executive member of the German National Committee for Physical Education, stated that physical discipline was the central theme of the "new German school's" approach to sport. Citing Diem, he stated that sport "is struggle with opponents and with opposition" and is "masculine joy in struggle and triumph." Similarly, in 1925, the rector of the German Academy for Physical Education, August Bier, saw sport building "an iron will, unbridled enthusiasm, true commitment, and a powerful masculinity." Ibid., 169.

16 Ibid., 171.

17 See George Eisen, "The Voices of Sanity: American Diplomatic Reports from the 1936 Berlin Olympiad," *Journal of Sport History* 11:3 (1984), 58 and note 7.

18 See ibid., 172.

19 Ibid.

20 Gleichschaltung – coordination – was the official term used to describe the process by which all German institutions were brought into line with the tenets of National Socialism.

> Gleichschaltung proceeded along two related paths: synchronization of all government institutions and mass mobilization of all citizens for the National Socialist cause. The first approach involved the eradication of all political opponents and parties and the second the creation of mass organizations of mass control
>
> Klaus Fischer, *Nazi Germany: A New History* (New York: Continuum Publishing Company, 1996), 278; see 278–84

21 Ibid., 174.

22 Ibid.

23 The significance and full context of the declaration of "total war" is discussed in Chapter Four. See also Iring Fetscher, *Joseph Goebbels im Berliner Sportpalast 1943* [Joseph Goebbels in the Berlin Sports Palace 1943] (Berlin: Europäische Verlagsanstalt, 1998); Ralf Reuth, *Goebbels* (New York: Harcourt Brace & Company, 1993), 293–330; and Albert Speer, *Erinnerungen* [Memoirs] (Berlin: Verlag Ullstein, 1969), 269–86.

24 See Fischer, *Nazi Germany,* 176–7.

25 Cited in ibid., 179.

26 See Arnd Krüger, "Viele Wege führen nach Olympia. Die Veränderungen in den Trainingssystemen für Mittel- und Langstreckenläufer (1850–1997) [Many Paths Lead to Olympia: the Changes in Training Systems for Middle and Long Distance Runers (1850–1997)]," in Norbert Gissel, ed., *Sportliche Leistung im Wandel* [Athletic Performance in Transition], (Hamburg: Czwalina, 1998), 41–56.

27 Thomas S. Kuhn, "Energy Conservation as an Example of Simultaneous Discovery," in Marshall Clagett, ed, *Critical Problems in the History of Science* (Madison, Wisconsin: University of Wisconsin Press, 1962), 321–56.

28 See Yehuda Elkana, *The Discovery of the Conservation of Energy* (Cambridge, Massachusetts: Harvard University Press, 1974); Kuhn, "Energy Conservation;" Cynthia Eagle Russett, *Sexual Science: The Victorian Construction of Womanhood* (Cambridge, Massachusetts: Harvard University Press, 1989), 106–7.

29 Written in 1748, Julien de la Mettrie's *L'Homme machine* was reissued in 1912 because it resonated with the scientific understanding of the human being at the time. See, Julien de la Mettrie, *Man a Machine* (La Salle, Il.: The Open Court Publishing Company, 1912); see also Russett, *Sexual Science*, 108–116.

30 Cited in ibid., 107.

31 Regarding physical education, see Paul Atkinson, "The Feminist Physique: Physical Education and the Medicalization of Women's Education," in James Anthony Mangan and Roberta J. Park, eds, *From 'Fair Sex' to Feminism: Sport and the Socialization of Women in the Industrial and Post-Industrial Eras* (London: Frank Cass, 1987), 38–57. The doctrine was even used to understand the relationship between the mind and soul, and the body's mysterious "vital forces" of instinctual, physical drives. See Kenneth L. Caneva, *Robert Mayer and the Conservation of Energy* (Princeton, New Jersey: Princeton University Press, 1993), 79–125.

32 Eberhard Hildenbrandt, "Milon, Marx und Muskelpille – Anmerkungen zur Kulturgeschichte des sportlichen Trainings [Milo, Marx, and Muscle Pills – Observations on the Cultural History of Training in Sport]," in Gabler and Göhner, *Für einen bessern Sport*, 264.

33 On Milo of Crotona, see Edward Gardiner, *Athletics of the Ancient World* (Oxford: Clarendon Press, 1955), 6 or David Willoughby, *The Super-Athletes* (New York: A.S. Barnes, 1970), 29–30.

34 See F. Hoole, *The Science and Art of Training. A Handbook for Athletes* (London: Trubner, 1888), 3, cited in Arnd Krüger, "Viele Wege führen nach Olympia." Similarly, see Montague Shearman, *Athletics and Football* (London: Longman, Green & Co., 1889), 7 – "there is no reason why an athlete who desires to get fit should lead other than a *natural life*."

35 Cited in Arthur Steinhaus, "Chronic Effects of Exercise," *Physiological Reviews* 13:103 (1933), 110.

36 Ibid., 104.

37 See Steve Bailey, "The Evolution of International Organisations in Physical Education and Sport," *Science in the Service of Physical Education and Sport* (Toronto: John Wiley & Sons, 1996), 16.

38 Alison Wrynn, "The Grand Tour: American Exercise Science and Sports Medicine Encounters the World, 1926–1966," *International Sports Studies* 24:2 (2002), 6–7. See also Thomas Neville Bonner, *Becoming a Physician: Medical Education in Britain, France, Germany, and the United States, 1750–1945* (New York: Oxford University Press, 1995).

39 See Thomas Levenson, *Einstein in Berlin* (New York: Bantam Books, 1994), 4–7.

40 Alison Wrynn, "The Grand Tour." The Deutsche Reichskomitee zur wissenschaftliche Erforschung der Leibesübungen changed its name to the Deutscher Artzbund zur Förderung der Leibesübungen (German Federation of Physicians for the Promotion of Physical Exercise) in 1924.

41 John Hoberman, "Prophets of Performance," *Mortal Engines: The Science of Performance and the Dehumanization of Sport* (Don Mills: Maxwell Macmillan Canada, 1992), 98.

42 See Hildenbrandt, "Milon, Marx und Muskelpille," 268. It was a small step from the principles of natural endowment to eugenics and the Nazi ideology of racial superiority. Track and field wisdom claimed that "The light, lanky, long headed, Nordic races, which constitute the main component of the Scandinavian and Anglo Saxon people, dominate the entire line [of competitive athletics]" (cited in ibid., 269). See also Ian Hacking, *The Taming of Chance* (New York: Cambridge University Press, 1990), 184–7

and Janine Marchessault, "David Suzuki's *The Secret of Life:* Informatics and the Popular Discourse of the Life Code," in Janine Marchessault and Kim Sawchuk, eds, *Wild Science* (New York: Routledge, 2000), 57–9.

43 The key text for Taylor is *The Principles of Scientific Management* (New York: Harper and Brothers, 1911), while for the Gilbreths they include Frank Gilbreth, *Bricklaying System* (New York and Chicago: The Myron C. Clark Publishing Co., 1909); Frank Gilbreth, *Motion Study* (New York: D. Van Nostrand Co., 1911); Frank Gilbreth, *Primer of Scientific Management* (New York: D. Van Nostrand Co., 1912); and Frank Gilbreth and Lillian Gilbreth, *Applied Motion Study* (New York: Sturgis & Walton Co., 1917).

44 Taylor, *Principles of Scientific Management*, 43–74. See also Daniel Bell, "Work and its Discontents: The Cult of Efficiency in America," *The End of Ideology* (Glenco, Il.: The Free Press, 1960), 223–36 and Harry Braverman, *Labor and Monopoly Capital* (New York: Monthly Review Press, 1974), 85–121.

45 See Arnd Krüger, "Viele Wege führen nach Olympia," 50. Nurmi described his guiding principle as the following: "When you race against time, you don't have to sprint. Others can't hold the pace if it is steady and hard all through to the tape." Cited in "Paavo Nurmi 100 Years," (1997) http://www.urheilumuseo.org/paavonurmi/life.htm.

46 Not surprisingly, German researchers dominated physiological research at this time – of the 266 citations in Steinhaus, "Chronic Effects of Exercise," 179 were from German periodicals, 78 English and the remaining nine primarily French. Though not quite as prevalent, Archibald Hill drew more than half of his citations from German sources in his review of leading edge research in muscle physiology – see Archibald Hill, "The Revolution in Muscle Physiology," *Physiological Reviews* 12 (1932), 54–66.

47 See ibid., and Alison Wrynn, "The Grand Tour," 8.

48 See, for example, S. Hoogerwert, "Elektrokardiographische Untersuchungen der Amsterdamer Olympiakämpfer [Electrocardiographic Studies of the Amsterdam Olympic Competitors," *Arbeitsphysiologie* [Physiology of Work] 2:61 (1929); W.W. Siebert, "Untersuchungen über Hypertrophie des Skelettmuskels [Studies on the Hypertrophy of Skeletal Muscle], *Zeitschrift der klinischen Medizin* [Journal of Clinical Medicine] 109 (1929); A. Vannotti and H. Pfister, "Untersuchungen zum Studium des Trainiertseins [Investigations on Studies of Being Trained], *Arbeitsphysiologie* [Physiology of Work] 7 (1934); and T. Petrén, T. Sjöstrand, and B. Sylvén, "Der Einfluss des Trainings auf die Haftigkeit der Capilaren in Herz- und Skelettmuskulatur [The Inflence of Training on the Absorption of Capillaries in the Heart and Skeletal Musculature]," *Arbeitsphysiologie* [Physiology of Work] 9 (1936).

49 See L. Pikhala, "Allgemeine Richtlinien für das athletische Training [General Rules for Athletic Training]," in C. Krümel, ed., *Athletik: Ein Handbuch der lebenswichtigen Leibesübengen* [Athletics: A Handbook of Essential Physical Exercises] (Munich: J.F. Lehmanns, 1930), 185–90.

50 See E.H. Christensen, "Beiträge zur Physiologie schwerer körperlicher Arbeit [Contributions to the Physiology of Heavier Physical Work]," *Arbeitsphysiologie* [Physiology of Work] 4:1 (1931).

51 See Steven Horvath and Elizabeth Horvath, *The Harvard Fatigue Laboratory: Its History and Contributions* (Englewood Cliffs: Prentice-Hall, 1973), 18–24, 74–9. It is also noteworthy that Elton Mayo, one of the leaders of the Harvard Business School's "human factors" approach was a co-founder of the Fatigue Lab with L.J. (Lawrence) Henderson.

52 Ibid., 3; see also 52, 106–17.

53 In their studies of fitness levels, the Lab reached identical conclusions as Christensen regarding fitness, workload, and the improvement of $VO_{2\ MAX}$ (see ibid., 116). The Lab's study of the impact of lactic acid on exercise and the mechanisms and importance for actively removing it from the muscle – "the removal of lactate could be accelerated if the subject continued working at a low metabolic level rather than resting" – were decades ahead of their application in athletic training; see ibid., 108–12.

54 See ibid., 104–22; see also 122–6 for a bibliography of Lab papers published on exercise. Although elite athletic performance was not a focus of the Fatigue Lab, general fitness was an interest. It was the Lab that developed the well-known Harvard Step Test as a simple, inexpensive and efficient means of assessing general fitness and was used by some coaches to measure fitness levels of their athletes.

55 Walter Cannon, *The Wisdom of the Body* (New York: W.W. Norton and Company, 1932), 25, see also vii–viii, 19–26 and Hildenbrandt, "Milon, Marx und Muskelpille," 278.

56 Cited in Wrynn, "The Grand Tour," 7.

57 George Stafford and Ray Duncan, *Physical Conditioning: Exercises for Sports and Healthful Living* (New York: A.S. Barnes and Company, 1942).

58 Ibid., 2.

59 See Steinhaus, "Chronic Effects of Exercise," 104 regarding the specificity of physiological adaptation to exercise and Olympic athletes.

60 Stafford and Duncan, *Physical Conditioning*, 11.

61 Ibid., 11–12.

62 Ibid., 15.

63 See, for example, Tudor Bompa, *Periodization: Theory and Methodology of Training*, fourth edition (Champaign, Il.: Human Kinetics, 1999), 27–52 and William Kraemer and Ana Gómez, "Establishing a Solid Fitness Base," in Bill Foran, ed., *High-Performance Sports Conditioning* (Windsor: Human Kinetics Press, 2001), 3–18.

64 Among the topics covered in Steinhaus, "Chronic Effects of Exercise," 103–40, are exercise specificity, overload, cardiac output, blood composition, vital capacity and respiration, and exercise metabolism. "Exercise," Steinhaus concludes,

> increases the capacity of the organism to perform work. Lindhard recognizes improvements in *strength*, in *endurance*, and in *sureness or perfection* of movement and attributes them *in general* to changes in the muscular system, respiro-circulatory system, and nervous systems, respectively. Further analysis discloses an interlocking of responsibilities.
>
> Ibid., 137; emphases in original

65 See George Bresnahan and Waid Wright Tuttle, *Track and Field Athletics*, second edition (St. Louis: C.V. Mosby Company, 1947); Dean Cromwell and Al Wesson, *Championship Technique in Track and Field*, Olympic Games Edition (Toronto: McGraw-Hill Book Company, 1949); and V-Five Association of America, *Track and Field*, revised edition (Annapolis, Maryland: United States Naval Institute, 1950).

66 Bresnahan and Tuttle, *Track and Field Athletics*, 20.

67 Ibid., 21.

68 Ibid., 31.

69 Ibid., 38–51.

70 Cromwell and Wesson, *Championship Technique*, 14, see 3–14 for their discussion of track success based on national conditions and traditions.

71 Ibid., 21, 24, 28.

72 V-Five Association of America, *Track and Field*, ix, 6.

73 Ibid., 8–9, see also "Basis of Conditioning," 14–17.

74 Roger Bannister, "The Meaning of Athletic Performance," in Ernst Jokl and Emanuel Simon, eds, *International Research in Sport and Physical Education* (Springfield, Il.: Charles C. Thomas Publishers, 1964), 71–2.

75 Ibid., 72–3.

76 Adolf Henning Frucht and Ernst Jokl, "The Future of Athletic Records," in *International Research in Sport and Physical Education*, 436.

77 Calvin Shulman, "Middle-Distance Specialists Committed to Chasing that Elusive Dream," (May 4, 2004), http://www.timesonline.co.uk/article/0,,13849-1097363,00.html.

78 See Neal Bascomb, *The Perfect Mile: Three Athletes, One Goal, and Less Than Four Minutes to Achieve It* (Boston and New York: Houghton Mifflin, 2004), 91. See also 90–4 concerning the oxygen deprivation experiments Bannister performed on himself and others.

79 John Bale, *Roger Bannister and the Four-Minute Mile* (London and New York: Routledge, 2004), 23–4, 54–5, 112–13.

80 John Fair, "Bob Hoffman, the York Barbell Company, and the Golden Age of American Weightlifting, 1945–1960," *Journal of Sport History* 14:2 (1987), 180.

81 John Ziegler, "Forward," in Goldman, *Death in the Locker Room*, 1–3; Goldman, *Death in the Locker Room*, 94.

82 Donna Haraway, "The Biological Enterprise: Sex, Mind and Profit from Human Engineering to Sociobiology," *Radical History Review* (Summer, 1979), 206–37.

83 Joseph Stalin, *Dialectical and Historical Materialism* (London: Lawrence and Wishart, 1943).

84 Friedrich Engels, *Dialectics of Nature* (New York: International Publishers, 1940).

85 See Trofim Lysenko, *Heredity and its Variability* (New York: Kings Crown Press, 1946) and Helena Sheehan, *Marxism and the Philosophy of Science: A Critical History* (Atlantic High Lands, NJ: Humanities Press, 1985).

86 See Paul E. Nowacki, "Vergangenheit, Gegenwart und Zukunft der deutschen Sportmedizin [Past, Present and Future of German Sport Medicine]," presented at the 37th German Congress for Sports Medicine and Prevention, Rotenburg, (September 28, 2001), http://www.uni-duesseldorf.de/awmf/fg/dksp/dksppr15.htm and http://www.dgsp.de/ueber_dgsp/historie/.

87 Per-Olaf Åstrand and Kaare Rodahl, *Textbook of Work Physiology* (Toronto: McGraw-Hill Book Company, 1970) see especially 375–430; Albert Taylor, *The Scientific Aspects of Sports Training* (Springfield, Illinois: Charles C. Thomas, 1975), especially ix, 5–45.

88 See http://www.csep.ca.

89 See http://www.casm-acms.org.

90 See http://www.dvs-sportwissenschaft.de.

91 See ibid., and http://www.hofmann-verlag.de/sw/index.php.

92 See http://journal.but.swi.uni-saarland.de/index.asp?lang=1.

93 Patrick Mignon, "The Tour de France and the Doping Issue," in Hugh Dauncey and Geoff Hare, eds, *The Tour de France, 1903–2003* (London: Frank Cass, 2003), 232.

94 Ibid., 233.

95 A number of nations, largely for fiscal reasons, have raised their qualifying standards above the IOC's minimum to ensure that they have "weed[ed] out the contenders from the pretenders." Canada, for example, sent only athletes ranked among the top 12 in the world to the 2004 Olympics. As a result, Nicole Stevenson, Canada's best marathoner, missed the marquee event in Athens even though the IAAF strongly encouraged countries to send more marathoners than they might normally. Canada's team was its smallest in decades; see Dave Feschuk, "Olympic Committee Raises Bar Impossibly High," *Toronto Star* (July 21, 2004), C3. See also Chapter Five, note 39, below.

Chapter 4

1 In many ways, the West German sport system served as the blueprint for the Canadian, Australian, and British sport systems that emerged in the 1970s, 1980s, and the 1990s respectively. Attempts to centralize and rationalize the American high-performance sport system in the 1980s drew from the experiences of the FRG, Canada and Australia, but had to blend those with the well-entrenched sport delivery system that already existed within the American educational system and, to a lesser extent, the local club or local sport organizations.

2 This view is shared by Becker *et al.*, who cite Niethammer's work as the guiding principle that directed their study of the development of sport in the Soviet Occupied Sector of Germany. "The history of the society in the GDR," Niethammer wrote,

> cannot be derived from its system alone; rather it must also take into account its specific situation as a successor society to the Third Reich, as the lost part of the division of Germany, and as the outpost of Soviet imperialism.
>
> Cited in Christian Becker, Wolfgang Buss, Sven Güldenpfenning, Arnd Krüger, Wolf-Dieter Mattausch, Lorenz Peiffer and Günther Wonneberger, "Die Vor- und Frühentwicklung der Sportentwicklung in der SBZ/DDR (1945–1956) [The Pre- and Early Development of Sport Development in the Soviet Occupied Zone/German Democratic Republic (1945–1956)]," *Bundesinstitut für Sportwissenschaft Jahrbuch 1998* (Karlsruhe: Präzis-Druck GmbH, 1999), 197

3 See Adolf Hitler, *Mein Kampf* [My Struggle], trans. Alvin Johnson (New York: Reynal and Hitchcock, 1939), 933–67, 389–455. Colonel-General von Richthofen, commander of the 4th Airfleet, noted in his diary in January 1943,

> I am again reading the chapter in [*Mein*] *Kampf* about Russian and eastern policies. Still very interesting and provides answers for almost all questions also in the present situation. Will take care to emphasize these arguments more strongly to the troops in the whole area.
>
> Cited in Omer Bartov, *Hitler's Army: Soldiers, Nazis, and War in the Third Reich* (New York: Oxford University Press, 1991), 132

4 Reinhard Rürup, ed., *Der Krieg gegen die Sowjetunion, 1941–1945: Eine Dokumentation zum 50. Jahrestag des Überfalls auf die Sowjetunion* [The War Against the Soviet Union, 1941–1945: Documentation on the 50th Anniversary of the Attack on the Soviet Union] (Berlin: Argon Publishers, 1991), 7; see also Omer Bartov, *Hitler's Army: Soldiers, Nazis, and War in the Third Reich* (New York: Oxford University Press, 1991), 120–30 and Anthony Beevor, *Stalingrad: The Fateful Siege, 1942–1943* (Toronto: Penguin Books, 1999), 15.

5 See Beevor, *Stalingrad*, 33–40.

6 The incalculable human tragedy, and some of the main reasons for it, that resulted from the transformation of the Russian campaign from Blitzkrieg into total war is clearly seen in Bartov, *Hitler's Army*, 28 and passim. See also Rürup, *Der Krieg gegen die Sowjetunion* and Omer Bartov, "Savage War: German Warfare and Moral Choices in World War II," and "From Blitzkrieg to Total War: Image and Historiography," *Germany's War and the Holocaust: Disputed Histories* (Ithaca: Cornell University Press, 2003), 3–32, 33–78.

7 Cited in, Beevor, *Stalingrad*, 379.

8 In the battle of Thermopylae (479 BC), a Greek army of 10,000 – including 300 Spartans – met a massive Persian army led by Xerxes. Drawing the Persians into a narrow pass, the Greeks inflicted enormous casualties until a Greek traitor, Ephialtes, showed Xerxes an alternate route around the pass. Leonidas could only withdraw the bulk of the Greek army by leaving the 300 Spartans – fighting to the last man – to hold off the Persians. By 480 BC, the Persians had moved into central Greece and overtaken Athens. Goering probably foreshadowed more than he had intended in his analogy.

9 Beevor, *Stalingrad*, 380.

10 See Rürup, *Der Krieg gegen die Sowjetunion*, 198; Bartov, *Hitler's Army*, 83. *Der Krieg gegen die Sowjetunion* presents vivid documentation of key aspects of the war in the Soviet Union including material on the Nazis' demonization of the Slavic people (11–30), the Nazis' oppressive occupation of eastern Europe and the USSR (80–139), the lives of German and Soviet soldiers throughout the campaign (155–67), and life in

Germany during the war (181–217). Data on war casualties have been systematically organized by Matthew White, "Source List and Detailed Death Tolls for the Twentieth Century Hemoclysm," http://users.erols.com/mwhite28/warstat1.htm#Second.

11 The full text of the speech may be found at http://www.nazi-lauck-nsdapao.com/ger-bon.htm (see Joseph Goebbels, Wollt Ihr den totalen Krieg? See also Iring Fetscher, *Joseph Goebbels im Berliner Sportpalast 1943* [Joseph Goebbels in the Berlin Sports Palace 1943] (Berlin: Europäische Verlagsanstalt, 1998). The accompanying CD was used in presenting the quotation. Albert Speer, *Erinnerungen* [Memoirs] (Berlin: Verlag Ullstein, 1969), 269, recalls that "not since Hitler's most successful public speeches had I experienced such an effectively fanaticized audience. Did you notice'? [Goebbels said to Speer] 'They reacted to even the slightest nuance and applauded at exactly the right spots. It was the best politically schooled public that one could find in Germany'." Wolfgang Richardt, "Joseph Goebbels: Rede im Berliner Sportpalast am 18. Februar 1943 [Joseph Goebbels' Speech at the Berlin Sports Palace on February 18, 1943]," http://www.wolfgang.richardt.info/2–4.htm, provides an excellent analysis of the rhetorical devices Goebbels employed in this speech.

12 See David Goldhagen, *Hitler's Willing Executioners: Ordinary Germans and the Holocaust* (New York: Knopf, 1996) and Christopher Browning, *Ordinary Men: Reserve Police Battalion 101 and the Final Solution in Poland* (New York: Harper Collins, 1992). On DORA and the use of slave labor in building German rockets, see Speer, *Erinnerungen*, 375–86; Klaus Fischer, *Nazi Germany: A New History* (New York: Continuum Publishing Company, 1995), 529–35; William Shirer, *The Rise and Fall of the Third Reich* (Greenwich, Conn.: Fawcett Publications, 1959), 1234–92.

13 The fear was well placed; Anthony Beevor, *The Fall of Berlin 1945* (Toronto: Penguin Books, 2002), 27–32,426–7, recounts some of the brutal treatment women – not just German women – suffered at the hands of the advancing Soviet forces. See also Anonymous, *A Woman in Berlin: Eight Weeks in the Conquered City*, trans. Philip Boehm (New York: Henry Holt and Company, 2005).

14 Beevor, *The Fall of Berlin*, 41–2.

15 Bartov, *Hitler's Army*, 76. Beevor, in *The Fall of Berlin*, 22–3, 27 recounts several egregious acts of destruction carried out by the Nazis. "Nothing was left but ruins and ashes covered by snow. Badly starved and exhausted residents" were all that was left of Warsaw following its levelling on January 17, 1945. See Speer, *Erinnerungen*, 409–15 on Hitler's "scorched earth" policy. Consistent with the Nazi Weltanscahauung, Speer was more concerned with, and attempted to disrupt, Hitler's plans in the western regions of Germany and did nothing to stop the destruction in the east.

16 Bartov, *Hitler's Army*, 94–5.

17 See Beevor, *The Fall of Berlin*, 4–6.

18 William R. Smyser, *From Yalta to Berlin* (New York: St. Martin's Press, 1999), 6–7.

19 The nine member "Ulbricht Group" consisted of Ulbricht, Richard Gyptner, who became head of the Central Secretariat of the Socialist Unity Party, Otto Winzer, an emotionless Stalinist who remorselessly carried through every directive on becoming head of the press and radio department in the Central Secretariat of the SED, Hans Mahle, who eventually managed all radio stations in the Soviet Sector of Occupation, Gustav Gundelach, President of the Central Directorate of Labour and Social Welfare in the Soviet Sector and later a member of the West German Bundestag as Communist Party Deputy, Karl Maron, the first Deputy Lord Mayor of Berlin and later deputy editor-in-chief of the Socialist Unity Party's newspaper, *Neues Deutschland*, Walter Koppe, Vice-Chairman of the German Communist Party in Berlin, Fritz Erpenbeck, a writer with no specific assignment, and Wolfgang Leonhard, the youngest member, who had grown up inside the Soviet Union. See Wolfgang Leonhard, *Die Revolution entlässt ihre Kinder* [The Revolution Dismisses its Children] (Cologne: Kiepenheuer and Witsch, 1955), 412–18.

20 See Smyser, *From Yalta to Berlin*, 27–56.

21 Clausewitz's original statement is that "war is not merely an act of policy but a true political instrument, a continuation of political intercourse, carried on with other means. What remains peculiar to war is simply the peculiar nature of its means" Carl von Clausewitz, *On War*, trans. M. Howard and P. Paret (Princeton, NJ: Princeton University Press, 1976), 87. It was the horrendous "peculiarity" of war from 1939–45 in general, but most particularly in the east, that created the inversion of Clausewitz's maxim.

22 See Office of the Chief of Staff, Supreme Headquarters, Allied Expeditionary Force, *Handbook for Military Government in Germany Prior to Defeat or Surrender* (1944), http://www-cgsc.army.mil/carl/download/books/handbkmilgov.pdf.

23 See Gerd Weißpfening, "Der Neuaufbau des Sports in Westdeutschland bis zur Gründung des Deutschen Sportbundes [The Rebuilding of Sport in West Germany up to the Founding of the German Sport Association]," in Horst Ueberhorst, ed., *Geschichte der Leibesübungen* [History of Physical Education] 3/2 (Berlin: Bartels and Wernitz, 1972), 765. Not all sports had the simple requirements of soccer, so took longer to emerge – see Weißpfening's discussion of gymnastics (765–6).

24 As an example of the French reluctance to grant permission for sports clubs to form in their Sector, Franz Nitsch, "'Berlin ist einer Bresche wert': Sportentwicklung unter geteilter Kontrolle [Berlin Will Lead the Way: Sport Development under Divided Control]," in Hartmut Becker and Giselher Spitzer, eds, *Die Gründerjahre des Deutschen Sportbund* [The Founding Years of the German Sport Association] (Vol. 1) (Schorndorf: Hofmann Verlag, 1990), 106–7, notes that even in 1947, the Americans approved 45 sports clubs in Berlin while the French only approved one single tennis club.

25 See Wolfgang Buss, "Sport und Besatzungspolitik [Sport and Occupation Politics]," in Hartmut Becker and Giselher Spitzer, eds, *Die Gründerjahren des Deutschen Sportbund* [The Founding Years of the German Sport Association] (Vol. 2) (Schorndorf: Hofmann Verlag, 1991), 9–10.

26 Ibid., 11.

27 Christian Becker *et al.*, "Die Vor- und Frühentwicklung der Sportentwicklung in der SBZ/DDR," 197–207.

28 "The tremendous success of the Berlin Games" Coubertin noted in an interview with the French Press, "has served the Olympic Idea beautifully." Cited in Hans Joachim Teichler, "Coubertin und das Dritte Reich: Zur Vorgeschichte eines unveröffentlichten Coubertin-Briefs an Hitler aud dem Jahr 1937 [Coubertin and the Third Reich: On the Background of an Unpublished Coubertin Letter to Hitler in 1937]," *Sportwissenschaft* 12 (1982), 35. See also Hajo Bernett, "Die innenpolitische Taktik des nationalsozialistischen Reichssportführers. Analysen eines Schlüsseldokuments [The Inner Political Tactics of the National Socialist Reich's Sport Officer: Analyses of a Key Document]," *Stadion* 1 (1975), 140–78.

29 Christine Peyton, "Sportstadt Berlin [Sport-City Berlin]," in Gertrud Pfister and Gerd Steins, eds, *Sport in Berlin: Vom Ritterturnier zum Stadtmarathon* [Sport in Berlin: From Jousting Tournaments to the City Marathon] (Berlin: Verlag Forum für Sportgeschichte, 1987), 96–123; Franz Nitsch, "Berlin is einer Bresche wert," 99.

30 Ibid., 100–3.

31 See Wolfgang Buss, "Sport und Besatzungspolitik," 5–11.

32 See *Handbook for Military Government*, 195–7 for the western Allies' policies on education.

33 See Control Council Directive Number 23, "Limitation and Demilitarization of Sport in Germany," http://www.loc.gov/rr/frd/Military_Law/Enactments/ 01LAW06.pdf, 140. The Allies had engaged in some earlier *ad hoc* regulation of sport, but these regulations were not at all comprehensive; see, for example, "Anweisung Nr. 2 der brit. MilReg., Erziehungskontrolle: 'Physical Training', July 18, 1945 [Instruction No. 2 of the British Military Government, Control of Education: 'Physical Training', July 18, 1945]," "Anordnung Nr. 221 der Alliierten

Kommandantur Berlin: 'Betrifft: Sport-Organisationen in Berlin', 19. Nov. 1945 [Order No. 221 of the Allied Commander Berlin: 'Concerning: Sport organizations in Berlin,' Nov. 19, 1945]," "Anweisung Nr. 17 der brit. MilReg., IA & C Division: 'Sportvereine und Versammlungen', 3. Dez. 1945 [Instruction No. 17 of the British Military Government, IA & C Division: 'Sport Associations and Meetings,' Dec. 3, 1945]," in. Lorenz Peiffer, ed., *Die erstrittene Einheit: Von der ADS zum DSB (1948–1950). Bericht der 2. Hoyaer Tagung zur Entwicklung des Nachkriegssports in Deutschland* [The Disputatious Unity. From the ADS to the German Sport Association (1948–1950). Reports from the Second Hoya Seminar on the Development of Post-War Sport in Gemany] (Duderstadt: Mecke 1989), 87–150. The Allies' regulations have also been published at http://www.rrz.uni-hamburg.de/sport/infodoc/digitale publikationen/tiedemann/AlliierteRechtsdokumente44–50.pdf.

34 Control Council Directive Number 23, 140–1.

35 Ibid., 141.

36 While the American and British Sectors permitted the Deutscher Arbeitsausschuß Turnen [German Turner Working Committee] to exist after September 1947, the Turners were not granted any official status in the French Sector. It was not until September 2, 1950 that the Deutsche Turner-Bund [German Gymnastics Federation] was officially founded in post-war West Germany – see also Gerd Weißpfening, "Der Neuaufbau des Sports in Westdeutschland," 770–1.

37 See Deutscher Sportbund, ed., *Sport in Deutschland* [Sport in Germany], http://www. dsb.de/fileadmin/fm-dsb/arbeitsfelder/wiss-ges/Dateien/Sport_in_Deutschland.pdf, 5.

38 See Ommo Grupe, "Der neue Weg im deutschen Sport: Über Sinn und Organisation des Sports [The New Direction in Geman Sport: On the Basic Ideas and Organization of Sport]," in *Die Gründerjahre* (Vol. 1), 17–18.

39 The following articles show the spectrum of influence that the western Allies exerted in the shaping of post-war sport in their respective Sectors: Julius Bohus, "Die Entwicklung in der amerikanischen Zone: München [Development in the American Sector: Munich];" Reiner Fricke, "Paul Keller (1884–1957);" Claus Tiedemann, "Die Entwicklung in der britischen Zone: Hamburg [Development in the British Zone: Hamburg];" Michael Joho, "Hamburger Sportverein gegen Lorbeer 06 – Bürgerlicher und Arbeiter-Fußball in Hamburg 1945 [Hamburg Sport Association Versus Lorbeer 06 – Bourgois and Worker Football in Hamburg];" and Gabi Langen and Giselher Spitzer, "Köln [Cologne]" in *Die Gründerjahre* (Vol. 2), 13–20, 21–24, 28–32, 42–8.

40 See Gerd Weißpfening, "Der Neuaufbau des Sports in Westdeutschland," 766–73.

41 A good example of such an Einheitsverband is the Volkssportverband Westfalen (Westphalia's People's Sport Association), organized by Hugo Grömmer, who had been involved with the Worker Sport Movement prior to the war and would play a prominent role in the debates and decisions that shaped sport in post-war Germany.

42 To take a single example, the Landessportbund Niedersachsen (Niedersachsen Provincial Sport Association) has 2.9 million members belonging to more than 9,500 sport clubs. LSB Niedersachsen is comprised of 4 Bezirkssportbünde which are made up of 48 Kreis- und Stadtsportbünde. There are an additional 57 Landesfachverbände (Single Sport Provincial Sport Associations). Sports clubs hold membership in the Kreis- und Stadtsportbünde as well as the Landesfachverbände; see http://www.lsb-niedersachsen.de/.

43 Gerd Weißpfening, "Der Neuaufbau des Sports in Westdeutschland," 766–7; see also the BLSV website, http://www.blsv.de/blsv/.

44 In response to criticisms made at a regional sport meeting in November 1946 that the military government was too restrictive in the building of a sport system, John Dixon replied that

Sports officers can approve regional sport associations [Bezirkssportverbände]. I will do all I can to facilitate the approval of individual sports clubs ... let's wait until the approval of the individual clubs is complete, then everything must be built from the bottom up. The reason for the unevenness is that the clubs have still not been approved.

Cited in German in Gerd Weißpfening, "Der Neuaufbau des Sports in Westdeutschland," note 47, 787.

45 Go to "Geschichte [History]" under "Wer wir sind [Who we are]," http://www.hamburger-sportbund.de/.

46 See, for example, the structure of Landessportbund Niedersachsen, http://www.lsb-niedersachsen.de/; the Landessportbund Hessen, http://www.landessportbund-hessen.de/de/ueberuns/struktur/; the Landessportbund Sachsen-Anhalt (under "Vereinsinformationssystem [Association Information System]" go to "Strukturen des Sports [Sport Structure] " under "Management"), http://www.lsb-sachsen-anhalt.de/o.red.c/home.php; or the Bayerischer Landes-Sport Verband (under "Verband"), http://www.blsv.de/blsv/.

47 Following 1990, there are now 16 Landessportbünde (including Landessportbund Berlin) – see Deutscher Sportbund, *Sport in Deutschland*, 13–14.

48 Deutscher Sportbund, *Sport in Deutschland*, 15. In 1952, in recognition of sport history in Germany, a proposal to change the name of the DSB to the Deutscher Turn- und Sportbund was defeated 53 to 31. The first sentence of the DSB's constitution was changed to read, "The DSB is a free association of the German Turner and Sport Associations and sport institutions." See Deutscher Sportbund, *Sport in Deutschland*, 16.

49 Gerd Weißpfening, "Der Neuaufbau des Sports in Westdeutschland," 775; see 773–6.

50 See Deutscher Sportbund, "Organisation des Sport in der Bundesrepublik Deutschland [Organization of Sport in the Federal Republic of Germany]," http://www.dsb.de/fileadmin/fm-dsb/arbeitsfelder/wiss-ges/Dateien/Organisation_des_Sports_in_Deutschland.pdf. At the time of its formation, there were 19,874 clubs comprised of 3.2 million members; in 2001 26.8 million members in 88,531 clubs (*Sport in Deutschland*, 77). It is due to the term Spitzenverbände that one often finds the term Spitzensport (top sport) used instead of Hochleistungssport (high-performance sport). Independent from Germany's National Olympic Committee, the Spitzenverbände oversee interprovincial level competitions, world and European championship teams, determine the rankings of German athletes and work with Stiftung DSH.

51 The Culture Committee of the Party's Executive Committee had a Sport Commission that included, among others, Adolf Buck, of the pre-War Central Commission for Workers' Sport, and Helmut Behrendt, from the Association for Red Sport Unity. Others involved with sport development in the SBZ who had been involved with the Worker Sport were Robert Riedel, Herbert Mank, Rudolf Friedrich, Erich Riedeberger, Joseph Schopp and Oskar Zimmermann – see Günther Wonneberger, "Sport im gesellschaftlichen Umbruch der Nachkriegszeit in der Sowjetischen Besatzungszone Deutschlands (1945–1949) [Sport during the Social Upheaval of the Post-War Period in the Soviet Occupied Zone of Gemany]," in André Gounot, Toni Niewerth and Gertrud Pfister, eds, *Spiele der Welt im Spannungsfeld von Tradition und Moderne* [Games of the World and the Tension between Tradition and Modernity] (Vol. 2), (St. Augustin: Academic Verlag, 1996), 209–14.

52 The Socialist Unity Party was established in 1946 by the forced amalgamation of the Communist Party of Germany and the Social Democratic Party. Documents released from the Soviet archives in the 1990s indicate the tension that existed because of this merger: the extant members of the German Communist Party felt that they, alone, should have become the central ruling authority in Germany. See, for example, Major General Sergei Tiulpanov's "Report at the Meeting of the Commission of the Central Committee of the CPSU to Evaluate the Activities of the Propaganda Administration of SVAG [Soviet Military Administration in Germany]," stenographic report

(September 16, 1946), http://www.wilsoncenter.org/index.cfm?topic_id=1409&fuse action=library.document&id=251.

53 See Gerald Carr, "The Involvement of Politics in the Sporting Relationships of East and West Germany, 1945–1972," *Journal of Sport History* 7:1 (1980), 40–1. See also Waldemar Borde, "Die Aufgaben unserer Demokratischen Sportbewegung [The Mission of our Democratic Sport Movement]," *Deutsches Sport-Echo* [German Sport Echo] (October, 1948), 3; Günther Wonneberger, *Die Körperkultur in Deutschland von 1945 bis 1961* [Physical Culture in Germany from 1945 to 1961] (East Berlin: Sportverlag, 1967).

54 Cited in Gerald Carr, "Involvement of Politics in the Sporting Relationships of East and West Germany," 41.

55 Ommo Grupe, "Der neue Weg im deutschen Sport: Über Sinn und Organisation des Sports [The New Path in German Sport: About Meaning and Organization of Sport]," in Hartmut Becker, Wolfgang Buss, Franz Nitsch and Giselher Spitzer, eds, *Die Gründerjahre des deutschen Sportbundes: Wege aus der Not zur Einheit* [The Founding Years of the German Sports Federation: Paths from Need to Unity] (Schorndorf: Karl Hofmann, 1990), 17–20. See also Franz Nitsch, "Traditionslinien und Brüche: Stationen der Sportentwicklung nach dem Zweiten Weltkreig [Traditions and Breaks: Stations in Sport Development in the post World War II Period]," in *Die Gründerjahre des deutschen Sportbundes*, 29–64.

Chapter 5

1 See George Orwell, *Animal Farm* (Harmondsworth, Middlesex: Penguin Books, 1945), 5–23.

2 See Giselher Spitzer, Hans Joachim Teichler, and Klaus Reinartz, eds, "Das Staatliche Komitee für Körperkultur und Sport übernimmt die wesentlichen Funktionen des Sportausschusses (1952) [The State Committee for Physical Culture and Sport Takes Over the Essential Functions of the Sport Committee (1952)]," *Schlüsseldokumente zum DDR-Sport. Ein sporthistorischer Überblick in Originalquellen. Schriftenreihe: Sportentwicklungen in Deutschland* [Key Documents in GDR Sport. A Historical Overview of Sport through Original Sources: Sport Development in Germany] (Vol. 4) (Aachen: Meyer & Meyer Verlag, 1998), 38–43.

3 Ibid., 40.

4 Ibid., 41.

5 See I. Boywitt, "Kindersportschulen – auch für unsere Jungen und Mädchen [Children's Sport Schools – Also for Our Boys and Girls]," *Körpererziehung in der Schule* [Physical Education in Schools] 4 (1952). By 1959, there were 23 Children and Youth Sport Schools in the GDR.

6 At the 1956 Olympic Winter Games in Cortina d'Empezzo, the East Germans provided 18 team members; the West Germans provided 58. At the 1956 Summer Olympic Games in Melbourne, the East Germans provided 37 team members, the West Germans 138. See Gerald Carr, "The Involvement of Politics in the Sporting Relationships of East and West Germany, 1945–1972," *Journal of Sport History* 7:1 (1980), 27. Combined German teams took part in the 1956, 1960 and 1964 Summer and Winter Games; see Deutscher Sportbund, ed., *Sport in Deutschland* [Sport in Germany], http://www.dsb.de/ fileadmin/fm-dsb/arbeitsfelder/wiss-ges/Dateien/Sport_in_Deutschland.pdf, 5.

7 See Hans-Joachim Teichler, ed., "Dokument 39: 'Entwicklung der Kinder- und Jugendsportschulen der DDR zu Spezialschulen des sportlichen Nachwuchses, 06.06.1963 [Document 39: 'Development of Children and Youth School of the German Democratic Republic to Special Schools for Developing Athletes]'," *Die Sportbeschlüsse des Politbüros: Eine Studie zum Verhältnis von SED und Sport mit einem Gesamtverzeichnis und Dokumentation ausgewählter Beschlüsse* [The Polit Bureau's Sport Resolutions: A Study of the Relationship Between the Socialist Unity Party and Sport

with a Complete Listing and Documentation of Selected Resolutions] (Köln: Sport und Buch Strauß, 2002), 432–47.

8 Horst Röder, *Von der 1. zur 3. Förderstufe* [From the First to the Third Stage of Development], http://www.sport-ddr-roeder.de/frame10.htm, cites "Maßnahmen zur Entwicklung der Kinder- und Jugendsportschulen der DDR zu Spezialschulen des sportlichen Nachwuchses. Vorlage an das Sekretariat des ZK der SED vom 6.6.1963 [Measures for the Development of Elementary and Intermediate Level Schools of the GDR to Special Schools for the Athletically Talented. A Bill for the Secretariat of the Central Committee of the SED, June 6, 1963]," 50–65.

9 Röder, *Von der 1. zur 3. Förderstufe,* cites "Beschluß des Politbüros der SED vom 10.8.1965 über die 'Weitere Entwicklung des Leistungssports bis 1972' [Resolution of the Politbureau of the SED on August 10, 1965 concerning the 'Further Development of High-Performance Sport into 1972']," 16.

10 Röder, *Von der 1. zur 3. Förderstufe,* cites "Information über die Durchführung des Beschlusses vom 6.6.1963 vor der LSK der DDR," internes Material vom 5.5.1969 ["Information on the Execution of the Resolution of June 6, 1963 by the LSK of the GDR," internal material from May 5, 1969]. According to Röder, the GDR had 69,000 young athletes training in 1,820 training centers by 1974. There were another 820 training support centers in which additional children and youths were cared for athletically. For 22 different sports, there were 121 regional training centers although the system was run largely on the basis of voluntary labor – the more than 8,000 training leaders were either volunteers or part-time coaches.

11 Cited in Asmuss Burkhard, "Die XX. Olympischen Sommerspiele in München 1972 [The 20th Olympic Summer Games in Munich, 1972]," German Historical Museum, http://www.dhm.de/~jarmer/olympiaheft/olympi11.htm.

12 Gesellschaft zur Förderung des olympischen Gedankens in der DDR, ed., *Spiele der XX. Olympiade, München 1972* [Games of the 20th Olympiad, Munich 1972] (East Berlin: GDR, 1972), 16.

13 Cited in Peter Kühnst, "Sportführer Manfred Ewald – Eine mentalitäsgeschichtliche Annärung zum Tod des ehemaligen DDR-Sportpraesidenten [An Attempt to Understand the Death of the Former DDR Sport President in Terms of the History of Mentalities]," *Das Sportgespräch* [Sport Talk], DeutschlandRadio, Berlin [German Radio, Berlin] (February 27, 2002), http://www.dradio.de/cgi-bin/es/neu-sport/27.html.

14 Franke and Berendonk, "Hormonal Doping and Androgenization of Athletes," identify K-H Bauersfeld, J. Olek, H. Meißner, D. Hannemann, and J. Spenke, "Analyse des Einsatzes u[nterstützende] M[ittel] in den leichtathletischen Wurf-/Stoßdisziplinen und Versuch trainingsmethodischer Abteilungen und Verallgemeinerungen [Analysis of the Use of 'Supporting Means' in Track and Field Throwing and Putting Disciplines and An Assay of the Methods of Training Divisions and Generalizations]," Scientific Report, German Athletic Association (DVfL) of the GDR, Science Center of the DVfL, 1973, as the source for the code term "unterstützende Mittel" or "u.M" for anabolic steroids. "Under u.M.," the authors wrote in footnote 1, page 3, "we refer exclusively to anabolic steroids."

15 See Werner Franke and Brigitte Berendonk, "Hormonal Doping and Androgenization of Athletes: a Secret Program of the German Democratic Republic Government," *Clinical Chemistry* 43:7 (1997), 1264. To substantiate the widespread usage claim, Franke and Berendonk cite Gary Wader and Brian Hainline, *Drugs and the Athlete* (Philadelphia: FA Davis Co., 1989), Charles Yesalis, ed., *Anabolic Steroids in Sport and Exercise* (Champaign, Il.: Human Kinetics Publishers, 1993), Joseph Biden, "Steroids in Amateur and Professional Sports – the Medical and Social Costs of Steroid Abuse," *US Senate Committee on the Judiciary Hearing,* J101–102 (Washington, DC: Government Printing Office, 1990), D.L. Breo, "Of MDs and Muscles – Lessons from Two 'Retired Steroid Doctors'," *Journal of the American Medical Association* 263 (1990), 1697–705, Charles Dubin, *Commission of Inquiry Into the Use of Drugs and Banned Practices Intended*

to *Increase Athletic Performance* (Ottawa: Canadian Government Publishing Centre, 1990), and Robert Voy, *Drugs, Sport, and Politics* (Champaign, Il.: Leisure Press, 1991). In footnotes 1 through 6, Franke and Berendonk also cite specific court cases involving drug use in sport. These include the 1984 conviction of Olympic weightlifting champion Karl-Heinz Radschinsky for the large-scale trafficking of prescription drugs, including 220,000 tablets of anabolic steroids, Jochen Spilker, national coach for the 200- and 400-meter women's sprints who was convicted in 1994 for using Anavar (oxandrolone) on his athletes, Karlheinz Steinmetz, sentenced in 1994 for steroid use and substituting his urine for that of one of his throwers in a doping control test; German shot-put champion Kalman Konya, sentenced to prison, with probation, for perjury concerning anabolic steroid use. See also Chapter One for additional evidence that the use of performance-enhancing substances was widespread by the 1960s.

16 See John Hoberman, "A Conspiracy So Vast: The Politics of Doping," *Mortal Engines* (New York: The Free Press, 1992), 229–65; John Hoberman, "Sports Physicians and the Doping Crisis in Elite Sport," *Clinical Journal of Sport Medicine* 202:12 (2002), 203–8; and Ivan Waddington, "The Other Side of Sports Medicine," *Sport, Health and Drugs* (New York: E & F Spon, 2000), 135–52 which demonstrate that as a systematic program involving a number of organizations and individuals, the East Germans were not doing anything that was particularly unique. See also note 43 in Chapter One.

17 Franke and Berendonk, "Hormonal Doping and Androgenization of Athletes," state that documents that became public after the fall of the Berlin Wall in 1989 and in court cases during the 1990s verify that the GDR's male athletes used steroids from the early 1960s and females from 1968. Among the documents they cite are the following, formerly classified, dissertations: W. Schäker, *Verbesserung des zentralnervalen und neuromuskulären Funktionsniveaus sowie sportartspezifischer Leistungen durch Oxytozin* [Improvement of the Level of Function of the Central Nervous and Neuromuscular Systems as well as Sport Specific Performance through Oxytocin], doctoral dissertation submitted to the Faculty for Military Medicine, Ernst-Moritz-Arndt-University, 1980, (the thesis was stored as classified material at Bad Saarow, Military Medical Academy in 1981); H. Riedel, *Zur Wirkung anaboler Steroide auf die sportliche Leistungsentwicklung in den leichtathletischen Sprungdisziplinen* [On the Effect of Anabolic Steroids on the Development of Athletic Performance in the Track and Field Jumping Disciplines], doctoral dissertation submitted to the Military Medical Academy, Bad Saarow, GDR, 1986; G. Rademacher, *Wirkungsvergleich verschiedener anaboler Steroide im Tiermodell und auf ausgewählte Funktionssysteme von Leistungssportlern und Nachweis der Praxisrelevanz der theoretischen und experimentellen Folgerungen* [A Comparison of the Effects of Various Anabolic Steroids in Animal Models and on Selected Functional Systems of High-Performance Athletes and Demonstration of the Practical Relevance of the Theoretical and Experimental Inferences], a doctor of science medical thesis submitted to the Military Medical Academy, Bad Saarow, GDR, 1989.

18 See Franke and Berendonk, "Hormonal Doping and Androgenization of Athletes," 1263.

19 Ibid.

20 John Hoberman, "The Transformation of East German Sport," *Journal of Sport History* 17:1 (1990), 63.

21 Franke and Berendonk, "Hormonal Doping and Androgenization of Athletes," 1265. Contrary to the popular misconception that all athletes in East Germany were forced to take steroids, Franke and Berendonk indicate that all performance-enhancing substances were tightly controlled in the GDR. As a result there was a "black market" for drugs like Oral–Turinabol and other compounds. These substances were in such demand that

the top-cadre athletes and their coaches often wanted more than the allotted dose, and second-class athletes and coaches of minors in so-called training centers (in some cases this involved 9- to 12-year-old boys and girls) tried everything to obtain "the stuff" unofficially on the black market

(1269–70)

22 Ibid., 1267–8.
23 Cited in ibid., 1264; translation supplied by the authors.
24 Ibid., note 4, 1264. Franke and Berendonk indicate that East German officials were aware of the increased viralizing effects of mestanolone on the basis of G. Hobe's work – "Untersuchungen zur Pharmakokinetik und Biotransformation von Oral-Turinabol im Vergleich zur Substanz XII und STS 646 beim Menschen [Investigations into the Pharmokinetic and Bio Transformation of Oral–Turinabol in Comparison to Substance XII and STS 646 [mestanolone] in Humans]," *Abschlußbericht* [Final Report] (Jena: ZI-MET, 1988).
25 See Giselher Spitzer, *Doping in der DDR: Ein historischer Überblick zu einer konspirativen Praxis* [Doping in the GDR: An Historical Overview of a Conspiratorial Practice] (Köln: Sport und Buch Strauß, 1998).
26 Brigitte Berendonk, *Doping Dokumente* [Doping Documents] (Berlin: Springer Verlag, 1991), 474–84 lists 130 studies that were classified as secret in the GDR. See also Franke and Berendonk, "Hormonal Doping and Androgenization of Athletes," 1277–8. Examples of the classified material include E. Kämpfe, *Untersuchungen zur Wirkungsdifferenzierung von Steroidhormonen am Trainingsmodell der unbelasteten und belasteten Ratte* [Investigations on the Differences in Effects of Steroid Hormones on the Model of Training in Stressed and Unstressed Rats], doctoral dissertation submitted to the Military Medical Academy, Bad Saarow, GDR, 1989; A. Müller, *Der Einfluß von Oral-Turinabol und einer Belastung auf das mischfunktionele Monooxygenasesystem der Rattenleber* [The Influence of Oral Turinabol and Stress on the Mixed Function of the Mono-oxygenase System of the Rat Liver], Lecture text, Z.I.M.E.T., (Jena, GDR 1987); W. Schäker, F. Klingberg, and R. Landgraf, "Wirkungsvergleich von Neuropeptiden im eletrophysiologischen Laborexperiment an männlichen Ratten [Comparison of Effects of Neuropeptides in Electrophysiological Laboratory Experiments on Male Rats]," in W. Schäker, ed, *Überprüfung weiterer u.M. auf ihre Anwendbarkeit in Training und Wettkampf* [Examination of Further Support Means Regarding Their Utility in Training and Competition] (F.K.S., Leipzig, 1981), 14–21. Among the studies published after 1989, see A. Müller, K. Hoffmann, E. Kämpfe and A. Barth, "Zur Beeinflussung des misch-funktionalen Monooxygenasesystems der Rattenleber durch koerperliche Belastung und Steroide [On influencing the mixed functions of the mono oxygenase system of the rat liver with bodily loads and steroids]," in R. Häcker and H. De Marees, eds, *Hormonelle Regulation und psychophysische Belastung im Leistungssport* [Hormonal Regulation and Psycho-Physical Stress in High-Performance Sport] (Köln, F.R.G.: Deutscher Aerzte-Verlag, 1991), 71–6. It is important to note that this research is now widely known within the scientific community and even passed on and cited in various internet bulletin boards or discussion groups; see, for example, the Biomch-L News Group run by the International Society of Biomechanics, http://isb.ri.ccf.org/biomch-l/archives/biomch-l-1996–08/00015.html.
27 See Hermann Bausinger, "Etappen des Sports nach den Gründerjahren [Stages of Sport following the Foundation Years]," in Hartmut Becker and Giselher Spitzer, eds, *Die Gründerjahre des Deutschen Sportbund* [The Founding Years of the German Sport Association] (Vol. 2) (Schorndorf: Hofmann Verlag, 1991), 213.
28 Stützpunkt may seem, at first glance, a curious choice of terminology but is, in fact, quite appropriate given the way in which the West Germans envisaged and used training centers. A Stützpunkt is a fulcrum, a starting point, a base, point of support, or a

foothold. Since Stützpunkte were not intended as permanent training sites for athletes, the idea that they were starting points for world-class development, footholds in
the process of complete athlete preparation, and simply bases from which athletes
would develop, was consistent with the image the DSB had to sell to local clubs to gain
the support needed for their implementation.

29 See Karl-Heinz Gieseler, "Das freie Spiel der Kräfte. Spitzensport in der
Industriegesellschaft [The Free Play of Powers. High Performance Sport in Industrial
Society]," in R. Andresen, ed., *Schneller, Höher, Stärker.... Chancen und Risiken im
Leistungssport* [Faster, Higher, Stronger ... Opportunities and Risks in High
Performance Sport] (Niedernhausen: Golling, Schors-Verlag, 1980), 33.

30 See Karl-Heinrich Bette and Friedhelm Neidhart, *Förderungseinrichtungen im
Hochleistungssport* [Mechanisms for the Promotion of High-Performance Sport]
(Schorndorf: Verlag Karl Hofmann, 1985), 52.

31 For complete information on the structure and goals of the DSH, see Stiftung
Deutsche Sporthilfe, "Verfassung der Stiftung Deutscher Sporthilfe [Constitution of
the German Foundation for Sport Assistance]," http://www.sporthilfe.de/doku-
mente/verfassung.pdf; see also the various information buttons on the main website
http://www.sporthilfe.de/; see especially, Förderung [Promotion], Finanzen [Finances],
and Facts and Figures. Summary information is also available on the Ivy Athletic Trust
website at http://www.dhatrust.org/about/exist/deutchsport.asp.

32 Bette and Neidhart, *Förderungseinrichtungen*, 98–101 and the "Events" section of the
DSH website, http://www.sporthilfe.de/.

33 Günter Pelshenke, *Die Stiftung Deutsche Sporthilfe: Die ersten 25 Jahre* [German
Foundation for Sport Assistance: The First 25 Years], 105–6; cited in Bette and
Neidhart, *Förderungseinrichtungen*, note 108, 95.

34 Ibid., 95–6.

35 Ibid. In 2004, 3,800 athletes were supported at a cost of almost 13 million euros.
Throughout its history, DSH has supported some 35,000 athletes at a cost of more than
310 million euros (personal email communication from Hans-Joachim Elz, head of
public relations for Stiftung Deutscher Sporthilfe, May 23, 2004). For a useful summary document of the DSH, see Stiftung Deutscher Sporthilfe, "Die Aufgaben und
Leistungen der Stiftung Deutscher Sporthilfe [The Duty and Performance of the
German Foundation for Sport Assistance]," 2002, http://www.sporthilfe.de/doku-
mente/aufgaben+leistungen.pdf.

36 Deutscher Sportbund, *Sport in Deutschland*, 33.

37 Deutscher Sportbund, *Sport in Deutschland*, 49.

38 See, for example, "'Goldener Plan Ost' fortführen ['Golden Plan East' Carries On],"
Blickpunk Bundestag [Focus on the Federal Parliament], (October 10, 2000),
http://www.bundestag.de/bp/2000/bp0010/0010050b.html; Winfried Hermann,
"*Goldener Plan Ost – Rot-Grün fördert Breitensport in den neuen Ländern [Golden Plan East
– Red–Green Coalition Supports Recreational Sport in the New Provinces],*"
http://www.winnehermann.de/sport/goldener_plan.html; *and* Bundesinnenministerium
des Innern [Federal Ministry of the Interior], "'Goldener Plan Ost' bis 2003 gesichert:
Über 14 Millionen Euro mehr für die Sportstättenförderung in den ostdeutschen
Ländern ['Golden Plan East' Until 2003 Assured: More than 14 Million Euros More for
the Support of Sport Facilities in the East German Provinces]," http://www.kommunal
web.de/news/anzeigen.phtml?category=218&thema=Freizeit+und+Sport. On the original Golden Plan, see Committee of German Physical Educators and the Federal
Institute for Sport Science, ed., "Der 'Goldene Plan,' [Golden Plan]," *Informationen zu
Sportwissenschaft, Sporterziehung, Sportverwaltung in Der Bundesrepublic Deutschland*
[Information on Sport Science, Education, and Administration in the Federal Republic
of Germany] (Schorndorf: Verlag Karl Hofmann, 1986), 21.

39 See, for example, Hermann, "*Goldener Plan Ost*," and Bundesinnenministerium des
Innern, "'Goldener Plan Ost' bis 2003 gesichert."

40 Canada, which developed its own high-performance sport system on a blue print that drew from both the East and West German sport systems, has followed exactly the same route in justifying the allocation of increasing funds to high-performance sport – see, for example, Canadian Olympic Committee, "Canadian Olympic Committee Launches $8.7 Million Excellence Fund," (February 25, 2003), http://www.olympic.ca/EN/organization/news/2003/0225.shtml; Canadian Olympic Committee, "The Evolution of Excellence: A Synopsis of COC Funding Initiatives," http://www.olympic.ca/EN/funding/files/evolution.pdf ; Department of Canadian Heritage, *Towards a Canadian Sport Policy: Report on the National Summit on Sport* (Ottawa, April 27-28, 2001), http://www.canadianheritage.gc.ca/progs/sc/pol/pcs-csp/sum-sum-e.pdf; Department of Canadian Heritage, *The Canadian Sport Policy* (May 24, 2002), http://www.pch.gc.ca/progs/sc/pol/pcs-csp/2003/polsport_e.pdf; see also Sport Canada's commentary on the *Sport Policy*, "The *Canadian Sport Policy* Presents a Powerful Vision for Sport in Canada," http://www.pch.gc.ca/progs/sc/pol/pcs-csp/index_e.cfm. For the United Kingdom, see, for example, Sport England, *Working Together for Sport* (London, July 18, 2000), http://www.sportdevelopment.org.uk/spengsummit.pdf; Department for Culture, Media and Sport, *A Sporting Future for All: The Government's Plan for Sport* (April 5, 2000), http://www.culture.gov.uk/NR/rdonlyres/A63A61D4-6F22-401B-8649-D0AAD85843E6/0/sportgovplan19.pdf; Department for Culture, Media and Sport, *The Government's Plan for Sport* (March 2001), http://www.culture.gov.uk/global/publications/archive_2001/governments_plan_for_sport+.htm?properties=archive%5F2001%2C%2Fsport%2FQuickLinks%2Fpublications%2Fdefault%2C&month=); Department for Culture, Media and Sport, *The Government's Plan for Sport: Second Annual Report* (April 2003), http://www.culture.gov.uk/global/publications/archive_2003/sport_2ndannualreport.htm; and The Prime Minister's Strategy Unit, *Game Plan: A Strategy for Delivering Government's Sport and Physical Activity Objectives* (December 2002), http://www.sportdevelopment.org.uk/html/gameplan.html.

41 See "Förderung [Promotion]," Stiftung Deutscher Sporthilfe [The German Foundation for Sport Assistance] homepage, http://www.sporthilfe.de/index.php?page=2.

42 "Stiftung Deutscher Sporthilfe: Erfolg möglich machen [The German Foundation for Sport Assistance: Making Success Possible]," Press Release of the Stiftung Deutscher Sporthilfe (July 2003), http://www.sporthilfe.de/dokumente/basistext.pdf.

43 See the discussion with Hans Wilhelm Gäb, member of the Executive Committee of the DSH, in "Wie viel Moral verträgt der Sport? [How Much Morality is Compatible with Sport?]," *Das Sportgespräch* [Sport Talk], DeutschlandRadio, Berlin [German Radio, Berlin] (November 25, 2001), http://www.dradio.de/cgi-bin/es/neu-sport/16.html. Thirty-five FRG medal winners received more than 631,000 euros in performance bonuses at Salt Lake City.

44 See the discussion with DSH President Hans-Georg Grüschow, in "Die Sporthilfe als Service-Gesellschaft für Spitzensport [Sport Assistance Foundation as a Social Service for High-Performance Athletes]," *Das Sportgespräch* [Sport Talk], DeutschlandRadio, Berlin [German Radio, Berlin] (January 19, 2003), http://www.dradio.de/cgi-bin/es/neu-sport/33.html.

45 See the discussion among Dagmar Freitag, Vice-President of the German Athletics Association and a Social Democratic Party member, Klaus Riegert, Sport Spokesperson for the Christian Democratic Union/Christian Social Union of Bavaria Party, Detlef Parr, Deputy Member of the Committee for Sport for the Free Democratic Party of Germany and Winfried Herrmann, Federation 90/The Green Party, Chair of the Federal Parliament's Committee for Sport and the Environment, "Die Sportpolitik in der neuen Legislaturperiode [Sport Politics in the New Session of the Legislature]," *Das Sportgespräch* [Sport Talk], DeutschlandRadio, Berlin [German Radio, Berlin] (November 24, 2002), http://www.dradio.de/cgi-bin/es/neu-sport/30.html.

46 See *Schule und Leistungssport – Verbundsysteme in den Ländern* [School and High-Performance Sport – Coordinated Systems in the Provinces], Bericht über den

Entwicklungsstand der pädagogischen Betreuungsmaßnahmen für jugendliche Leistungssportlerinnen und Leistungssportler im Rahmen der Kooperationsprojekte "Sportbetonte Schule" und "Partnerschule des Leistungssports" in den Ländern [Report on the Status of the Pedagogical Mechanisms that Protect the Welfare of Young High-Performance Athletes in the Framework of the Projects "Sport Oriented Schools" and "High-Performance Sport Partnership Schools" in the Provinces], (November 3, 2000), http://www.kmk.org/doc/publ/leistung.pdf, 13.

47 *Schule und Leistungssport*, 15–16.

48 See, for example, The Sports Factor, "Athlete Talent Search Programs," (September 19, 1997), http://www.ausport.gov.au/fulltext/1997/sportsf/sf970919.htm; Australian Institute of Sport, "Talent Search," http://www.ais.org.au/talent/index.asp; Tim Ackland, "Talent Identification: What Makes a Champion Swimmer," *Coaches' Info Service: Sport Science Information for Coaches*, http://www.coachesinfo.com/category/swimming/166/; Istvan Balyi, "System Building and Long-term Athletic Development in British Columbia," a paper presented on the Irish Sport Council's National Coaching and Training Centre website, http://www.msysa.net/CoachingArticles/NewCoaching/SportsSystemBuildingbyDrIstvanBalyi.pdf and Istvan Balyi, "Sport System Building and Long Term Athlete Development," http://www.talentladder.org/tl_res.html.

49 Udo Merkel, "The German Government and the Politics of Sport and Leisure in the 1990s: An Interim Report," in Scott Fleming, Margaret Talbot and Alan Tomlinson, eds, *Policy and Politics in Sport, Physical Education and Leisure* (Eastbourne: Leisure Studies Association, 1995), 100.

50 See Wolf-Dietrich Brettschneider, "Unity of the Nation – Unity in Sports?" in Ralph Wilcox, ed., *Sport in the Global Village* (Morgantown: Fitness Information Technology, 1994), 252. See also R. Burgess, "Talent Identification," The Australian Sports Commission, http://www.ausport.gov.au/info/topics/talentid.asp, Tudor Bompa, "Talent Identification," *Sports Periodical On Research and Technology in Sport* (February 1985), 1–11, and Clive Rushton, *Talent Detection, Identification, and Development: A Swimming Perspective* (New Zealand: Swimming New Zealand, 2003), http://www.ausport.gov.au/info/topics/talentid.asp.

51 Arnd Krüger, "Breeding, Rearing and Preparing the Aryan Body: Creating the Complete Superman the Nazi Way," in James Anthony Mangan, ed., *Shaping the Superman: Fascist Body as Political Icon*, (London: Frank Cass Publishers, 1999), 44.

52 See Arnd Krüger, "A Horse Breeder's Perspective: Scientific Racism in Germany, 1870–1933," in Norbert Finzsch and Dietmar Schirmer, eds, *Identity and Intolerance: Nationalism, Racism, and Xenophobia in Germany and the United States* (Cambridge: Cambridge University Press, 1998), 371–95, especially 395.

53 See Brettschneider, "Unity of the Nation – Unity in Sports?" 252.

54 See Ackland, "Talent identification: What makes a champion swimmer?"

55 For example, the Australian Institute of Sport offers a three-level certification program in anthropometry; see Australian Institute of Sport, "Accredited Anthropometry Courses," Laboratory Standards Assistance Scheme, http://www.ais.org.au/lsas/courses.asp. See also Jan Bourgois, Albrecht Claessens, Jacques Vrijens, Renaat Philippaerts, Bart Van Renterghem, Martine Thomis, Melissa Janssens, Ruth Loos, and Johan Lefevre, "Anthropometric Characteristics of Elite Male Junior Rowers," *British Journal of Sports Medicine* 34:3 (2000), 213–16; J. Maestu and J. Jurimae, "Anthropometrical and Physiological Factors of Rowing Performance: A Review," *Acta Kinesiologiae* (2000), 130–50; A.M. Williams and T. Reilly, "Talent Identification and Development in Soccer," *Journal of Sports Sciences* 18:9 (2000), 657–67; P.A. Hume, W.G. Hopkins, D.M. Robinson, S.M. Robinson, and S.C. Hollings, "Predictors of Attainment in Rhythmic Sportive Gymnastics," *Journal of Sports Medicine and Physical Fitness* 33:4 (1993), 367–77; K.L. Quarrie, P. Handcock, A.E. Waller, D.J. Chalmers, M.J. Toomey, and B.D. Wilson, "The New Zealand Rugby Injury and Performance Project. III. Anthropometric and Physical Performance Characteristics of

Players," *British Journal of Sports Medicine* 29:4 (1995), 263–70; or L. Pavicic, V. Lozovina, M. Zivicnjak and E. Tomany, "The Nature of Groupings of the Young Water Polo Players Described by the Anthropometric Indicators," and S. Dacres-Mannings, "Anthropometry of the NSW Rugby Union Super S 12 Team," papers presented at the Australian Conference of Science and Medicine in Sport, Adelaide, Australia, October 1998. See also M. Bracko, C. Geithner and K. Rundell, "Performance and Talent Identification of Female Ice Hockey Players: What We Know – How Do We Use It?" *Medicine & Science in Sports & Exercise* 34:5 (Supplement, May 2002), 296; C. Geithner, R. Malina, J. Stager, J. Eisenmann and W. Sands, "Predicting Future Success in Sport: Profiling and Talent Identification in Young Athletes," *Medicine & Science in Sports & Exercise* 34:5 (Supplement, May 2002), 88.

56 See Thomson and Beavis, "Talent Identification in Sport."

57 Victor Zilberman, "German Unification and the Disintegration of the GDR Sport System," in *Sport in the Global Village*, 273.

58 See Michael Vitelli and Darwin Semotiuk, "Elite Sport in a United Germany: A Study of the German Sports Union November 9, 1989 – October 3, 1990," in *Sport in the Global Village*, 289–304.

59 See Berendonk, *Doping Dokumente*, 91–113.

60 Orwell, *Animal Farm*, 120.

Chapter 6

1 During his illustrious career, Salazar set one world and six US records, broke a 12-year-old record at the New York Marathon in 1981 and the Boston Marathon record in 1982, won three straight New York Marathons (1980–2), qualified for the 1980 and 1984 US Olympic teams, and was known as a gutsy performer who as a college runner competing against Bill Rodgers in heat and high humidity at the 1978 Falmouth 7.1-mile race collapsed at the finish in a state of exhaustion so severe he was given last rites in the medical tent.

2 Andrew Tilin, "The Ultimate Running Machine," *Wired Magazine* (Online) (August, 2002), http://www.wired.com/wired/archive/10.08/nike.html.

3 The Oregon Project is not an isolated instance of cutting-edge science and technology being made available to athletes. Well-funded national training centers exist around the world. The Australian Institute for Sport, for example, notes on its webpage that

> [t]he AIS leads the development of elite sport and is widely acknowledged in Australia and internationally as a world best practice model for elite athlete development. The AIS is a pre-eminent elite sports training institution in Australia with world class facilities and support services.
>
> See http://www.ais.org.au/

There are also private sector facilities that rival the AIS. Athletes' Performance, a private sector training facility, commits itself to providing "the finest methods, specialists and facilities [that are] seamlessly integrated to efficiently and ethically enhance our athletes' performance." See http://www.athletesperformance.com/. Finally, athletes in endurance sports in several countries have in recent times made use of a "GO2 Hypoxicator," an oxygen mask worn during rest periods that simulates a high altitude, low pressure oxygen environment. See Barrie Sheply, "Technology helps athletes get fitter, sitting down," the *Globe and Mail* (May 18, 2004), A17; http://www.peakaltitude.com; http://www.go2altitude.com.

4 See Stanley Z. Koplik, Executive Director, Kansas Board of Regents, "Forward," in Ray Tricker and David L. Cook, eds, *Athletes at Risk: Drugs and Sport*, (Dubuque, Ia.: Wm. C. Brown), xi.

5 Ibid., x.
6 Ibid., xi.
7 Bruce Woolley, "History and Evolution of Drugs in Sport," in Tricker and Cook, *Athletes at Risk*, 21.
8 Ibid., 16. The quotation, in context, reads as follows:

> Many people have expressed that drug use to achieve greater athletic achievement is a new phenomenon and that we should revert back to the good old days, but that is a simplistic outlook. The use of substances for performance enhancement has existed since the dawn of man's history. Even the most primitive people have developed potions that could induce changes in their bodies and thoughts.

9 Ibid., 18–24.
10 Ibid., 18.
11 Charles E. Yesalis and Michael S. Bahrke, "History of Doping in Sport," *International Sports Studies* 24:1 (2002), 43. Yesalis and Bahrke, it should be noted, are not sympathetic to the use of performance-enhancing substances in high-performance sport. Like Woolley, they are opponents of their use. As research scientists, however, they appear to be more precise and careful in their analyses.
12 Ibid., 46.
13 See Chapter One, page 20, as well as A.J. Ryan, "Athletics," in Charles Kochakian, ed., *Handbook of Experimental Pharmacology* (Vol. 43, *Anabolic–Androgenic Steroids*) (New York: Springer-Verlag, 1976), 516–17 or Terry Todd, "Anabolic Steroids: The Gremlins of Sport," *Journal of Sport History* 14:1 (1987), 93–4. See also John Ziegler, "Forward," in Bob Goldman, *Death in the Locker Room: Steroids and Sports* (South Bend, Indiana: Icarus Press, 1984), 1–3; Goldman, *Death in the Locker Room*, 73, 94.
14 See also Ivan Waddington, "The Development of Sports Medicine," *Sociology of Sport Journal* 13:2 (1996), 189.
15 See Ivan Waddington, *Sport, Health and Drugs* (New York: E & FN Spon, 2000), 147.
16 Ibid., 146–51.
17 Yesalis and Bahrke, "History of Doping in Sport," 53.
18 Ibid., 54.
19 Charles L. Dubin, *Commission of Inquiry Into the Use of Drugs and Banned Practices Intended to Increase Athletic Performance* (Ottawa, Canada: Canadian Government Publishing Centre, 1990), xxii.
20 World Anti-Doping Agency, *World Anti-Doping Code* (Version 3.0, 2003), 3, www.wada-ama.org/docs/web/standards_harmonization/code/code_v3.pdf.
21 Ibid.
22 Ibid.
23 The moment the "spirit of sport" gives even the slightest importance to the contest per se and the goal of winning, then the attendant "legitimate enhancement" of athletes' talents and performance immediately grounds the ideal in the real world of material history and the politics of power. Winning a contest becomes a legitimate goal and enhancing performance equally justified. This explains how even a former IOC president could state that "[a]nything that doesn't adversely affect the health of the athlete, for me isn't doping." See "La polémicia propuesta de Samaranch [Samaranch's Polemical Proposal]," *El Mundo* (July 26, 1998), 4 or Steve Rushin, "Throwing in the Towel: Beating a Hasty Retreat in the War on Drugs," *Sports Illustrated* (August 10, 1998), 17. From the vantage point of the real world of high-performance sport, Samaranch was focused on the immediate outcome of the Tour de France, where performance is the decisive criterion, and the contest is fair only to the extent that each athlete is free to choose how far, and by what means, he will develop his talents, skills and prowess.
24 Dubin, *Commission of Inquiry*, xxii.

25 Roland Barthes, *Mythologies*, trans. Annette Lavers (New York: Hill and Wang, 1972), 151.

26 Ibid.

27 Roland Barthes, "The Tour de France as Epic," in *The Eiffel Tower and Other Mythologies*, trans. Richard Howard (New York: Hill and Wang, 1979), 87–8.

28 On Coubertin's knowledge and use of public relations, see John Slater, "Modern Public Relations: Pierre Coubertin and the Birth of the Modern Olympic Games," in Kevin B. Wamsley, Robert K. Barney and Scott G. Martyn, eds, *The Global Nexus Engaged: Past, Present, Future Interdisciplinary Olympic Studies* (Proceedings for the Sixth International Symposium for Olympic Research) (London, On., 2002), 149–60. See also Allen Guttmann, *The Olympics: A History of the Modern Games*, second edition (Urbana and Chicago: University of Illinois Press, 2002), 7–20.

29 On the concrete problems Coubertin faced convincing the different national delegations to support his project, see Guttmann, *The Olympics*, 14–20.

30 Pierre Coubertin, "Why I Revived the Olympic Games" [original 1908], in Pierre Coubertin, *Olympism: Selected Writings*, ed. Norbert Müller (Lausanne: International Olympic Committee, 2000), 543, 545.

31 Ibid., 545.

32 Ibid., 543.

33 See Bruce Kidd, "The Myth of the Ancient Games," in Alan Tomlinson and Garry Whannel, eds, *Five Ring Circus: Money, Power and Politics at the Olympic Games* (London and Sydney: Pluto Press, 1984), 76 or Public Broadcasting Service, *The Real Olympics: A History of the Ancient and Modern Olympic Games* (Alexandria, Va.: PBS Home Video, 2004).

34 Immanuel Kant distinguished between the phenomenal world – things as we know them through our senses – and the noumenal world – things as they are in themselves.

35 Cited in Jan Todd and Terry Todd, "Significant Events in the History of Drug Testing and the Olympic Movement: 1960–1999," in Wayne Wilson and Edward Derse, eds, *Doping in Elite Sport: The Politics of Drugs in the Olympic Movement*, (Champaign, Il.: Human Kinetics Press, 2001), 68; their footnote refers to A.H. Beckett and D.A. Cowan, "Misuse of Drugs in Sport," *British Journal of Sports Medicine* 12 (1979), 185–94.

36 John Munro, *A Proposed Sports Policy for Canadians* (Ottawa: Department of National Health and Welfare, 1970), 4–5.

37 See Rob Beamish, "The Persistence of Inequality: An Analysis of Participation Patterns Among Canada's High Performance Athletes," *International Review for the Sociology of Sport* 25:2 (1990), 143–57.

38 Anthony Giddens, *The Constitution of Society: Outline of the Theory of Structuration* (Berkeley and Los Angeles: University of California Press, 1984), especially 16–25 on the rules of social structure.

39 Ibid., 19.

40 Ibid., 20–1; regarding the "Laws of Soccer," see *The Rules of the International Football Association Board*, http://www.drblank.com/slaws.htm.

41 See Mary Glendon, Michael Gordon, and Christopher Osakwe, *Comparative Legal Traditions* (St. Paul, Minnesota: West Publishing Co., 1982).

42 Giddens, *Constitution of Society*, 21. See also Anthony Giddens, *Central Problems in Social Theory* (London: The Macmillan Press, 1979), 81–5.

43 Giddens, *Constitution of Society*, 22.

44 Charles Lemert, *Social Things: An Introduction to the Sociological Life*, second edition (Lanham: Rowman & Littlefield Publishers, 2002), 5.

45 See Tom Donohoe and Neil Johnson, *Foul Play: Drug Abuse in Sport* (Oxford: Basil Blackwell, 1986), 61; Todd, "Anabolic Steroids," 70–3.

46 See also Todd and Todd, "Significant Events," 69, or Yesalis and Bahrke, "History of Doping in Sport," 53–4.

47 The Canadian Olympic Committee's recent *Own the Podium – 2010*, for example, explicitly ties funding to increasingly stringent performance criteria and the use of science and technology in the enhancement of performance (see also Chapter Five, note 38, for the same phenomenon in the FRG). The GDR was not the only country that kept its scientific programs "Top Secret." The Canadian report mentions its own "Top Secret" program that will give Canadian athletes "a technological 'edge' over other nations." See Canadian Olympic Committee, *Own the Podium – 2010*, http://www.olympic.ca/EN/organization/news/2005/files/otp_final.pdf, 22.

48 In his book *Speed Trap*, published just after the Ben Johnson scandal and ensuing Dubin Inquiry in Canada, Johnson's coach Charlie Francis provided useful insights regarding the practices that constitute the world of international track and field. However, Franke and Berendonk document that the practices that constituted the East German system were much more systematic and show that Francis had seen only the tip of the iceberg. See Charlie Francis, *Speed Trap* (Toronto: Lester and Orpen Dennys 1991), 105–8; Brigitte Berendonk, *Doping Dokumente von der Forschung zum Betrug* [Doping Documents: From Research to Cheating] (Berlin: Springer-Verlag, 1991); Werner Franke and Brigitte Berendonk, "Hormonal Doping and Androgenization of Athletes: A Secret Program of the German Democratic Republic Government," *Clinical Chemistry* 43:7 (1997), 1262–79.

49 Francis, *Speed Trap*, 84.

50 "Ben Johnson, Drugs and the Quest for Gold," *W5* (CTV, July 10, 2004).

51 Francis, *Speed Trap*, 83.

52 Angella Issajenko, *Running Risks* (Toronto: Macmillan of Canada, 1990), 53.

53 Bernard Suits, *The Grasshopper: Games, Life and Utopia* (Toronto/Buffalo: University of Toronto Press, 1980).

54 Suits, *The Grasshopper*, 41. Suits' definition also applies to games but Suits differentiates between games and sports by noting that the constitutive rules of sport require some act of physical prowess or skill. See also Bernard Suits, "The Elements of Sport," in William J. Morgan and Klaus V. Meier, eds, *Philosophic Inquiry in Sport*, (Champaign, Il.: Human Kinetics, 1988), 39–48 and Klaus V. Meier, "On the Inadequacies of Sociological Definitions of Sport," *International Review of Sport Sociology*, 2:16 (1981), 79–102. Suits' constitutive rules are the shallow, discursive, formalized and strongly sanctioned codified rules that Giddens acknowledges as important to social life but are not where he invests the depth of his analysis.

55 See also Sheryle Bergmann Drewe, *Why Sport? An Introduction to the Philosophy of Sport* (Toronto: Thompson Educational Publishing, 2003), 156–7.

56 It may be important to distinguish Robert Millar from David Millar: the latter is the British time trial specialist who was banned from the 2004 Tour de France over allegations of EPO use; see "Millar dans la tourmente [Millar inside the storm]," *L'Équipe* [*The Team*] (June 25, 2004), http://www.lequipe.fr/Cyclisme/20040625_091924 Dev.html, or Randy Starkman, "More Drug Bombshells Revealed," *Toronto Star* (June 25, 2004).

57 Originally appearing in the UK's *Guardian*, this citation is from Robert Millar, the *Globe and Mail* (July 31, 1998). The article may also be seen in "Cycling News and Analysis," http://www.cyclingnews.com/results/1998/aug98/aug1.shtml.

58 Dubin, *Commission of Inquiry*, xxii.

59 Kevin B. Wamsley, "Violence and Aggression in Sport," in Jane Crossman, ed., *Canadian Sport Sociology*, (Scarborough: Thomson Nelson, 2003), 94. See also Kevin B. Wamsley, "The Public Importance of Men and the Importance of Public Men: Sport and Masculinities in Nineteenth-Century Canada," in Philip White and Kevin Young, eds, *Sport and Gender in Canada*, (Don Mills, On.: Oxford University Press, 1999), 24–39.

60 Richard Gruneau and David Whitson, *Hockey Night in Canada: Sport, Identities and Cultural Politics* (Toronto: Garamond Press, 1993), see especially "Violence, Fighting, and Masculinity," 175–96.

61 See Wamsley, "Violence and Aggression in Sport," 96. Two examples of constantly replayed egregious sport violence were the McSorely–Brashier and Bertruzzi–Moore incidents; see Scott Carpenter, "Above the Law," http://www.enterstageright.com/archive/articles/0300mcsorley.htm concerning McSorley and Brashier and Jamie Fitzpatrick, "The NHL's Public Profile Takes Another Beating. So What?" *Your Guide to Pro Ice Hockey* (March 19, 2004), http://proicehockey.about.com/cs/businessofhockey/a/nhl_image.htm regarding Bertruzzi and Moore.

62 W. M. Brown, "As American As Gatorade and Apple Pie: Performance Drugs and Sport," in William J. Morgan, Klaus V. Meier and Angela J. Schneider, eds, *Ethics in Sport,* (Champaign, Il.: Human Kinetics, 2001), 146.

63 Terry Roberts and Dennis Hemphill, *Banning Drugs in Sport: Ethical Inconsistencies* (Submission to the Senate Standing Committee on Environment, Recreation and the Arts, Australia, July, 1988), 2.

64 Waddington, "The Development of Sports Medicine," 177.

65 Ibid., 179.

66 See Roberts and Hemphill, *Banning Drugs in Sport,* 2.

67 Gerald Dworkin, "Paternalism," *The Monist* 56 (1972), 65.

68 See International Olympic Committee, *Olympic Movement: Anti-Doping Code,* http://www.medycynasportowa.pl/download/doping_code_e.pdf, 3.

69 See World Anti-Doping Agency, *World Anti-Doping Code* (v. 3) (March, 2003), http://www.wada-ama.org/rtecontent/document/code_v3.pdf, 1 (italics in the original). The *Olympic Charter* is clear that the WADA *Code,* as of September 2004, governs the Olympic Games; see International Olympic Committee, *Olympic Charter* (Lausanne: International Olympic Committee, 2004), 82.

70 W. M. Brown, "Paternalism, Drugs, and the Nature of Sports," *Journal of the Philosophy of Sport* XI (1985), 15.

71 See International Olympic Committee, *Olympic Movement: Anti-Doping Code,* 5.

72 World Anti-Doping Agency, *World Anti-Doping Code* (v. 3), 8 (italics in the original).

73 Ibid., italics in the original.

74 Among the most comprehensive, objective, and informative scholarship concerning the use of performance-enhancing substances in the GDR are Giselher Spitzer, *Doping in der DDR: Ein historischer Überblick zu einer konspirativen Praxis* [Doping in the GDR: An Historical Overview of a Conspiracy] (Köln: Sport und Buch Strauß, 1998) and Werner Franke, "Funktion und Instrumentalisierung des Sports in der DDR: Pharmakologische Manipulationen (Doping) und die Rolle der Wissenschaft [Function and Instrumentalization of Sport in the GDR: Pharmacological Manipulation (Doping) and the Role of Science]," in Deutscher Bundestag [German Parliament], ed., *Enquete-Kommission "Aufarbeitung von Geschichte und Folgen der SED-Diktatur in Deutschland": Materialien* [Commission of Inquiry, "Contributions to Understanding the History and Consequences of the SED Dictatorship in Germany:" Materials] (Vol. 3), (Frankfurt am Main: Suhrkamp Verlag, 1995).

75 On the cyclical nature of steroid protocols in the GDR, see Berendonk, *Doping Dokumente,* 334–6, 392–408, 409–15, 416–26.

76 For a discussion of the effects athletes receiving steroids would experience and the sophisticated knowledge that circulated widely in the high-performance sport subculture, see Lee Monaghan, *Bodybuilding, Drugs and Risk* (New York: Routledge, 2001), 95–128. A personal interview with a former GDR high-performance athlete in 1990 indicated that the athlete (identity protected by confidentiality agreement) knew about the substances she or he was taking and that others did too. The athlete was also aware of what "pills" western athletes were taking.

77 In his psychoanalytical analysis of the impact the Stalinist state had upon the emotions of the GDR's citizens, Hans-Joachim Maaz, *Der Gefühlsstau: Ein Psychogramm der DDR* [Repressed Emotions: A Psychogram of the GDR] (Berlin: Argon Verlag, 1990) demonstrates that despite their repressive life–world, East Germans were more than passive

dupes to the system. Works by Chris Harman, *Class Struggles in Eastern Europe: 1945–83* (London: Pluto Press, 1983); Bruce Allen, *Germany East: Dissent and Opposition* (Montreal: Black Rose Books, 1989); Günter Johannes and Ulrich Schwarz, *DDR: Das Manifest der Opposition* [GDR: Manifesto of the Opposition] (Munich: Wilhelm Goldmann Verlag, 1978); Ralph Giordano, *Die Partei hat immer recht: Ein Erlebnisbericht über den Stalinismus auf deutschem Boden* [The Party is Always Right: A Report of Experiences under Stalinism on German Soil] (Vienna: Verlag Herder Freiburg, 1990); Stefan Heym, *Wege und Umwege* [Paths and Detours] (Frankfurt am Main: Fischer Taschenbuch Verlag, 1980), 181–380; and Stefan Heym, *Stalin verläßt den Raum* [Stalin Left the Room] (Leipzig: Recalm Verlag, 1990) indicate the numerous ways in which citizens registered covert and overt, passive and active, dissent and resistance to the GDR state.

78 See Giddens, *Constitution of Society*, 1–16.

79 Rob Beamish conducted extensive interviews with each of these individuals, and many more, in November 1990. On Bahro, see Rudolf Bahro, *Alternative in Eastern Europe*, trans. David Fernbach (London: New Left Books, 1987) and *Building the Green Movement*, trans. Mary Tyler (London: New Society Publishers, 1986).

80 Franke and Berendonk, "Hormonal Doping and Androgenization of Athletes," 1264.

81 Ibid., 1270.

82 Robert L. Simon, "Good Competition and Drug-Enhancing Performance," *Journal of the Philosophy of Sport* XI (1984), 8.

83 Brown, "Paternalism, Drugs, and the Nature of Sports," 140.

84 See World Anti-Doping Agency, *The 2004 Prohibited List: International Standard* (March 17, 2004), http://www.wada-ama.org/docs/web/standards_harmonization/code/list_standard_2004.pdf.

85 Substances such as glutamine, trypthophan (or 5HT, which might boost adrenaline production), and creatine monohydrate, which pose no serious health risks while, according to the scientific literature, possibly enhancing performance, are not included on the banned list.

86 Concerning female use of steroids, there has also been a tendency to overstate the virilizing side effects of steroids. Kopera, "The History of Anabolic Steroids and a Review of Clinical Experience with Anabolic Steroids," *Acta Endrocrinologica* 110 (1985), 16 indicates that they "are usually reversible, with the exception of growth and voice disturbances." He also notes that "[a]ll androgenic [i.e. virilizing] side-effects are dependent on the dose and the androgenicity of the compound." See also Richard Strauss and Charles Yesalis, "Additional Effects of Anabolic Steroids on Women," in Charles Yesalis, ed., *Anabolic Steroids in Sport and Exercise*, (Champaign, Il: Human Kinetics Press, 1993), 151–60.

87 James Wright, "Anabolic–Androgenic Steroids," in Tricker and Cook, *Athletes At Risk*, 65. It is important to note that *Athletes at Risk* was prepared by the state of Kansas to properly inform athletes about the risks attendant in the use of performance-enhancing substances and to discourage their use among athletes.

88 See Roberts and Hemphill, *Banning Drugs in Sport*, 3–4; Simon, "Good Competition and Drug-Enhancing Performance," 9–10. For a different analysis of the "harm to the athlete" argument and the role of paternalism, which reaches similar conclusions to the argument presented here, see Angela J. Schneider and Robert B. Butcher, "An Ethical Analysis of Drug Testing," in Wilson and Derse, *Doping in Elite Sport*, 129–52.

89 Regarding the cost of policing the current system, see Dubin, *Commission of Inquiry*; or Terry Black and Amelia Pape, "The Ban on Drugs in Sports: The Solution or the Problem?" *Journal of Sport and Social Issues* 21:1 (1997), 83–92. Concerning commissions of inquiry: in Canada, see Dubin, *Commission of Inquiry*; in Australia, see J. Black, *Drugs in Sport: An Interim Report*, Senate Standing Committee on Environment, Recreation and the Arts (Canberra: Australian Government

Publishing Service, 1989) and J. Black, *Drugs in Sport: Second Report*, Senate Standing Committee on Environment, Recreation and the Arts (Canberra: Australian Government Publishing Service, 1990); in the United States, see Joseph Biden, *Steroids in Amateur and Professional Sport: The Medical and Social Costs of Steroid Abuse* (Hearing before the Senate Committee on the Judiciary, 101st Congress, April 3 and May 9, 1989); in Germany, see "Druck von oben: Die Doping-Kommission des Deutschen Sportbundes empfiehlt die Entlassung von rund 100 Trainern und Funktionären [Pressure from above: The Doping Commission of the German Sport Federation recommends the dismissal of about 100 coaches and officials]," *Der Spiegel* 50 (1991), 238. For independent studies, see for example Berendonk, *Doping Dokumente*; Donohoe and Johnson, *Foul Play*. For reports in the press, see *Der Spiegel*, "Aufforderung zum Doping [Invitation to Doping]" 46 (1989), 258–9; *Der Spiegel*, "Anabolika im Vatikan besorgt: Interview mit dem kanadischen Leichtathletik-Trainer Charlie Francis über die weltweiten Dopingpraktiken [Steroids Procured in the Vatican: an Interview with Canadian Track Coach Charlie Francis About Doping Practices Worldwide]" 46 (1990), 236–42; Michael Janovsky, "Prominent U.S. Coach Describes Steroid Use," the *Globe and Mail* (April 4, 1989), A12; Leonard Stern, "Is There a Case for Drugs in Sports?" the *Citizen Weekly* (September 10, 2000), C3–C6. For academic treatments, see Brown, "As American As Gatorade and Apple Pie;" John Hoberman, "How Drug Testing Fails: The Politics of Doping Control," in Wilson and Derse, *Doping in Elite Sport*, 241–74; Waddington, "The Development of Sports Medicine;" Yesalis and Bahrke, "History of Doping in Sport."

90 See Patrick Bird, "Keeping Fit, Column 37: Eliminating Steroids from the System" (University of Florida, College of Health and Human Performance, 1991), http://www.hhp.ufl.edu/keepingfit/ARTICLE/elim.HTM; Craig Kammerer, "Drug Testing and Anabolic Steroids," in Charles Yesalis, ed., *Anabolic Steroids in Sport and Exercise*, (Champaign, Il.: Human Kinetics Press, 1993), 283–308; or Jeff Everson, "Steroids: Muscle Miracle or Dangerous Myth," *Planet Muscle Magazine*, http://www.bodybuilding.com/fun/planet9.htm.

91 Robert Voy with Kirk D. Deeter, *Drugs, Sport, and Politics* (Champaign, Il.: Leisure Press, 1991), 19.

92 See "The Death of Birgitt Dressel," *Der Spiegel* (May, 1987), Berendonk, *Doping Dokumente*, 244–48, 448–51; Steve Buffery, "Why Pro-style Hypocrisy No Solution to Doping," *Toronto Sun* (July 24, 2000), http://slam.canoe.ca/2000Games Columnists/buffery_jul24.html presents a summary of the *Spiegel* story. It is important to note that deaths associated with drug use among athletes have tended to arise from alcohol or other recreational drugs or dietary aids like ephedra – not banned, performance-enhancing drugs. The unfortunate deaths of Pelle Lindburg of the Philadelphia Flyers, Augustinius Jaspers of Clemson University, Len Bias of the University of Maryland, Don Rogers of the Cleveland Browns, David Croudin of the Atlanta Falcons, and Korey Stringer of the Minnesota Vikings all fall under these categories (see Woolley, "History and Evolution of Drugs in Sport," 21–2). Amy Coutee, "Healthy Athletes Die Without Warning Signs," the *Orion* (September 25, 1996) shows that even under the best of conditions, athletes are no more exempt from sudden, unanticipated, unexplained death than anyone else.

93 A. Ryan, "Causes and Remedies for Drug Misuse and Abuse by Athletes," *Journal of the American Medical Association* 252: 4 (1984), 517–19; R. J. Strauss, G. Finerman, and D. Catlin, "Side Effects of Anabolic Steroids in Weight-trained Men," *The Physician and Sports Medicine* 11: 12 (1983), 87–96 and H. Kopera, "The History of Anabolic Steroids," *Acta Endocrinologixia* 271 (1985), 11–18.

94 See for example H. Haupt and G. Rovere, "Anabolic steroids: a review of the literature," *The American Journal of Sports Medicine* 12:6 (1984), 469–84 or C. Kochakian, ed., "Anabolic-Androgenic Steroids," *Handbook of Experimental Pharmacology* (1976), 43.

95 See Charles Erlich, "The Wandering Rowing Coach: Drug Testing" (October 2000), http://www.widomaker.com/~ehrlich/letter/oct00.html.

Conclusion

1 Roger Bannister, "The Meaning of Athletic Performance," in Ernst Jokl and Emanuel Simon, eds, *International Research in Sport and Physical Education*, (Springfield, Il.: Charles C. Thomas Publishers, 1964), 72–3; Pierre Coubertin, *Olympism: Selected Writings*, ed. Norbert Muller (Lausanne: International Olympic Committee, 2000), 252.

2 Bannister, "The Meaning of Athletic Performance," 71–2.

3 See Adolf Henning Frucht and Ernst Jokl, "The Future of Athletic Records," in *International Research in Sport and Physical Education*, 436.

4 See Neal Bascomb, *The Perfect Mile: Three Athletes, One Goal, and Less Than Four Minutes to Achieve It* (Boston and New York: Houghton Mifflin, 2004) on the competition between Bannister, Landy and Santee to break the four-minute barrier.

5 David Powell, "Blessed be the Pacemakers, For They Got Away With It," *Times*online (May 5, 2004), http://www.timesonline.co.uk/article/0,,13849–1098019,00.html. Powell points out that Bannister's record run 11 months earlier (4:02 at the Surrey Schools meet) was disallowed because he had used a pacemaker (see also Bascomb, *The Perfect Mile*, 130–3, 139 on the race and the decision). Swedish rival Gunder Hägg and others had also used this tactic. Bannister's pacemakers during the record breaking run were Chris Brasher and Chris Chataway.

6 On physiological treadmill experiments, see Bascomb, *The Perfect Mile*, 90–5. On other performance-enhancing techniques and devices used by Bannister, see John Bale, *Roger Bannister and the Four-Minute Mile* (London and New York: Routledge, 2004), 23–4, 53–5, 75–6, 112–13.

7 Bale, *Roger Bannister*, 136.

8 See Owen Slot, "Problems of Unique Training Regime," *Times*online (May 4, 2004), http://www.timesonline.co.uk/article/0,,13849–1097367,00.html and Bascomb, *The Perfect Mile*, 5–6, 12–16, 41–56, 115.

9 Calvin Shulman, "Middle-Distance Specialists Committed to Chasing that Elusive Dream," *Times*online (May 4, 2004), http://www.timesonline.co.uk/article/0,,13849–1097363,00.html.

10 See John Berger, *Ways of Seeing* (New York: Penguin, 1977).

11 See also Harvey J. Krahn and Graham Lowe, eds, *Work, Industry and Canadian Society*, fourth edition (Scarborough, Ontario: Thomson Nelson Learning, 2002); Dietrich Rueschemeyer, *Power and the Division of Labour* (Stanford, California: Stanford University Press, 1986); Ann H. Stromberg and Shirley Harkness, eds, *Women Working: Theories and Facts in Perspective*, second edition (Mountain View Ca.: Mayfield Publishing Company, 1988); or Paul Thompson, *The Nature of Work: An Introduction to the Debates on the Labour Process* (London: The Macmillan Press, 1983) for additional descriptions of this type of work.

12 For complete documentation of the above material, see, inter alia Rob Beamish and Janet Borowy, *Q: What Do You For A Living? A: I'm An Athlete* (Kingston: The Sport Group, 1988); Bernard Cahill and Arthur Pearl, eds, *Intensive Participation in Children's Sports* (Champaign, Il.: Human Kinetics Press, 1993); Michael Klein, ed., *Sport und soziale Probleme* [Sport and Social Problems] (Hamburg: Rowohlt Taschenbuch Verlag, 1989); Peter Becker, ed., *Sport und Hochleistung* [Sport and High-Performance] (Hamburg: Rowohlt Taschenbuch, 1987); Udo Steiner, ed., *Kinderhochleistungssport* [Children's High-Performance Sport] (Heidelberg: C.F. Müller Juristischer Verlag, 1984).

13 CanWest News Service, "A Bittersweet Day: Canadian Rowers Disqualified, Women's Water Polo Team Upsets Yanks," *The Kingston Whig Standard* (August 19, 2004), 21.

14 For a sample of some academic treatments of athlete identity creation, see the articles in "Experience and Identity: Becoming an Athlete," in Jay Coakley and Peter Donnelly, eds, *Inside Sports* (London and New York: Routledge, 1999), 61–126, especially Christopher Stevenson, "Becoming an International Athlete: Making Decisions About Identity," 86–95. Much of the elite athlete identity literature has studied the process of retirement at the end of athletes' careers while the creation of elite athletes' identity remains less studied and understood.

15 The closest parallel to the life of a high-performance sportsperson is that of the ballet dancer, but even here there are demands faced by athletes, the most obvious being the need to perform at a world-class level each and every time that even dancers do not have to confront in every performance. On September 28–9, 2001, the Centre for Sport Policy Studies at the University of Toronto hosted a conference, "Talented Children in Sport, Music and Dance: How Can We Nurture Talent Without Exploiting or Abusing Children?" The conference was an exception to the rule; there have been very few serious attempts to study or understand elite child athletes, their rights or working lives.

16 The sometimes deleterious effects of this process on young female figure skaters and, in particular, gymnasts, are recounted in Joan Ryan, *Little Girls in Pretty Boxes: The Making and Breaking of Elite Gymnasts and Figure Skaters* (New York: Doubleday, 1995).

17 See Elk Franke, "Kinderleistungssport oder Wie relativ sind soziale Probleme im Sport [Children's High Performance Sport or How Relative are Social Problems in Sport?]," in Michael Klein, *Sport und soziale Probleme*, 121–38; Herbert Hartmann, ed., *Emanzipation im Sport?* [Emancipation in Sport?] (Giessen/Collar: Verlag Andreas Achenbach, 1975); Thomas Kutsch und Karl-Heinrich Bette, "Doping im Hochleistungssport [Doping in High-Performance Sport]," in Thomas Kutsch und J. Wiswede, eds, *Sport und Gesellschaft: Die Kehrseite der Medaille* [Sport and Society: The Other Side of the Medal] (Knigstein: Verlag Anton Hain, 1981), 71–82; Friedhelm Neidhardt, "Zeitknappheit, Umweltspannungen und Anpassungsstrategien im Hochleistungssport [Time Shortages, Environmental Tensions and Adaptive Strategies in High-Performance Sport]," in Kutsch and Wiswede, *Sport und Gesellschaft* 55–70; L. Rose, "Die Angst der Pedagogen vor den unkindlichen Kinder: Die Debatte zum Kinderleistungssport [The Anxiety of the Pedagogues over Unchildlike Children: The Debate over Children's High-performance Sport]," in Becker, *Sport und Hochleistung*, 51–62; or H. Ulrich, "Zur sozialen Situation des professionalisierten Leistungssportlers [On the Social Situation of the Professionalized High-Performance Athlete]," *Leistungssport* [High-Performance Sport] 1:3 (1975), 386–91.

18 In *The Gulag Archipelago: 1918–1956* (New York: Harper and Row Publishers, 1974, 168), Alexander Solzhenitsyn makes a remarkably similar point with respect to good and evil in human behavior.

> If only it were all so simple! If only there were evil people somewhere insidiously committing evil deeds, and it were necessary only to separate them from the rest of us and destroy them. But the line dividing good and evil cuts through the heart of every human being. And who is willing to destroy a piece of his own heart? During the life of any heart this line keeps changing place; sometimes it is squeezed one way by exuberant evil and sometimes it shifts to allow enough space for good to flourish. One and the same human being is, at various ages, under various circumstances, a totally different human being. At times he is close to being a devil, at times to sainthood. But his name doesn't change, and to that name we ascribe the whole lot, good and evil.

Later Solzhenitsyn (175) writes:

Evidently evildoing also has a threshold magnitude. Yes, a human being hesitates and bobs back and forth between good and evil all his life. He slips, falls back, clambers up, repents, things begin to darken again. But just so long as the threshold of evildoing is not crossed, the possibility of returning remains. But when, through the density of evil actions the result either of their own extreme degree or of the absoluteness of his power, he suddenly crosses that threshold, he has left humanity behind, and without, perhaps, the possibility of return.

Though we have developed insights about health and pathology in high-performance sport completely independently of Solzhenitsyn's description of good and evil, there is a striking parallel in our analyses.

19 Barrie Houlihan, "Civil Rights, Doping Control and the World Anti-Doping Code," *Sport in Society* 7:3 (Autumn 2004), 421–2.
20 Ibid., 422.

Index

Adidas 24, 151n59
ADS (Arbeitsgemeinschaft Deutscher
     Sport) 81–2
advertising 16, 23–4
amateurism 14–15, 25–6, 151n68;
     (alleged) breaches of 17, 18–19, 27,
     152n79; change of policy on 27–30;
     Code, 150n46; objections to 15,
     16–17, 18
anabolic steroids see steroids
Andrianov, Constantin 25, 37
anthropometry 100, 101, 176n55
Aristotle 51
Arnold, Thomas, Rev. 12
art, parallel with high-performance sport
     142
Åstrand, Per-Olaf 62
athletes: awareness of actions/situation 3,
     4, 130–1, 181n75; best interests, as
     legislative criterion 126; choices made
     by 129–31; demands of lifestyle 9–10,
     65, 122–3, 125, 139–40, 142–4;
     finances, 143; identity creation
     185n14; (lack of) stake in Games 143;
     responsibilities (with regard to banned
     substances) 126–7; scientific study
     52–6, 63–5
Athletes at Risk: Drugs and Sport 107–8
Australian Institute for Sport 177n3
Averoff, George 16

Bahrke, Michael 109
Bahro, Rudolf, *The Alternative in Eastern
     Europe* 129
Baillet-Latour, Henri 149n27
BALCO (Bay Area Laboratory Co-
     operative) 3, 4, 147n19
ballet, comparison with athletics 185n15
banned substances 9; athletes' required
     awareness of 126–7;

counterproductivity of ban 132–4, 142;
     court cases involving 172n15; deaths
     resulting from 124, 183n91; failure to
     distinguish between harmful and
     innocuous 134; inefficacy of ban 4–5,
     92, 130, 141; lack of danger from
     131–2; (publication of) lists 2, 3, 26,
     118, 131–2, 134; selectivity/omissions
     141, 182n84
Bannister, Sir Roger 59–60, 136–7,
     164n78, 184n5
Barthes, Roland 112–13
Bartov, Omer 71
Bascomb, Neal 60
Beckett, Arnold 38
Behrendt, Helmut 169n51
Berendonk, Brigitte 26, 91, 103, 172n17,
     172n21
Berger, John, *Ways of Seeing* 138–9
Berlin: blockade (1948) 73, 85; as centre
     for sports 75–6; postwar occupation 72,
     75–6; Wall, crossings/fall of 31, 93, 129
Bernett, Hajo 50, 51, 159n6
Bertruzzi, Todd 181n61
Bias, Len 183n92
Bier, August, 53 160n15
Biermann, Wolf 128, 129
biology 62–2
black market 129–30, 133–4, 142,
     172n21
Bonds, Barry 147n20
Bouin, Jean 54
Bourgeois Sport Movement 49–50, 76, 82
Boy Scouts 41
Boys/Girls Clubs 75
Brasher, Chris 184n5
Brashier, Donald 181n61
Breo, Dennis 156n32
Bresnahan, George 58
Brodeur, Martin 117

"broken time" payments 16–17

Brown, W.M. 124

Brundage, Avery 18–19, 21, 24–6, 140, 149n27, 152n78

Buck, Adolf 169n51

Bundesinstitut für Sportwissenschaft (Federal Institute for Sport Science) 95–6

Bunge, R.G. 44

Burghley, David 19

The Cabinet of Dr Caligari (1920) 32–3

caffeine 3, 132

Calder, David 139

Canada: government inquiry vi, 47, 48, 111, 146n11; National Olympic Committee 180n47; Olympic qualifying standards 164n95; sports ethos 124; sports science 62–3; sports system/funding 175n40; testing program 3

Canon, Walter 56

Cantelon, Hart 16

Castro, Fidel 37

Catlin, Don 3

Chamberlain, Houston Stewart 154n12

Chataway, Chris, 184n5

"cheating," use of performance enhancers as 107, 108–9, 117

child athletes 89; identification/ development 98–9, 100–1; lack of legal protection127–8, 131; use of steroids 93; *see also* education; sport schools

choice, freedom of 128–30

Christensen, E.H. 55, 57, 60

Churchill, Sir Winston 30, 71, 72

Ciba Pharmaceutical Company 20, 109

Clausewitz, Carl von 72, 167n21

Clay, Lucius D., General 72

Coca-Cola 16

Cofidis (cycling team) 4

cold remedies 131–2

cold war, impact on sports 8, 31–2

Cole, Cheryl 40

commercial interests: conflict with Coubertinian ideal 15–17, 23–5, 29; progressive takeover of Games 103–4; role in development of high-performance sport 67

condition, (in)equality of 116–17

Connolly, Harold 20

Connolly, Pat 26

contact sports 123–4; injuries/deaths resulting from 124

Conte, Victor 3

Cooper, Chris 147n20

corticosteroids 3

Coubertin, Pierre de, Baron: attitude to women 40–1; departures from aims/principles 9, 19, 27, 28, 29, 49, 66, 86, 103, 104, 136, 144; manipulation of Olympic image 32, 113; musical tastes 149n9; obstacles facing 113; partial adoption of ideas 49, 51; upholding of principles 18, 21–2, 25; vision of Olympic ideal 7–8, 11, 12–15, 28–9, 113–14, 140, 148nn6–8, 149n17, 151n68

Cowan, David 38

Cowart, Virginia 38–9

creatine monohydrate 182n85

Cromwell, Dean 58

Croudin, David 183n92

Crump, Jack 17

cyling 64, 124–5; *see also* Tour de France

Dassler, Adolf/Rudolf 24, 151n59

Deutsche Hochschule für Körperkultur (German Academy for Physical Culture) 62, 87

Deutsche Vereinigung für Sportwissenschaft (German Union of Sport Science) 63

Dianabol 20, 61, 109

Diem, Carl 50–1, 140

Dietlen, H. 53

"Directive 23" 77–9, 81–2, 84, 97–8

disqualifications 1, 27, 108, 139

Dixon, John 168n44

Dominican Republic 4

Dressel, Birgit 133–4

drugs *see* banned substances; performance-enhancing substances; steroids; *names of specific preparations*

DSB (Deutscher Sportbund: German Sport Federation, FRG) 23, 81, 94, 96–9, 169n48

DSH (Stiftung Deutscher Sporthilfe: German Foundation for Sport Assistance, FRG) 94–5, 98, 174n35

DTSB (Deutscher Turn- und Sportbund: German Gymastics and Sport Federation, GDR) 22, 88–9

Dubin, Charles, Chief Justice 26, 47, 48, 111, 122, 146n11

Dumitru, Daniel 39

Duncan, Ray 57

East Germany *see* GDR
Edstrøm, Sigfrid 18–19, 149n27
education, role of sport in 12–13, 41–2
Eichmann, Adolf 45
Eisenhower, Dwight D. 72
Ekelund, Bo 18
Eligibility Code 25–6, 95;
    introduction/wording 28
elitism (role in Olympic ideal) 14
endorsement payments 27
energy, scientific theories of 52, 161n31
Engels, Friedrich 61, 85
EPO (erythropoietin) 1, 4, 122
Erlich, Charles 135
Erpenbeck, Fritz 166n19
European Championships 19
Ewald, Manfred 22, 90–1, 151n53

Fair, John 61
fairness 115–16, 119–20; distinguished
    from equality 116–17
fashion industry 138–9
Festina (cycling team) 1, 145n6
FIFA (Fédération Internationale de
    Football Association) 16–17
Flexner, Abraham 53
Forschungsinstitut für Körperkultur und
    Sport (Research Institute for Physical
    Culture and Sport, GDR) 92, 95
four-minute mile, quest for 59–60, 137
France, actions against rule-breakers 1
Francis, Charlie 26, 119–20, 180n48
Franke, Werner 26, 91, 172n17, 172n21
Freitag, Dagmar 175n45
Fremantle Overseas and TV Incorporated
    24
FRG (Federal Republic of Germany) 8–9;
    combined teams with GDR 23, 88,
    170n6; competition with eastern bloc
    23, 95–6, 98–9; governmental role
    94–5; high-performance sport system
    23, 95–9, 102–3, 104; mass sport system
    51, 74, 78–9, 81–2, 84, 94–5, 96, 97–8;
    as model for western methods 23, 66,
    164n1; National Olympic Committee
    83, 86–7; sports education 94, 98–9;
    sports investment/expenditure 101–2;
    sports science 63; training centers 94,
    173–4n28
Friedrich, Rudolf 169n51
Frucht, Adolf Henning 59

Gäb, Hans-Wilhelm 175n43
Gaines, Chryste 147n20

GDR (German Democratic Republic),
    8–9; (alleged) coercion of
    athletes/citizens 127–31, 181–2n77;
    (alleged reasons for) Olympic successes
    67, 91; athletes' support for system 91;
    influence on developments worldwide
    67; investment in high-performance
    sport 86; as model of eastern bloc
    methods 66; and Munich Games
    (1972) 89–92; National Olympic
    Committee 83, 86–7, 88; (non-)
    recognition by IOC 83, 86–7, 88,
    89–90, 102–3; numbers of sports staff
    93, 101–2; postwar genesis 74–7;
    rivalry with FRG/west 67, 85–6, 92;
    rivalry with USSR 22, 73, 86, 92;
    secrecy policy 92; sports education
    87–9, 100–1, 170n5; sports
    expenditure 101–2; sports medicine 62,
    93; sports policy/system 22, 51, 73,
    82–3, 84, 86–9, 100–2, 103–4; training
    centers/methods 89, 170n10; use of
    performance-enhancing substances 26,
    90–3, 172n17
German–Soviet war 68–72; brutality of
    methods 69, 70–1, 83, 166n13, 166n15
Germany: accused of professionalism 17;
    postwar conditions 74; reunification
    93, 101–2; scientific research 53–4,
    162n46; sporting history 8, 48–51;
    sports medicine 125; *see also* FRG;
    GDR; Nazism; Sectors of Occupation
Giambi, Jason 147n20
Giddens, Anthony 117–18, 121, 128–9
Gilbreth, Frank/Lillian 54, 55
Gleichschaltung 160n20
glutamine 182n85
Goebbels, Joseph 32, 39, 51, 69–70,
    166n11
Goering, Hermann 69, 165n8
Goldhagen, Daniel 153n6
Goldman, Bob 20
Graham, Trevor 3
Greece, Ancient: elitism 14; (idealised)
    modern view of 12–13, 113–14, 148n6,
    149n14; social reality 114; use of
    performance enhancers 107, 108
Grömmer, Hugo 168n41
Gruneau, Richard 16, 124
Grüschow, Hans-Georg 98, 175n44
Gubar, Susan 158n57
Gundelach, Gustav 166n19
gymnastics 15, 93
Gyptner, Richard 166n19

Hägg, Gunder 184n5
Hamann, Brigitte 154n12
Haraway, Donna
Harvard Fatigue Lab 55–6, 57,
    162–3nn53–4
Haupt, Herbert 39
Hayden, Mike, Governor 108
health (of athletes) 112, 122–5, 126,
    141–2; risks to (arising from IOC
    policy) 132–4
Hébert, Georges 54
Helmholtz, Hermann von 52
Helms, Paul 16
Hemphill, Dennis 125
Herrmann, Winfried 175n45
Hetherington, Chris 147n20
Heym, Stefan 128
high-performance sport: nature/practices
    137–8, 142–4; repression 95;
    similarities between systems 66, 99,
    104, 138; *see also* names of countries
Hildenbrant, Eberhard 54
Hill, Archibald 55, 60, 162n46
Hirsch, C. 53
Hitler, Adolf 32, 33–5, 39, 43, 68, 69, 86,
    154n12, 154n13, 154–5n20, 156n32
Mein Kampf 165n3
Hobe, G. 173n24
Hoberman, John 2, 54, 91, 157n38
hockey: drugs testing 3; travelling routines
    147n23; violence, 124 181n61
Hodge, Russ 20
Hoffman, Bob 20, 61
Holocaust 36, 71, 155n24
Honecker, Erich 22, 83, 84, 86–7, 92,
    150n51
Hoogerwert, S. 55
Höppner, Manfred 92–3
Hoth, Hermann, General 68
Houlihan, Barrie 143
human growth hormone 1
HVfL (Hamburger Verband für
    Leibesübungen: Hamburg Association
    for Physical Education) 80
"hypobaric house" 105–6

IAAF (International Amateur Athletic
    Association) 17, 19
ice hockey *see* hockey
International Swimming Association 1
IOC (International Olympic Committee)
    11; *Anti-Doping Code* 126–7;
    conferences 2, 18, 21, 25–6; dealings
    with NOCs 83, 86–7; impact of

decisions 102–3; Medical Committee
    21; policy on amateurism 16–17, 25–6,
    27–8, 29–30; projected image of
    "sport" 6–7; stance on doping 1–2, 21,
    26, 30, 115–16, 119, 141; substances
    banned by 9, 126
ISFs (International Sport Federations) 2,
    7, 9, 11, 17
Issajenko, Angella 119–20

Jahn, Friedrich Ludwig, Fr 49
Janowitz, Hans 33
Japan 93
Jaspers, Augustinius 183n92
Jaspers, Karl 51
Jensen, Knud 20, 123
Johnson, Ben vi, 1, 108, 120
Jokl, Ernst 56–7, 59
Jones, Marion 147n20
Joule, James Prescott 52

Kant, Immanuel 179n34
Kee, Robert 70
Kelvin, Lord 56
Kennedy, John F. 45
Kerr, Robert 44
Khrushchev, Nikita 43, 45
Kidd, Bruce, 159n7
Kingsley, Charles, Canon 12
KJSs (Kinder- und Jugendsportschulen:
    Children and Youth Sport Schools)
    88–9, 94, 101, 170n5
Kolehmainen, Hannes 54
Kolko, Gabriel 153n5
Konya, Kalman 172n15
Kopera, H. 134, 182n86
Koppe, Walter 166n19
Kracauer, Siegfried 32–4, 153n7
Krüger, Arnd 100
Krümmel, Carl 50

la Mettrie, Julien de, *L'Homme machine*
    161n29
Landessportbund Niedersachsen (Lower
    Saxony sport federation) 168n42
Landy, John 60, 136, 137
Laqueur, Thomas 40
Lemert, Charles 118, 121
Lempart, Tomasz 27
Lenin, Vladimir Ilyich (Ulyanov) 71
Leonhard, Wolfgang 166n19
"level playing field" argument 115, 117,
    119–20
Lindburg, Pelle 183n92

List, Guido von 154*n12*
Ljungqvist, Arne 3
Lupien, Gilles 147*n23*
Lysenko, Trofim Denisovitch 61–2

MacAloon, John 2
Macfarlane, Helen 31
Madden, Terry 3, 4
Mahle, Hans 166*n19*
Major League baseball; testing program 3–4
Makosky, Lyle 146*n11*
Mallwitz, Arthur 53
Manhattan Project 103
Mank, Herbert 169*n51*
Manstein, Erich von, General 68
marijuana 3
Maron, Karl 166*n19*
Marx, Karl 85, 129; *The Communist Manifesto* 31, 39, 45
May, Elaine Tyler 42
Mayer, Carl 33
Mayer, Julius Robert 52
Mayo, Elton 162*n51*
McSorely, Marty 181*n61*
Mellion, M.B. 39
Mengele, Joseph 45
mestanolone 93, 173*n24*
methandieone *see* Dianabol
middle-distance running 59–60, 136–7
Mignon, Petrick 64
Mikhailov, Andrei 1
Millar, David 4, 180*n56*
Millar, Robert 122–3, 124–5, 180*n56*
Milo of Crotona 53
Montgomery, Tim 147*n20*
MOOC (Melbourne Olympic Organizing Committee) 24
Moore, Barrington 14
Moore, Steve 181*n61*
Morell, Theodor 156*n32*
Moritz, F. 53
Morton, Johnnie 147*n20*
Müller, Franz 76
Munro, John, Hon. 116–17
myth, theories of 112–13

nandrolone 91
Naval Institute 58–9
Nazis(m) 8, 160*n20*; political ideology 161–2*n42*; popular support 69–70, 153*n6*; propaganda 154*n13*; rise to power 50; sports policy 50–1; *see also* German-Soviet war; Hitler; Holocaust; World War Two

Neufeld, Renate 91
Niethammer, Lutz 165*n2*
Nike 24, 105–6
Nixon, Richard M. 43
NOCs (National Olympic Committees) 7, 17
Nurmi, Paavo 54

Ochs, Phil 129
Olympic Charter 18, 45, 126; Rule 26 (on amateurism) 11, 12, 25–6, 28, 29, 150*n46* (*see also* Eligibility Code); Rule 28 (on performance-enhancing substances) 21; Rule 49 (on television rights) 24–5
Olympic Games: 1896 (Athens) 15; 1900 (Paris) 16; 1904 (St. Louis) 16; 1908 (London) 16; 1928 (Amsterdam) 16; 1936 (Berlin) 7, 24, 31, 32, 34–5, 75–6; 1948 (London) 19; 1952 (Helsinki) 8, 19–20, 37, 38, 109, 125, 137; 1956 (Melbourne) 24; 1964 (Tokyo) 21, 23, 93; 1968 (Mexico City) 94, 109; 1972 (Munich) 7, 9, 23, 89–92, 93–4, 102–3; 1976 (Montreal) 7; 1980 (Moscow) 7; 1984 (Los Angeles) 7, 109; 1988 (Seoul) 108; 2002 (Salt Lake City) 98; disenfranchisement of athletes 143; global profile 7; image manipulation 31, 32; mythical significance 113–14; national qualifying standards 164*n95*; political significance 7
Olympic Movement: founding 12–15; motto 14
Olympic Oath 15, 149*n17*
opportunity, (in)equality of 116–17
Oral-Turinabol 91, 93, 172*n21*
Oregon Project 105–6, 177*n3*
Orwell, George 46, 138; *Animal Farm* 85, 104
Owens, Jesse 35
oxygen, control of amount in atmosphere 105–6

pacemakers, use of 136, 184*n5*
Pallain, Richard, Judge 4
Pan American Games 63
Parr, Detlef 175*n45*
paternalism 44, 125–8, 130, 131–2
Paulus, Friedrich, Field Marshal 68–9
performance-based awards/funding 18–19, 24, 98, 175*n43*
performance-enhancing substances: assumptions regarding 106–9, 120; role

in sport systems 5, 30, 118–19, 137–8; *see also* steroids
Petrén, T. 55
Pfister, H. 55
physiology, study of 52–6
Pikhala, L. 55, 57, 60
Plato 112
Poland 71
policy (official), discrepancy with practice 5–6, 115, 141
politics, relationship with sport 5–6, 67
Porritt, Sir Arthur 21
Portland, Oregon *see* Oregon Project
Pound, Richard vii, 30, 46, 47, 146*n12*
Press, Tamara/Irina 43
Preuß, Max 76
Priem, Cees 1
pseudoephedrine 3, 132
Puma 24

Radschinsky, Karl-Heinz 172*n15*
Ratjen, Hermann "Dora" 43
records, pursuit of 6, 26, 119, 135, 137–8, 141; *see also* four-minute mile
reinfusion, performance-enhancing technique 109–10
Richthofen, Colonel-General von 165*n3*
Riedeberger, Erich 169*n51*
Riedel, Ropbert 169*n51*
Riefenstahl, Leni 34–5, 36, 154*n19*
Riegert, Klaus 175*n45*
Ritola, Ville 54
Roberts, Terry 125
Rodahl, Kaare 62
Rogers, Don 183*n92*
Romanov, Aleksei 37
Roosevelt, Franklin D. 71
Roux, W. 53
Rovere, George 39
rowing 101–2, 135, 139
rules, types of 117–18; constitutive vs. regulative 121–2; related to banned substance use 118–22
Ryan, A. 134

Salazar, Alberto 105, 177*n1*
Samaranch, Juan Antonio 1–2, 146*n8*, 151*n53*, 178*n23*
Santee, Wes 60, 136
SCC (Sport-Club Charlottenburg) 76–7
schools, physical education in, 41–2, 75, 100–1; *see also* sport schools
Schopp, Joseph 169*n51*
Schranz, Karl 27

Schulman, Calvin 60, 137
Sectors of Occupation (in postwar Germany) 72, 73, 74–83; Allied policies 74, 83–4, 102; Allied sports policy 77–9, 167–8*n33*; sport in 75, 76–82; sports clubs 78–9, 168–9*n44*, 169*n50*; sports federations 79–80, 82, 168*n42*; variations in policy 75, 79–80, 167*n24*
SED (Sozialistische Einheitspartei Deutschland: German Social Unity Party) 22, 51, 73, 84, 87–8, 128–30, 169*n52*
Senn, Alfred 155*n23*
Sereny, Gitta 155*n24*
sex tests 43–4, 45
Shumilov, Mikhail, General 68
Sickinger, Anton 160*n15*
Siebert, W.W. 55
Simon, Robert 131
Simpson, Tommy 21
Sjöstrand, T. 55
skiing 27
"slippery slope" argument 134–5
soccer 16–17; in postwar Germany 75, 80–1
Solzhenitsyn, Alexander 185–6*n18*
Speer, Albert 35, 36–7, 166*n11*, 166*n15*
Spilker, Jochen 172*n15*
"spirit of sport": Coubertinian view of 13–15; (misplaced) appeals to 107, 111–12, 115, 138, 141, 178*n23*
Spitzenverbände (top sport unions) 169*n50*
Spitzer, Giselher 93
sport: (fallacies of) universal conception 6, 47–8, 65, 111–15; medicine 62, 63, 125; (problems of) definition 46–7, 159*n6*; schools 22–3, 87–9, 94, 98–9, 100–1, 170*n5*; science 52–6, 61–5; *see also* high-performance sport; "spirit of sport"
Stafford, George 57
STAKO (Staatliches Komitee für Körperkultur und Sport: State Committee for Physical Culture and Sport) 22, 87–8
Stalin, Joseph 8–9, 18, 22, 61–2; plans for Germany 71–3, 75, 76, 84, 85
Stalingrad, battle of 68–9
Stasi (Ministerium für Staatssicherheit: State Security Ministry, GDR) 26, 92–3, 128–30
State Plan Subject 14, 25 (GDR), 103
Steinhaus, Arthur 55, 57, 60, 163*n64*

Steinmetz, Karlheinz 172n15
steroids: cessation of effects 132;
    consumption levels 93; detection,
    attempts to avoid 3, 132–3; fears of
    use/effects 8, 31, 38–40, 44, 106;
    GDR's success ascribed to 67; impact
    on running times 120; impossibility of
    winning without 120; oil-based vs.
    water-based 132–3; on/off cycles of use
    128; potential risks 132–3; proscription
    45, 92, 106, 118; research into 92, 93;
    (rumored) use by combat troops 31–2,
    38–9; statistical impact on
    performance 93, 120; test for 118; use
    of 20, 26, 90–3, 110, 118–19, 182n86;
    see also corticosteroids
Stevenson, Nicole 164n94
Strauss, R.J. 134
Strenk, Andrew 151n68
Stringer, Korey 183n92
Stubblefield, Dana 147n20
Stützpunkte (training centers) 94,
    173–4n28
Suits, Bernard, *The Grasshopper* 121,
    180n53
Sylvén, B. 55

Taylor, Bert 62
Taylor, Frederick Winslow 54, 55
Taylor, William 156n32
television, 24–5 67; liking for violence
    124, 181n61
testing, required by IOC/WADC 2, 118,
    135; counterproductivity 132–3
testosterone 20, 36, 91
Thermopylae, battle of 69, 165n8
THG (tetrahydrogestrinone) 3
Todd, Jan 26
Todd, Terry 26, 38, 156n32
Toth, Kevin 147n20
Tour de France 1, 21, 112–13, 122–3,
    125
training; centers 89, 94, 171n10,
    173–4n28, 177n3; evolution 52,
    53–65; experimental techniques 60;
    manuals 56–9; "natural method" 54;
    regimes 27; systematization 63–5; time
    spent on 26–7; young athletes 27
Truman, Harry S. 72
tryptophan 182n85
Turner Sport Movement 15, 48–50, 78,
    79, 82
Tuttle, W.W. 58

Ulbricht, Walter 8–9; political operations
    72, 73, 83, 84; political vision 67, 73,
    76, 82, 85–6; relations with USSR 73;
    sports policy 22, 73, 84, 86–7;
    "Ulbricht Group" 72, 74, 75–6,
    166n19
uM (unterstützende Mittel: supplementary
    materials) 90–1, 92–3, 171n14
Ungerleider, Steven, 39
United States: accused of professionalism,
    17, 18; attitudes to women 41–3; child
    performers 101; Olympic successes
    19–20; physical education 41–2; sport
    system 164n1; sports science 55–6, 61,
    62; training methods/manuals 56–9,
    61; use of performance-enhancing
    substances 3, 20, 109–10
USADA (United States Anti-Doping
    Agency) 3
USSR: collapse 31; contravention of
    international rulings 18–19; entry into
    IOC/Games 19, 37; Olympic successes
    19–20, 37, 109; postwar ambitions in
    Germany 72–3, 74–5; scientific
    research 61–2; sports system/policies
    18–19, 22–3, 61, 62; (stereotypical)
    view of female athletes 39–40, 43,
    44–5; (suspected) steroid use 20,
    38–40; Western fears of 8

Van Dyken, Amy 147n20
Vannotti, A. 55
victory, importance of 6, 17, 119, 135,
    137, 138
Vietnam War 45
violence (in sport) 123–4;
    injuries/fatalities 124; media appeal
    124, 181n61
Virenque, Richard 145n6
Voet, Willy 1
Voy, Robert 123

WADA (World Anti-Doping Agency) 9,
    11, 111, 130, 134; activities 2–3, 4;
    establishment 2; scale of operation 7
Waddell, Tom 26
Waddington, Ivan 125
Wade, Nicholas, Dr 38–9
Wagner, Richard 149n9
Wamsley, Kevin 123, 124
Warhol, Andy 138
weight-regulated sports 139–40
weightlifting 19, 20, 61, 109
Wesson, Al 58

West Germany *see* FRG
Wheatley, Tyrone 147n20
Whitson, David 124
Wiene, Robert 33
Windsor, Robert 39
Winzer, Otto 166n19
Wolff, Christa 128
women: eastern domination of events 20,
   40; exclusion from Olympiads 40–1;
   (feared effects of) steroid use 8, 32, 36,
   40, 106, 182n86; "men dressed as,"
   rumors of 36, 40, 43, 106; new events
   for 89; physical education 41–2; socio-
   political attitudes to 40–3; *see also* sex
   tests
Woolley, Bruce 108–9, 177–8n8
Worker Sport Movement 49–50, 76, 78,
   82
World Anti-Doping Code 47, 48, 111;
   development/ratification 2; provisions
   126–8

World War One 33–4
World War Two: events 36, 68–72; impact
   on sports 17–18, 32, 110; military
   methods 31–2; political/psychological
   after-effects 9, 36–7, 153n5; *see also*
   German-Soviet war
World Weightlifting Championships 19,
   109
Wright, James E. 39, 132, 134

Yesalis, Charles 109
Young, David 148n6
Yuan Yuan 1

Zhou Zhewen 1
Ziegler, John 20, 40, 61, 109
Zimmermann, Oskar 169n51

eBooks – at www.eBookstore.tandf.co.uk

A library at your fingertips!

eBooks are electronic versions of printed books. You can store them on your PC/laptop or browse them online.

They have advantages for anyone needing rapid access to a wide variety of published, copyright information.

eBooks can help your research by enabling you to bookmark chapters, annotate text and use instant searches to find specific words or phrases. Several eBook files would fit on even a small laptop or PDA.

NEW: Save money by eSubscribing: cheap, online access to any eBook for as long as you need it.

Annual subscription packages

We now offer special low-cost bulk subscriptions to packages of eBooks in certain subject areas. These are available to libraries or to individuals.

For more information please contact webmaster.ebooks@tandf.co.uk

We're continually developing the eBook concept, so keep up to date by visiting the website.

www.eBookstore.tandf.co.uk